# Introducing Phonetic Science

This accessible new textbook provides a clear and practical introduction
to phonetics, the study of speech. Assuming no prior knowledge of the
topic, it introduces students to the fundamental concepts in phonetic
science, and equips them with the essential skills needed for
recognising, describing and transcribing a range of speech sounds.
Numerous graded exercises enable students to put these skills into
practice, and the sounds introduced are clearly illustrated with examples
from a variety of English accents and other languages. As well as looking
at traditional articulatory description, the book introduces acoustic and
other instrumental techniques for analysing speech, and covers topics
such as speech and writing, the nature of transcription, hearing and
speech perception, linguistic universals, and the basic concepts of
phonology. Providing a solid foundation in phonetics, *Introducing Phonetic
Science* will be invaluable to all students beginning courses in linguistics,
speech sciences, language pathology and language therapy.

MICHAEL ASHBY is Senior Lecturer in Phonetics at University College London,
and an experienced teacher of phonetics at both undergraduate and
graduate level. He is the Phonetics editor of the *Oxford Advanced Learner's
Dictionary* and other ELT dictionaries, and has published various papers
on both English and general phonetics.

JOHN MAIDMENT is Lecturer in Phonetics at University College London, and
an experienced teacher of phonetics at both undergraduate and graduate
level. He is co-author of *English Transcription Course* (2000), and has been
Director of an HEFCE-funded project on teaching and learning in
phonetics. He has published various papers on both English and general
phonetics.

## Cambridge Introductions to Language and Linguistics

This new textbook series provides students and their teachers with accessible introductions to the major subjects encountered within the study of language and linguistics. Assuming no prior knowledge of the subject, each book is written and designed for ease of use in the classroom or seminar, and is ideal for adoption on a modular course as the core recommended textbook. Each book offers the ideal introductory material for each subject, presenting students with an overview of the main topics encountered in their course, and features a glossary of useful terms, chapter previews and summaries, suggestions for further reading, and helpful exercises. Each book is accompanied by a supporting website.

Books published in the series:
*Introducing Phonology* David Odden
*Introducing Speech and Language Processing* John Coleman
*Introducing Phonetic Science* John Maidment and Michael Ashby

Forthcoming:
*Introducing Sociolinguistics* Miriam Meyerhoff
*Introducing Morphology* Maggie Tallerman and S. J. Hannahs
*Introducing Historical Linguistics* Brian Joseph
*Introducing Second Language Acquisition* Muriel Saville-Troike
*Introducing Language* Bert Vaux

# Introducing Phonetic Science

MICHAEL ASHBY
AND
JOHN MAIDMENT

CAMBRIDGE
UNIVERSITY PRESS

CAMBRIDGE UNIVERSITY PRESS
Cambridge, New York, Melbourne, Madrid, Cape Town, Singapore, São Paulo,
Delhi, Dubai, Tokyo

Cambridge University Press
The Edinburgh Building, Cambridge CB2 8RU, UK

Published in the United States of America by Cambridge University Press, New York

www.cambridge.org
Information on this title: www.cambridge.org/9780521808828

First published 2005
Fifth printing 2010

Printed in the United Kingdom at the University Press, Cambridge

*A catalogue record for this book is available from the British Library*

*Library of Congress Cataloguing in Publication data*

Ashby, Michael.
Introducing phonetic science / Michael Ashby and John Maidment.
    p.   cm. – (Cambridge introductions to language and linguistics)
Includes bibliographical references and index.
ISBN 0-521-80882-0 (alk. paper) – ISBN 0-521-00496-9 (pb. : alk. paper)
1. Phonetics.   I. Maidment, John A.   II. Title.   III. Series.

P221.A778 2005                                        2004054642
414'.8–dc22

ISBN 978-0-521-80882-8 hardback
ISBN 978-0-521-00496-1 paperback

# Contents

# 1 Introduction to speech

## CHAPTER OUTLINE

In this chapter you will learn about: the basic distinction between spoken and written language; the ways in which languages of the world are written; the units from which speech is composed: syllables, vowels and consonants; phonetic symbols as a means of representing speech; speech considered as an acoustic signal; the similarities and differences in the speech sounds used in languages of the world.

## Introduction

The way we usually represent and describe speech depends on a powerful idea that is already known by everyone who is literate in a language with an alphabetic writing system. Human listeners can hear speech as a sequence of sounds, and each sound can be represented by a written mark. In this chapter we look at how this idea can be the basis of a comprehensive system of phonetic symbols, suitable for representing reliably the sounds of any language – and at how this is different from the many existing writing systems for particular languages.

## Sounds and symbols

Although there are estimated to be 5,000 to 8,000 languages in the world, each with its own particular selection of sounds, the total number of symbols required to represent all the sounds of these languages is not very large – it is somewhere around two to three hundred. This, of course, is because many sounds are found again and again in languages. The human speech apparatus, which produces sounds, and the hearing mechanism, which perceives them, are exactly the same all over the world. Languages make their selection from the stock of humanly possible sounds – and some sounds are so common and basic that they are found in almost all languages.

From surveys that compare the sounds employed in hundreds of languages, we know that almost all languages have consonant sounds like those at the beginnings of the English words *tea*, *key*, *pea*, *see*, *fee*, *me* and *knee*, and vowel sounds resembling those heard in *seat* and *sat*. Although English has quite a large system of sounds, none of the sounds is very unusual when seen in a global perspective. The most unusual sounds in English are probably the so-called *th*- sounds heard at the beginning of *think* and *this*. It's interesting that some varieties of English don't use these sounds, but replace them with others that are more frequent in the world's languages. Speakers from London, for instance, often say *fink* rather than *think*.

### The International Phonetic Alphabet

The International Phonetic Alphabet (IPA) aims to provide a separate symbol for every sound used distinctively in a human language (see Figure 1.1). Using symbols from the IPA, we should be able to represent the pronunciation of any word or phrase in any human language. The IPA has grown and evolved over more than a century of international collaboration, with new symbols being added when new sounds turned up in languages that had not previously been described.

## CONSONANTS (PULMONIC)

| | Bilabial | Labiodental | Dental | Alveolar | Postalveolar | Retroflex | Palatal | Velar | Uvular | Pharyngeal | Glottal |
|---|---|---|---|---|---|---|---|---|---|---|---|
| Plosive | p b | | | t d | | ʈ ɖ | c ɟ | k g | q ɢ | | ʔ |
| Nasal | m | ɱ | | n | | ɳ | ɲ | ŋ | N | | |
| Trill | ʙ | | | r | | | | | R | | |
| Tap or Flap | | | | ɾ | | ɽ | | | | | |
| Fricative | ɸ β | f v | θ ð | s z | ʃ ʒ | ʂ ʐ | ç ʝ | x ɣ | χ ʁ | ħ ʕ | h ɦ |
| Lateral fricative | | | | ɬ ɮ | | | | | | | |
| Approximant | | ʋ | | ɹ | | ɻ | j | ɰ | | | |
| Lateral approximant | | | | l | | ɭ | ʎ | ʟ | | | |

Where symbols appear in pairs, the one to the right represents a voiced consonant. Shaded areas denote articulations judged impossible.

## CONSONANTS (NON-PULMONIC)

| Clicks | | Voiced implosives | | Ejectives | |
|---|---|---|---|---|---|
| ʘ | Bilabial | ɓ | Bilabial | ʼ | Examples: |
| ǀ | Dental | ɗ | Dental/alveolar | pʼ | Bilabial |
| ǃ | (Post)alveolar | ʄ | Palatal | tʼ | Dental/alveolar |
| ǂ | Palatoalveolar | ɠ | Velar | kʼ | Velar |
| ǁ | Alveolar lateral | ʛ | Uvular | sʼ | Alveolar fricative |

## OTHER SYMBOLS

| | |
|---|---|
| ʍ Voiceless labial-velar fricative | ɕ ʑ Alveolo-palatal fricatives |
| w Voiced labial-velar approximant | ɺ Alveolar lateral flap |
| ɥ Voiced labial-palatal approximant | ɧ Simultaneous ʃ and x |
| ʜ Voiceless epiglottal fricative | |
| ʢ Voiced epiglottal fricative | Affricates and double articulations can be represented by two symbols joined by a tie bar if necessary.  k͡p t͡s |
| ʡ Epiglottal plosive | |

## VOWELS

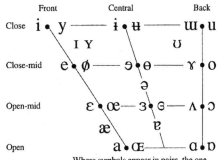

Where symbols appear in pairs, the one to the right represents a rounded vowel.

## SUPRASEGMENTALS

| | |
|---|---|
| ˈ | Primary stress |
| ˌ | Secondary stress    ˌfoʊnəˈtɪʃən |
| ː | Long    eː |
| ˑ | Half-long    eˑ |
| ˘ | Extra-short    ĕ |
| ǀ | Minor (foot) group |
| ‖ | Major (intonation) group |
| . | Syllable break    ɹi.ækt |
| ‿ | Linking (absence of a break) |

## DIACRITICS

Diacritics may be placed above a symbol with a descender, e.g. ŋ̊

| | | | | | | | |
|---|---|---|---|---|---|---|---|
| ̥ | Voiceless | n̥ d̥ | ̤ | Breathy voiced | b̤ a̤ | ̪ | Dental | t̪ d̪ |
| ̬ | Voiced | s̬ t̬ | ̰ | Creaky voiced | b̰ a̰ | ̺ | Apical | t̺ d̺ |
| ʰ | Aspirated | tʰ dʰ | ̼ | Linguolabial | t̼ d̼ | ̻ | Laminal | t̻ d̻ |
| ̹ | More rounded | ɔ̹ | ʷ | Labialized | tʷ dʷ | ̃ | Nasalized | ẽ |
| ̜ | Less rounded | ɔ̜ | ʲ | Palatalized | tʲ dʲ | ⁿ | Nasal release | dⁿ |
| ̟ | Advanced | u̟ | ˠ | Velarized | tˠ dˠ | ˡ | Lateral release | dˡ |
| ̠ | Retracted | e̠ | ˤ | Pharyngealized | tˤ dˤ | ̚ | No audible release | d̚ |
| ̈ | Centralized | ë | ̃ | Velarized or pharyngealized | ɫ | | | |
| ̽ | Mid-centralized | e̽ | ̝ | Raised | e̝  (ɹ̝ = voiced alveolar fricative) | | | |
| ̩ | Syllabic | n̩ | ̞ | Lowered | e̞  (β̞ = voiced bilabial approximant) | | | |
| ̯ | Non-syllabic | e̯ | ̘ | Advanced Tongue Root | e̘ | | | |
| ˞ | Rhoticity | ɚ a˞ | ̙ | Retracted Tongue Root | e̙ | | | |

### TONES AND WORD ACCENTS

| LEVEL | | | CONTOUR | | |
|---|---|---|---|---|---|
| e̋ or ˥ | Extra high | | ě or ˩˥ | Rising | |
| é ˦ | High | | ê ˥˩ | Falling | |
| ē ˧ | Mid | | e᷄ ˧˥ | High rising | |
| è ˨ | Low | | e᷅ ˩˧ | Low rising | |
| ȅ ˩ | Extra low | | e᷈ ˧˩˧ | Rising-falling | |
| ↓ | Downstep | | ↗ | Global rise | |
| ↑ | Upstep | | ↘ | Global fall | |

FIGURE 1.1
The International Phonetic Alphabet.

The IPA, then, is intended to contain all the sounds of human languages. But where do the symbols come from? In a sense, any shapes would do, provided they were distinctive and available in sufficient numbers – and some early attempts at phonetic alphabets did involve complicated invented shapes.

The IPA takes the familiar Latin alphabet as its starting point. The twenty-six letters of the alphabet are all used, mostly with values that seem very natural to us, and further symbols are obtained in a variety of ways:

- by using small capital letters with different meanings from the lower case ones; for example, [g] and [ɢ] stand for different sounds, so do [n] and [ɴ]. Notice how square brackets are put around phonetic symbols.
- by turning or inverting existing letter shapes, as in [ə], [ɹ] [ɯ] [ʁ]
- by using diacritics, which are dots, hooks, and other small marks added to symbols, as in [n̥], [ã]
- by using some letters from the Greek alphabet, such as [ɸ] and [ɣ], (though the values attached to the symbols are not necessarily Greek sounds)
- by inventing new shapes, such as [ɥ], [ɲ]. The new shapes mostly look like existing letters, or have some logical feature in them that highlights resemblances among sounds.

It's useful to consider some devices the IPA *doesn't* generally use in forming new symbols. Differences between fonts – the mere appearance of a letter – don't matter. In particular, it doesn't matter whether letters have serifs (little cross strokes at the ends of lines). So [n] (with serifs) and [n] (without) stand for the same sound. In the same way, *italic* or **bold** are never used to make different symbols.

## Normal speech and pathological speech

As you see from Figure 1.1, the chart of the IPA fits on one page. It provides nearly everything that is required to represent speech in any language – at least, in the normal adult pronunciations of those languages. But speakers who have speech disorders sometimes employ types of sound different from those used by any normal speaker. The IPA provides a supplementary chart, and further diacritics, which may be needed to cope with the range of sounds encountered in pathological speech.

## Transcribing sounds

After phonetic training, we can listen analytically to words or phrases, imitate them, and record them with symbols. We can start from zero with a language we do not know at all, transcribing words with the help of a co-operative speaker who is willing to repeat words for us and listen to our imitations. For instance, in the first session with a speaker of the language Divehi (Maldive Islands), the first word asked for was the one for 'hand'. The response was transcribed as [aeʔ]. The two symbols [ae] represent a particular gliding vowel sound (roughly like that in English *eye*), and [ʔ] represents a glottal stop. The native speaker of Divehi would not accept [ae] without the glottal stop as a version of 'hand', which showed that she regarded the glottal stop as an essential sound in the word.

The next word asked for was that for 'finger'. This time the response was noted down as [iŋgiliʔ]. Here the [i] symbols represent vowels approximately like those in English *beat*, and again there is a final glottal stop. The symbol [ŋ] represents a sound which is encountered commonly in English but spelled with *n* in conjunction with other letters (commonly *k* or *g*). It is the nasal sound before the [k] of *think*, or the final sound of *thing* for most speakers. Actually the English word *finger* contains exactly the same sequence [ŋg] noted in the Divehi word. The next word asked for was 'head' and this was noted down as [bɔ]. Here the symbol [ɔ] represents a vowel somewhat like that in English *saw*. There seemed to be no glottal stop at the end, but as the other two words noted so far had finished with a glottal stop, the investigator pointed to his head and tried a version [bɔʔ]. This produced laughter from the informant. It turns out that [bɔʔ] is a separate word meaning 'frog'. This established that the glottal stop was not just an automatic termination for Divehi words, but a significant sound capable of marking distinctions between words.

If this process of imitation and transcription were continued, we could expect to encounter all of the vowels and consonants employed in the language, and select suitable symbols for transcribing them all. It makes no difference to this process whether the language under investigation happens already to have a written form. As a matter of fact, Divehi *is* a written language, with a unique alphabet of its own; and the speaker in question was literate in both Divehi and English – but these facts have no relevance to the process of listening, imitating and transcribing.

> *A glottal stop (or more fully a glottal plosive) is the speech sound that often replaces the [t] of a word such as* better *in a London pronunciation, or the [t] of words such as* football *quite generally in both British and American pronunciation. As we will see, it is formed by a momentary closure of the vocal folds, located in the larynx. Within a word such as* better, *a glottal stop is heard as a brief interval of silence. A glottal stop which follows a vowel, as in this Divehi example, is heard as an abrupt termination of the vowel sound.*

## Types of transcription

Once a phonetic transcription has been made, it should sound right when we read it aloud again. But people often have a wrong idea about how precise phonetic transcription can be. The IPA symbols may look a bit like mathematical symbols, but they are not used with mathematical precision. Learning to transcribe is not at all like learning formal logic or algebra – it is more like learning how to make a recognisable sketch of a face or an object (one kind of transcription is even called impressionistic). Different observers can make somewhat different transcriptions of the same sample of speech, without either of them being necessarily 'wrong'. And however detailed we make our transcription, it remains only a rough approximation compared with a sound recording, or a film of the speaker's actions in producing the speech.

### Symbols for particular languages

The symbols needed to represent the sounds of any particular language – whether it's English or Divehi, or any other – will be a selection from (a subset of) the IPA. As an illustration, symbols for representing one type of English are given in the table below. This is followed by a specimen of transcription for you to try reading.

COPY THIS
UP.

| | Keyword | | Keyword |
|---|---|---|---|
| p | pie | j | yes |
| t | tie | h | hat |
| k | key | iː | pea |
| b | buy | ɪ | pit |
| d | die | e | pet |
| g | guy | æ | pat |
| m | my | ɑː | pa |
| n | no | ʌ | pup |
| ŋ | sing | ɒ | pot |
| f | fee | ɔː | paw |
| v | van | ʊ | put |
| θ | thigh | uː | too |
| ð | though | ə | so<u>da</u> |
| s | so | ɜː | bird |
| z | zoo | eɪ | pay |
| ʃ | she | aɪ | pie |
| ʒ | measure | ɔɪ | boy |
| tʃ | chip | aʊ | now |
| dʒ | jam | əʊ | no |
| w | wet | ɪə | near |
| r | red | eə | hair |
| l | let | | |

The mark ' indicates that the following syllable is stressed, and | indicates a slight pause at the end of a phrase.

ðə 'nɔːθ 'wɪnd ən ðə 'sʌn wə dɪ'spjuːtɪŋ wɪtʃ wəz ðə 'strɒŋgə |
wen ə 'trævlə 'keɪm ə'lɒŋ | 'ræpt ɪn ə 'wɔːm 'kləʊk |
ðeɪ ə'griːd ðət ðə 'wʌn huː 'fɜːst sək'siːdɪd ɪn 'meɪkɪŋ ðə 'trævlə
'teɪk ɪz 'kləʊk ɒf | ʃʊd bɪ kən'sɪdəd 'strɒŋgə ðən ðɪ 'ʌðə |
'ðen ðə 'nɔːθ 'wɪnd 'bluː əz 'hɑːd əz iː 'kʊd | bət ðə 'mɔː hiː 'bluː |
ðə mɔː 'kləʊslɪ dɪd ðə 'trævlə 'fəʊld ɪz 'kləʊk ə'raʊnd hɪm | ən ət
'lɑːst ðə 'nɔːθ 'wɪnd 'geɪv 'ʌp ðɪ ə'tempt | 'ðen ðə 'sʌn 'ʃɒn aʊt
'wɔːmlɪ | ən ɪ'miːdjətlɪ ðə 'trævlə 'tʊk 'ɒf ɪz 'kləʊk | ən səʊ ðə 'nɔːθ
'wɪnd wəz ə'blaɪdʒd tə kən'fes | ðət ðə 'sʌn wəz ðə 'strɒŋgər əv
ðə 'tuː |

(The orthographic version of this text is given at the end of the answers section for this chapter.)

The IPA does not provide fixed transcription systems for particular languages. It provides a stock of symbols, and principles and conventions for using them – but there can be perfectly legitimate differences between transcription systems for one and the same language. As a simple illustration, consider the vowel in a Southern British pronunciation of a word such as *dress*. It is somewhere between the sounds represented [e] and [ɛ] in the IPA. We could use a diacritic added to one of these symbols to show an intermediate quality – for instance [e̞]. But how inconvenient would it be, all the way through a book on English pronunciation, or in a dictionary that shows pronunciations, to add the diacritic each time? Far better to choose either [e] or [ɛ] for regular use, and give a once-for-all statement that the actual quality is something like [e̞]. In fact, some transcription systems for English use [e] while others use [ɛ].

## Syllables

Though both speaker and listener may have the impression that speech is a sequence of sounds, the shortest stretch of speech that a speaker can actually pronounce in a fairly natural way is not the individual sound, but the syllable. If a person is asked to speak very slowly, splitting words up into sections (e.g. for dictation), division will usually be into syllables. Thus the word *signal* can be spoken as two chunks separated by a pause: *sig - nal*. This is because *signal* is a word of two syllables. By contrast the word *sign* is a one-syllable word (a monosyllable). It cannot be divided into two individually pronounceable parts. It begins like *sigh*, but the remainder is the single sound represented by *n*, which we can only pronounce in an unnatural and disjointed way. The middle part of *sign* is also clearly the same as *I* or *eye*, but removing that portion leaves us with two sounds represented by *s* and *n*, separated by a gap. The conclusion is that *sign, sigh* and *eye* are all monosyllables.

A syllable is like one pulse of speech. It always contains one loud or prominent part (almost always a vowel sound), and may optionally have consonant sounds preceding or following the vowel. If we compare the pronunciations of the three syllables *be*, *eat* and *beat* we can hear that they all contain the same vowel sound, which we can represent with its phonetic symbol [i]. In *be*, the vowel is preceded by a consonant sound [b], but nothing comes after the vowel, giving [bi]. In *eat* there is nothing before the vowel, but a consonant sound [t] follows. *Beat* [bit] has both preceding and following consonants.

## Segments: vowels and consonants

The term segment is another way of referring to the individual speech sounds that make up syllables. Segments are of two kinds: vowels and consonants. Typical vowel segments are [i a u]; a few examples of typical consonants are [m b k f s]. Using V to stand for any vowel and C for any consonant, the structure of a syllable or word can be shown as a string of Vs and Cs. So, for example, the word *book*, pronounced [bʊk], is CVC. This means a sequence of one consonant followed by one vowel which in turn is followed by one consonant. This sort of representation is called a CV-skeleton.

Here are some examples of CV-skeletons for English, together with some words that conform to each of them. Remember that we are dealing with pronunciations, not spellings. The double -oo- in the conventional spelling of *book* doesn't mean that the word contains two vowel sounds. To take

| V | eye, oh |
| CV | be, my, see, saw, tea, you |
| VC | eat, each, aim |
| CVC | book, chip, thumb, top, win |
| CCV | draw, glue, stay |
| CVCCCC | texts |
| CCCV | straw |
| CVCVC | unit |
| CVCCVC | signal |
| CVVC | going |

another example, look at the skeleton for *unit*. This word is spelt with a vowel letter at the beginning, but it is pronounced with a consonant segment in initial position, exactly like the word *you*. Notice also that in *win* and *you* the letters *w* and *y* stand for consonant sounds, whereas in *my*, *saw*, *draw*, *stay*, *straw* they are used as part of the representation of the vowel.

As we see in these examples, when we represent careful pronunciations of whole words with CV-skeletons, there must be one V element for each syllable. The three-syllable word *banana* has the skeleton CVCVCV. In addition to simple vowels, like those heard in *book*, *bit* or *cat*, there are also diphthongs, which are vowels of changing or 'gliding' quality like those heard in *voice* or *house*. Since *voice* and *house* are one-syllable words, English diphthongs must count as one V element rather than two. Both *voice* and *house* have the structure CVC, rather than CVVC. But *going* has two syllables: one is the stem *go*, which contains a diphthong, the second is the ending *-ing*, which contains a further vowel followed by the consonant [ŋ].

Some languages also permit certain consonants to be syllabic – that is, to form a syllable by themselves. In English, [l] and [n] may be syllabic, as in the second syllables of certain pronunciations of *settle* [setl̩] or *sudden* [sʌdn̩]. (The IPA diacritic added to the relevant consonants means 'syllabic'.) These words can be represented CVCC̩. But notice that there are also alternative pronunciations [setəl], [sʌdən] in which the second syllables of these words contain a V element followed by a non-syllabic consonant, giving the structure CVCVC.

## Syllables and words

In a sense, spoken words are composed of syllables. The shortest possible words are words of one syllable. The English words *hand*, *arm*, *head*, *eye*, *mouth* are all monosyllables, as are *have*, *be*, *go*, *do*, *make*, *eat*, *die*. Of course, English words may have two, three or more syllables. For example, the English words *mother*, *husband*, *river*, *heaven*, *berry* have two syllables, while *description*, *musical*, *prominent* have three, *applicable* has four, *characteristic* has five, and so on.

But syllables are units of pronunciation rather than elements of word structure. Notice that the word *dog* is a monosyllable, and so is its plural, *dogs*; but the plural clearly consists of two elements of word structure: one is the stem, *dog-*; the other is the ending indicating 'plural'. There are thus two elements of word-structure within the one syllable. On the other hand, *banana* has three syllables, but just one element of word structure (a stem), as the word isn't made up of separate meaningful parts.

## Suprasegmentals

Segments aren't the whole story. We also have to pay attention to features that are not themselves segments, and that seem to spread across several successive segments (often a whole syllable). Such properties are called suprasegmentals. Stress and tone are in this category. In English, for example, the noun *import* and the verb *import* have exactly the same segments. But the words are distinguished according to which of the two syllables is stressed: the noun is IMport but the verb is imPORT. Here we've used capitalisation to give an indication of which syllable is stressed, but as you will see from the chart, the IPA provides symbols for suprasegmentals too, and we will return to these in a later chapter.

## Speech as an acoustic signal

Like any sound, speech can be picked up with a microphone, recorded and analysed. Sound is a rapid variation of pressure travelling through some physical medium (such as air). The velocity of sound in air is about 330 metres per second (about 740 miles per hour). When variations in pressure arrive at the eardrum, or at a microphone, they cause vibration (tiny to-and-fro movements) of the eardrum or the diaphragm of the microphone. The human listener experiences hearing a sound, and the microphone produces an electrical signal which can be measured.

A graph showing variation of pressure (or equivalently, movements of the eardrum) as a function of time gives the waveform of a sound. In a perfectly quiet place, a microphone picks up no sound, and the resulting waveform will be flat, showing no up and down movement at all. In most locations there will generally be background or ambient noise (traffic or aircraft noise from outside, wind, sounds from appliances, and so on) and this will show as constantly fluctuating energy on a waveform. Speaking reasonably close to a microphone results in a waveform that is much bigger than the ambient noise level.

Because the pressure variations in sound are very rapid, the amount of detail we can see in a waveform depends on the scale on which it is plotted. If a lot of time is shown in a small space, the details of the waveform are lost, and we just see blocks of activity.

The amplitude of a wave is a measure of the size of the pressure variations (or eardrum movements). The auditory property that is correlated with amplitude is loudness. Other things being equal, a wave with larger variation in air pressure will correspond to a louder sound. In Figure 1.2 we can see that the vowels have more energy (are louder) than the consonants.

*While English has plenty of basic vocabulary items that are single syllables, not all languages actually permit monosyllabic words. In most indigenous Australian languages, for example, words have to have at least two syllables, following the formula CV(C)CV(C). The brackets show that the consonants in those positions may be present, but are not obligatory. So the formula covers CVCV, CVCCVC, CVCCV and CVCVC.*

FIGURE 1.2

The waveform for *Peter Piper picked a peck of pickled pepper*. The phrase has been specially chosen so that the twelve syllables of the utterance can be counted. The consonant sounds that separate the syllables have low amplitude, making the prominent sounds at the centre of the syllables easy to see.

Zooming in on the waveform, so that only a small fraction of a second is shown, reveals the detailed pressure variations and can tell us something about the sound of individual segments. It is generally convenient to measure time not in whole seconds, but thousandths of a second. One millisecond (ms) = 1/1000 second.

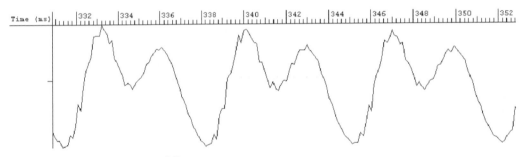

FIGURE 1.3

A short sample (about 22 milliseconds long) from the first vowel of *Peter* in the utterance shown above. The time scale shows milliseconds from the start of the recording. At this point, the waveform has a regular repeating pattern. Listening to this sample, we hear a very short but recognisable vowel [i].

## Writing systems

The writing systems used by the languages of the world are many and various and it needs a whole book considerably larger than this one to deal with them in detail. We will give a simple account here, which should give you an idea of the amount of diversity in writing systems. Ways of writing fall into three basic categories: (1) alphabetic systems, (2) syllabaries and (3) logographic systems.

### Alphabets

If you are reading this book, you are of course familiar with at least one alphabetic writing system. The writing system of English is a development of the Latin alphabet, as are many writing systems used for languages of Europe and in many other parts of the world. Each of these languages has adapted the alphabet used in classical Rome to suit its own needs. Some languages have needed to add letters to the alphabet to suit their needs – English, for instance, has added *w*.

Languages often differ in the value, or range of values, given to a particular letter. So, for instance, the English letter *c* represents the sounds [s] as in *cinema* or [k] as in *cow*, whereas in the writing system of Zulu the same letter represents a click sound. In English, *x* commonly represents a sequence of consonants [ks], as in *six* or *tax*, but in some languages (Maltese is an example) the same letter is used to represent the sound [ʃ], which is the consonant at the beginning of the English word *shop*.

There are alphabetic writing systems that have not come directly from the Latin alphabet. You may be familiar with the Greek alphabet: αβγδεζηθικλμνξοπρστυφχψω or with the Cyrillic alphabet, which is a development of it, used to write Russian and some other Slavonic languages: абгдеёжзийклмнопрстуфхцчшщъыьэюя. Some of the letters in both of these resemble Latin letters. However, there are alphabets used around the world where the letters look very different from the Latin ones. Here is part of the alphabet used to write modern Hebrew: עסנןמםלךיטחזוהדגבא. The direction of writing can vary, too: the writing system of Hebrew and some other languages such as Arabic runs from right to left.

Despite their very different appearances, all alphabets are thought to be developments of just one. And all alphabetic writing systems have in common the fact that by and large each letter is an attempt to represent a segment. Clearly, this is exactly the same principle that is used for phonetic transcription, and the IPA can be thought of as a development of the roman alphabet, adapted and extended to represent the sounds of all languages.

## Syllabaries

If spoken language consists of syllables, one way to write a language is to provide one symbol for each possible syllable. This is what is done in the type of writing system called a syllabary. Many different syllabaries have evolved at different times in different parts of the world. A portion of the Linear B syllabary, used to write an early form of Greek about 1500 BC, is shown in Figure 1.4. You can see that most of the symbols represent a CV syllable. But the symbols that represent syllables sharing the same vowel do not appear to resemble each other. The same is true for symbols that represent syllables that share a consonant. So the symbol representing [di] looks nothing like that representing [ki] and the symbol for [ka] is completely different to that for [ku]. Each symbol therefore represents a complete syllable, which is not analysed into its component segments.

A syllabary works well if the total number of different syllables that need to be represented is reasonably small – say of the order of 100. Some languages do have highly constrained syllable inventories and hence lend

*Writings in an unknown script were found on clay tablets during an archaeological excavation on the island of Crete around 1900, and termed 'Linear B'. No-one could decipher them, or even be sure what language they were in, until the 1950s, when an Englishman called Michael Ventris showed that attaching certain syllabic values to the marks led to readings that were overwhelmingly likely to be an archaic form of Greek.*

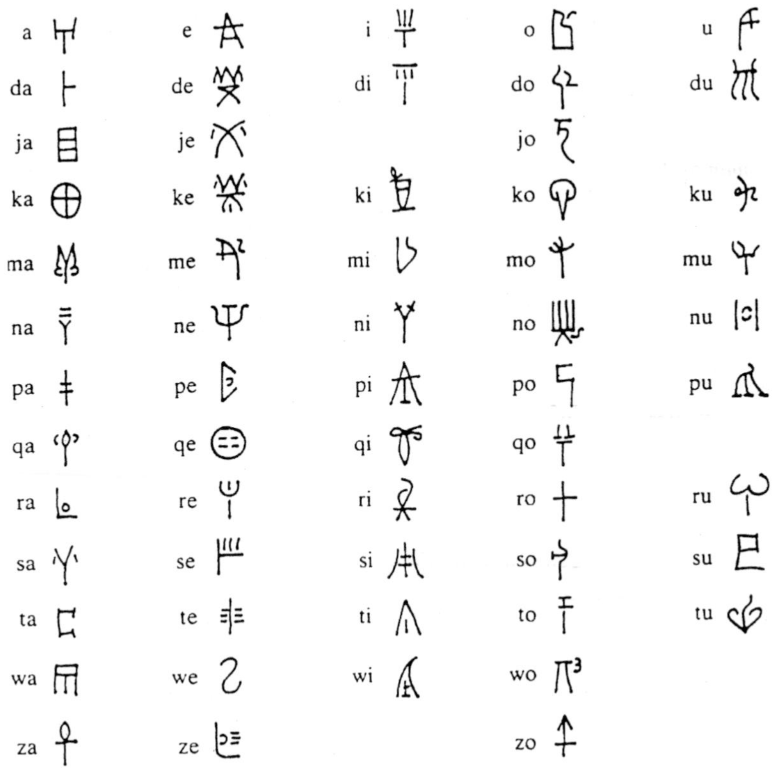

| a | ⊢ | e | ⋀ | i | Ⱶ | o | ⟨ | u | ⟨ |
|---|---|---|---|---|---|---|---|---|---|
| da | ⊢ | de | ⋈ | di | ⊤⊤ | do | ⊱ | du | ⋔ |
| ja | ⊟ | je | ⋋ | | | jo | ⋝ | | |
| ka | ⊕ | ke | ⋈ | ki | ⊞ | ko | ⬭ | ku | ⋎ |
| ma | ⋈ | me | ⋔ | mi | ⫭ | mo | ⋏ | mu | ⋔ |
| na | ⫶ | ne | ⋔ | ni | ⋎ | no | ⫽ | nu | ⎮○⎮ |
| pa | ⊹ | pe | ⫽ | pi | ⋔ | po | ⟆ | pu | ⋔ |
| qa | ⟨⟩ | qe | ⊜ | qi | ⟆ | qo | ⋕ | | |
| ra | ⊾ | re | ⊻ | ri | ⋜ | ro | ⊹ | ru | ⋓ |
| sa | ⋎ | se | ⊨ | si | ⋔ | so | ⋟ | su | ⊟ |
| ta | ⊏ | te | ⋕ | ti | ⋀ | to | ⊤ | tu | ⋓ |
| wa | ⊞ | we | ⊋ | wi | ⋀ | wo | ⋂³ | | |
| za | ⟊ | ze | ⊭ | | | zo | ⟊ | | |

FIGURE 1.4
Part of the Linear B syllabary, used to write an archaic form of Greek about 1500 BC (from G. Sampson, *Writing Systems*, London: Hutchinson, 1985).

themselves to representation in this way. But the number of possible English syllables is in tens of thousands; and the number of different syllables that a human being can in principle make or recognise is perhaps of the order of a million. So syllabic writing is not suitable for all languages, and would certainly not form a satisfactory basis for a general system of phonetic transcription.

## Logographic writing

A logographic writing system does not attempt to represent the pronunciation of words at all. The best known example is the one used in Chinese. Each logogram (or character) represents a complete word and basically it is up to the reader to know how the word is pronounced. There is just no way of working out the pronunciation from the logogram. To illustrate this here are two Chinese characters:

木 = *tree*, pronounced [mu]   本 = *root*, pronounced [bən]

It is easy to see the connection between the meanings of the two words and why the characters resemble each other, but the pronunciations have absolutely nothing in common. This means that there really is no equivalent of spelling in this type of system. As a further illustration, here is the character meaning *good*. It is pronounced [hau].

好

The left-hand side of this exists as a character in its own right. It means *woman* and is pronounced in a way that can be transcribed [ny] (the symbol [y] means a vowel like that in French *lune* meaning 'moon'). The right-hand side of the character can also be used independently. It means *child* and is pronounced [dz]. So there is no way of working out that *good* = [hau] in Chinese from the character used to represent the word.

Finally, there are writing systems that are mixtures of the above types. Ancient Egyptian hieroglyphics are a mixture of alphabetic writing and logograms. Modern Japanese is written with a mixture of Chinese logograms and two different syllabaries.

## The relationship between speech and writing

If we think of a language as a system for communication, then speech and writing are the two main channels through which communication can pass. Speech is the original channel for which human language evolved, and all written languages have (or once had) a spoken form. Writing, the preservation of language messages with visible marks, is a much later development (from about the Bronze Age) and many languages today still have no written form.

Speech and writing are obviously good for different things. Speech is fast and interactive, and we can talk and listen while at the same time getting on with something else (such as working or eating). Talking is a social activity, and when we talk to other people we are doing much more than communicate linguistic messages. But like all sounds reaching our ears, speech is fleeting. Writing is permanent, and gives human beings the power to keep records. It also helps us organise ideas that would be too complex to keep in our heads at once. Writing is in fact the most fundamental invention in the field we now call information technology.

People who do not make use of writing can pass stories, songs and poems from one generation to the next by oral tradition – that is, by memorisation and repetition. But in our society oral tradition has just about died out, because it is assumed that everyone will learn to read and write. Writing is used for law, religion, literature and science, and as a result has become the basis of almost all education.

Within limits, we can swap messages between speech and writing. For instance, we can write down the words somebody used when they were speaking. This may preserve the 'literal meaning' of what was said, but we will lose the intonation, loudness, voice quality, local accent – and the information that enables us to tell whether the speaker is a man, woman or child, and whether the speaker is someone we know. Equally, we can make an attempt at speaking aloud anything that is written – but here we have to supply all the characteristics that are not specified in writing. And there certainly isn't a spoken equivalent for everything that's written.

Taking away the visual organisation of a written document may make it more or less useless: think of the difficulties we would face in using a purely spoken version of something like a telephone directory.

Writing is not simply a representation of speech. Admittedly, speech was probably an important factor in the original development of writing, and it remains true that in most writing systems, the way to write a word has some connection with its pronunciation. But once writing has become established, it tends to develop all kinds of peculiarities that do not directly reflect speech, and which in fact have very little to do with the language system either. The insistence on standardised spelling, punctuation and the use of capital letters in the writing of English are examples. A schoolchild who writes *beleeve* will have the spelling crossed out and corrected, even though it indicates the intended word quite as clearly as the conventional spelling *believe* (and was in fact used in the first printed version of Shakespeare's plays). The insistence on one spelling rather than the other, and on a single spelling rather than two or more spellings used interchangeably, is simply arbitrary. Conventions like this seem very important to most educated people (perhaps because they have had to work very hard to learn them) but they are entirely artificial.

We have just shown that writing is not simply a representation of speech. Much more obviously, speech is not in any sense a version of writing. People sometimes have quite powerful prejudices, believing that speech should really be modelled on written language, or that spelling somehow shows us how we should pronounce. We need to keep spoken language and written language separate in our minds, and study each on its own terms.

## Homophones

A good example of the independence of speech and writing in the representation of language comes from looking at homophones (different words that are pronounced the same way). Consider, for example, the English words that are conventionally written *see* and *sea*. They are pronounced in exactly the same way [si]. Without the assistance of a meaningful context the spoken words are completely indistinguishable. We can go further, because there are at least two English words spelt *see*. One is the verb meaning 'to perceive with the eyes', the other a noun meaning 'the area of authority of a bishop'. (These two words have entirely separate origins.) The same pronunciation is also used for the name of the letter C, which is also used as a word (*I tried hard in my exam, but I only got a C*). So the language has four words: *see* (verb), *see* (noun), *sea* and *C*. The four words are absolutely identical in speech. The writing system makes a three-way distinction, which may be useful, but has nothing to do with pronunciation.

Homophones are found scattered randomly – but fairly commonly – in the vocabularies of languages. They are certainly not restricted to languages that happen to have a written form. If we were learning any unwritten language we would almost certainly come across some examples before very long. Of course, young children meet and cope with homophones such as *see/sea* or *vin/vingt* long before they learn to read and write.

*Homophones are of course not just found in English. A simple example from French is* **vin** *meaning 'wine' and* **vingt** *meaning 'twenty' both are pronounced* [vɛ̃] *(the diacritic [˜] means a nasalised vowel).*

## Sign languages

We have described speech and writing as the two channels for language. Don't the sign languages used by the deaf show us a third channel? Certainly signing represents another mode of communication, which is neither speech nor writing. But sign languages (such as British Sign Language, BSL) don't operate by giving a word-for-word version of an otherwise written or spoken language (such as English). The system underlying the signs is a language in its own right. A message that has been originated in BSL has to be *translated* into English, not merely transposed into speech or writing, to make it accessible to a person who doesn't know BSL. So signing isn't an extra channel for the thousands of conventional languages like English, which have spoken (and possibly written) forms.

## Problems with syllables and segments

Although segments and syllables are important in the description of speech, it is only fair to point out that there are some problems in defining and making use of these notions.

Sometimes the number of syllables in a word is uncertain or variable. For example, the English word *science* may seem to be two syllables or one. It can be pronounced in a way that clearly has two syllables, or in another that seems to have only one. There are also various intermediate pronunciations over which people would not agree. The problem in words like this is caused by adjacent vowel sounds without a consonant to separate them. Adding the consonant [l] between the two vowels (and keeping the other sounds the same) gives the word *silence*, and we have no doubt that this has two syllables. Sometimes there are alternative pronunciations of a word, which differ in the number of syllables. For example *camera* can be pronounced as three syllables or two. The word *prison* has two syllables, but *prisoner* can be pronounced as three or as two. When we hear particular examples of words such as *camera* or *prisoner* we can't always decide whether we hear two syllables or three.

Our perception of syllables is partly governed by our language experience. To a Japanese listener, the English syllable [bi] (*be* /bee) seems to consist of two units rather than one, because it contains a vowel that is long in duration. The first unit is a syllable [bi] with a short example of vowel [i], the second unit is another [i], needed to account for the length of the vowel. So the Japanese perception is [bi – i]. Add a consonant to give *beat* and a Japanese listener now perceives three units: [bi – i – tu], because syllables in Japanese cannot end with a consonant such as [t].

Some caution is needed with segments, too. Although they are essential for phonetic description and transcription, we should beware of thinking that segments are 'real' in any simple sense, or that they necessarily form the basis of the production and perception of speech. Although recordings of speech can be cut up reasonably well into syllables, the same is not true for segments. And the movements we make in producing speech are smooth and continuous, without abrupt joins between successive segments. Some people even go so far as to claim that segments are complete illusions which we believe in only because of the alphabet. It is certainly true that when we hear a stretch of speech in an unfamiliar language we may have real doubts about what segments it contains. The same is true if we hear words of a familiar language (such as English) spoken by a young child, or by an adult who has suffered a stroke. And if short snippets of casual speech are taken out of context and played to listeners, the listeners make wild attempts to make sense of what they hear and differ greatly from each other in how many segments they seem to hear and what they are.

## Chapter summary

Phonetic science is concerned with the objective description and analysis of all aspects of speech. The representation of speech depends upon treating it as a succession of sounds. The International Phonetic Alphabet (IPA) aims to provide a symbol for any sound in any language.

The sounds in speech are of two kinds: vowels and consonants. Vowels may be simple or diphthongal. Segments are grouped into syllables, which are the smallest units that can be pronounced in a natural way. Recording speech with a microphone enables us to display a waveform, on which certain aspects of speech can be observed and measured.

Speech and writing are separate channels through which language messages can be passed. The two channels have different uses and different characteristics. Writing is important in our culture but we must avoid the mistake of believing that written language can somehow show us what speech is really like (or how it ought to be).

## Exercises

### Exercise 1.1

How many segments have the following words? Represent each word as a string of Xs, one X for each segment. (Remember you are looking for sounds, not letters.)

1  box X X X X
2  sorry X X X X
3  possess X X X X X
4  knees X X X
5  quickly X X X X X X
6  rhyme X X X
7  climb X X X X
8  gnaw X X
9  mushroom X X X X X X
10 elephants X X X X X X X X

### Exercise 1.2

Represent the following English words using the symbols C and V to make CV-skeletons.

1  damp C V C C
2  fox C V C C

3 friend CCVCC ✓
4 unit CVCVC ✓
5 talker CVCV ✓
6 physics CVCVCC ✓
7 knowledge CVCCVC ✗ CVCVC
8 spaghetti CCVCCVCV ✗ CVCVCV
9 columnist CV.CVCCVCC ✗ CVCVCVCC
10 ghastliness CVCCCVCVC ✓

## Exercise 1.3

For each of the CV-skeletons you have found in 1.2, find at least one other English word that will fit it.

## Exercise 1.4

Examine the short English passage below and then list all the words you can find in it that conform to each of the CV-skeletons given. Treat the sound [tʃ] as at the beginning of *chew*, and the sound [dʒ] as at the beginning of *jazz*, as single C elements rather than CC.

He tried to alter the height of the ladder, but it still would not reach the window. 'You aren't having a lot of success, are you?' said the old man. Colin shook his head and smiled. He patted his pockets again, but he knew he had lost the keys. He would have to try and break in, but he wanted to avoid causing too much damage.

1 CV  he to the you
2 CVC  height but still would not reach areit lot said man shook his head and but knew had have
3 CVCC  ladder lost keys
4 VC  of it are old
5 VCC  alter
6 CVCV  window
7 CCVC  tried
8 CCVCC  smiled pockets
9 CVCVC  having colin
10 CVCCVC  success patted

## Exercise 1.5

Here is a short passage of English. Determine the number of segments in each word and count the number of words with one segment, with two segments and so on. Then draw a bar chart with number of segments on the horizontal axis and number of words on the vertical axis. Keep a record of any words where the number of segments is problematic.

The first time I drove a car abroad was in Italy. We picked up a car at the airport and drove to where we were staying. It took us about five and a half hours. I had a bit of trouble with the gears and spent the first couple of miles stuck in third, but after I got the hang of it, we got along fine. The next day was a different matter. I suppose it was overconfidence or something, but we nearly had a terrible disaster. We set off to see some sight or other, I forget now where we were going. Suddenly my wife screamed out that I was driving on the wrong side of the road. I managed to get back to the correct side just in time to miss a large lorry which appeared round the bend in front of us. It would have been a very nasty accident and I was extremely careful for the rest of the holiday.

**Exercise 1.6**

Use the passage in exercise 1.5 (or take 100 consecutive words from any other text or from a sample of recorded speech). Determine the number of words pronounced with one syllable, two syllables, etc. Keep a list of problematic cases. Again, draw a bar chart to show the results. Try this with texts and recordings of different types and styles.

**Exercise 1.7**

Try to make up a short passage of English using only monosyllables. There is actually at least one complete novel written this way (Launcelot Hogben, *Whales for the Welsh*, London: Rapp and Carroll, 1967). Here is a specimen:

All the same, he was not a bad clerk as clerks go, and as clerks go he went home in good time each night to the small house where he slept and took his one meal of the day. There he could cash in on the thoughts which came to him at his desk . . .

(p. 7)

**Exercise 1.8**

[Needs access to a computer, with soundcard and microphone.] Using Windows Sound Recorder, record some samples of speech into the computer and replay them. Record a stretch of speech that does not have long pauses in it. Sound Recorder shows you the duration of a recording (in seconds). By counting the number of syllables in the recording, you can work out the rate of speaking, expressed in syllables per second. In a similar way, you can arrive at an estimation of the number of segments produced per second. [Note: Sound Recorder records and replays sound perfectly well, but the 'waveforms' it displays are not accurate. Software to display waveforms correctly can be downloaded free. See website link.]

**Exercise 1.9**

Two speech waveforms A and B are shown below. One is *potato*, while the other is *pepper*. Say which is which, and give reasons for your choice.

Waveform A

Waveform B

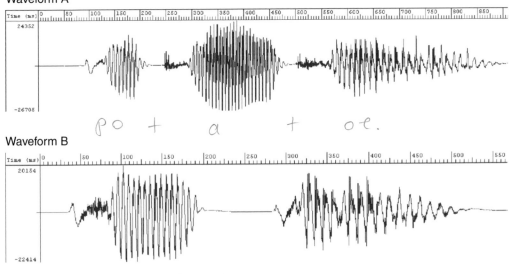

**Further reading**

Most of the topics introduced in this chapter will be considered in greater depth later in the book. If you're just beginning the study of phonetics, the best advice on further reading, once you've tried the exercises to this chapter and looked at the accompanying website, is to continue with the other chapters. You may like to look at the *Handbook of the International Phonetic Association*, Cambridge: Cambridge University Press, 1999, for a comprehensive guide to the IPA, and examples of its application to around thirty languages.

Some of the background areas we have touched on in this introduction won't come up again, and we wouldn't recommend getting sidetracked onto them at this early stage. But you may at some point in the future want to know more about them. On writing systems, we'd recommend Florian Coulmas, *Writing systems: An introduction to their linguistic analysis*, Cambridge: Cambridge University Press, 2003. You can learn about the spelling system of English in Edward Carney, *English spelling*, London: Routledge, 1997. If you are interested in the decipherment of old scripts like Linear B, a good start is Maurice Pope, *The story of decipherment: From hieroglyphs to Maya script*, London: Thames and Hudson, rev. edn 1999.

# 2 Voice

## CHAPTER OUTLINE

In this chapter you will learn about: the structure of the larynx; how the larynx is used to produce voiced and voiceless sounds; how larynx activity can be observed and monitored; the role of voice in the languages of the world; the waveforms of voiced and voiceless sounds.

## Introduction

The basis of all normal speech is a controlled outflow of air from the lungs. Air flows up the trachea (windpipe) and out of the body through the mouth or the nose. On the way it must pass through the larynx, a structure formed of cartilages and visible on the outside of the neck as the 'Adam's apple'. The airway from the larynx to the lips, and the side-branch via nasal cavities to the nostrils, contain all the organs that control the production of speech sounds, and are known as the vocal tract.

## The larynx

We cannot see directly into the larynx, but it can be observed in a mirror placed right at the back of the mouth (a laryngoscope mirror) – for this, the subject must keep the mouth wide open. Another way is with a fibrescope, which can be inserted via the nose and does not prevent the subject from speaking. Both methods give a top view of the larynx, and this is how it is usually shown in pictures and diagrams.

The cartilages of the larynx together form a short section of tube through which air must flow on its way to and from the lungs. The two main cartilages are the cricoid (which is a ring-shaped cartilage at the base) and the thyroid cartilage, which forms the prominence which can be seen and felt in the neck. The larynxes of males and females are essentially similar, though the male larynx is generally larger and more prominent.

## Vocal folds

Contained within the cartilages are the two vocal folds (vocal cords in older terminology), one at the left and one at the right. Looking down on the larynx from above we see the top surfaces of the folds. The folds are fixed adjacent to each other at the front, but at the back they are attached to the two moveable arytenoid cartilages. If the back ends of the folds are held apart, a roughly triangular space opens up between the folds. The space between the folds is called the glottis. As the back ends of the folds are brought together, the glottis can be narrowed to a slit, and then closed completely as the folds are pressed together. In this position, they prevent any air flowing through the larynx.

For normal breathing, the glottis is open and air passes in and out silently. For certain speech sounds, too, the glottis is open. For the sound [f], for example, air flows out rapidly through the open glottis (but is obstructed as it leaves the vocal tract through a narrow gap between upper teeth and lower lip).

## Voiced and voiceless sounds

There is another adjustment of the glottis that is of great importance in the production of speech. If the vocal folds are held gently together and air under pressure from the lungs is pushed between them, the folds can be made to vibrate evenly to produce the tone we call voice. If we sustain a vowel sound such as [i] or [a], the tone we hear is contributed by the vibrating folds. A sound of this type is said to be voiced. The rapid vibration of the folds can be felt with fingertips applied to the neck on the outside of the larynx. It is not only vowels that are voiced, but many consonants such as [m] [v] [z]. If we sing a vowel, or one of these voiced consonants, we can change the pitch of the note we are singing by varying the rate of vocal fold vibration.

Sounds like [f] and [s], which are made without vocal fold vibration, are said to be voiceless. The airflow is converted into sound energy not at the larynx, but elsewhere in the vocal tract. There is no tone from the larynx, and nothing will be felt with fingertips applied there.

All vowels are normally voiced. Consonant sounds come in both voiced and voiceless kinds, and in fact voicing versus voicelessness is the only difference between certain pairs of consonants. For example, comparing [f] and [v] we find that the only difference between them is that [v] is voiced while [f] is voiceless. The position of the rest of the vocal tract is the same. With a little practice, it is possible to hold the position for [f] and continue to produce sound, while switching voicing on and off. This gives a sequence [fvfv . . . ]. The sounds [s] and [z] are related in the same way and a similar alternating sequence [szsz] should be tried.

## Vibration of the vocal folds

The way in which the vocal folds vibrate for voice is quite similar to the way that the lips can be made to vibrate by blowing air between them (the lips are made to vibrate this way by the player of a brass instrument such as a trumpet or trombone, or by anyone making the sound known as a

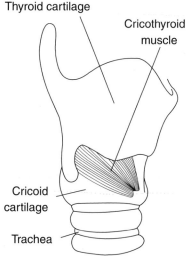

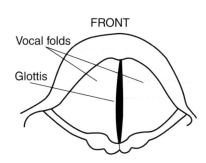

FIGURE 2.1
The cartilages of the larynx, seen from the right-hand side.

FIGURE 2.2
View of larynx from above.

'raspberry'). The series of events for one complete cycle of vibration of the vocal folds is as follows:

- First the vocal folds are together, and stop the airflow.
- Air from beneath pushes up between the folds, forcing them apart near the middle.
- A burst of air flows through, but this begins to be cut off as the folds recoil back to the closed position.
- As the opening gets smaller, the rapid airflow through the narrowing gap leads to suction which helps to complete the closure rapidly and effectively.
- Once the folds are closed completely, the cycle of vibration begins again, and the folds are once again forced open.

It is important to understand that the openings which appear as part of the cycle of vibration at not at all like the stationary open glottis position that is obtained by moving the arytenoid cartilages apart. During voicing, the arytenoids remain still and close together. The process of vibration will repeat for as long as air under pressure is supplied from the lungs, and as long as the tension and position of the folds is suitable.

This is a simplified account of vocal fold vibration. Because the folds have vertical thickness, they do not necessarily close face-to-face all at once. Commonly they close at the bottom first, and the closure then rolls up through the folds. And the 'closure' doesn't have to be totally complete – vibration can take the form of alternating more-open and more-closed positions.

## Observing vocal fold vibration

It is very useful for many purposes to observe what actually happens when the vocal folds are vibrating. For instance, if a speaker is having trouble with producing vocal fold vibration normally, observation of the vibratory pattern may give a clue to what is wrong with the larynx. Also, as we shall see in Chapter 10, some languages use different types of vocal fold vibration to signal the difference between one word and another. It is obviously a good idea to see how these differences are actually produced. We will now have a look at two techniques for observing vocal fold vibration.

### The Laryngograph

Vocal fold vibration can be detected and measured with a device called the laryngograph. It works by passing a tiny high frequency electric current across the larynx from one fold to the other. The degree of contact between the folds controls the current, which can be measured and turned into a waveform showing the vibration. The device is completely non-invasive and harmless: the electrodes are simply placed comfortably on the outside of the neck, either side of the thyroid cartilage.

## Time (milliseconds)

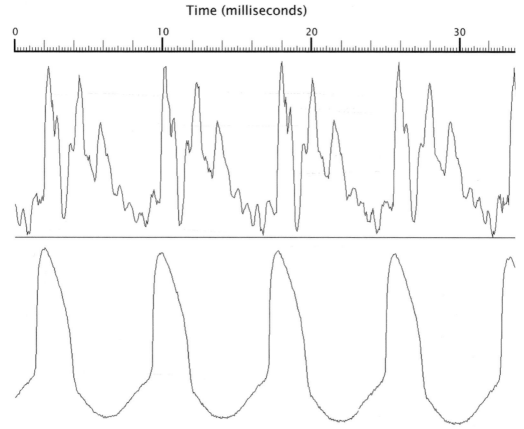

FIGURE 2.3
Laryngograph (lower) and microphone waveforms.

In Figure 2.3, the lower waveform, obtained with a laryngograph, shows five closures of the vocal folds from a stretch of voicing. Up corresponds to contact, down to opening. If heard, this wave is just a buzzing sound. The upper simultaneous waveform is from a microphone and shows the result of modification of the voicing tone by the rest of the vocal tract. This sounds like the vowel of *bird*, which is the voiced sound that the speaker was producing. Notice that the two waveforms have the same repetition rate. This rate, as we shall see below, is what determines the pitch of the sound we hear. As the repetition rate of the speech waveform (the output of the vocal tract) is identical with that of the laryngograph waveform (the contact pattern of the vibrating vocal folds and therefore related to the input to the vocal tract), we must conclude that the rate of vocal fold vibration determines the pitch of voiced sounds.

## Stroboscope
The vibrating vocal folds can be filmed, but a very high film speed is needed to show the details of vibration (ordinary film runs at 24 pictures

per second, and even a low-pitched male speaker will have completed 2 or 3 vibrations in 1/24 of a second). An alternative is to use a stroboscope – a flashing light of the sort used to slow down or freeze the appearance of rotating machinery – together with a suitable camera. A refinement is to trigger a stroboscope from the laryngograph waveform, which allows us to see the appearance of the folds at precisely determined points in the waveform (see Figure 2.4).

## Voicing in languages

Voiced and voiceless sounds are to be heard in all languages, and for the most part languages make use of differences between voiced and voiceless consonants like that already pointed out for English. There are, however, certain languages where the voicing or voicelessness of consonants can't make a difference to meaning, because it is largely an automatic consequence of the position of a consonant within a word. Many indigenous languages of Australia are like this. In the language Dyirbal, for example, the word for 'stone' is generally [tiban] with a voiceless consonant at the beginning, and a voiced one within the word. But the initial sound can be made voiced with no change of meaning, giving [diban], and, though it is less usual, the consonant within the word can be voiceless, giving two further versions [tipan] and [dipan]. It is not unusual for children acquiring English speech to go through a stage of context-sensitive voicing which resembles this.

## Whisper

When we whisper a sound, there is no vocal fold vibration, and so no musical pitch. But whisper is not the same as voicelessness. To whisper a sound, we make a narrow opening between the folds (the glottis becomes a small opening) and air flows noisily through that opening. The noise from airflow takes the place of the tone produced by voicing, and is applied to just those speech sounds that would normally be voiced. If we whisper a whole utterance, what we do is to use the whisper position for the voiced sounds, and the voiceless position for the voiceless ones, so we are still switching back and forth between two adjustments of the larynx.

To prove that whisper and voicelessness are different, try comparing the sequences [afa] and [ava]. In the ordinary way, they are distinct because [f] is voiceless and [v] is voiced. But are they still different when whispered? There seems to be a clearly audible difference, so the attempt at [v] which turns up in whispered speech cannot be identical with the voiceless sound [f]. In the whispered [v], there is a narrowed glottis, and airflow noise is being generated there as well as at the lip-teeth constriction. But for [f], whether it occurs in ordinary speech or in a whispered context, the glottis is open allowing air to flow freely.

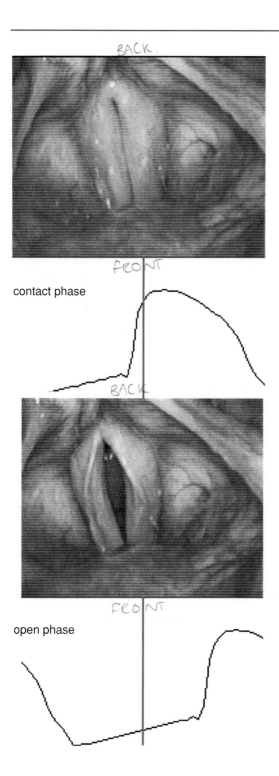

contact phase

open phase

FIGURE 2.4
Stroboscopic photographs
showing two instants
during the vocal fold
vibratory cycle. The front
of the larynx is at the
bottom of the pictures.
Compare the
laryngograph waveform
with that shown in
Figure 2.2 (courtesy of
Laryngograph Ltd).

## Periodic waves  –voiced

The waveforms of voiced and voiceless sounds are quite different. A wave that has a pattern that repeats regularly in time is called periodic. A period runs from one clearly identifiable point on the wave (e.g. an upwards-going zero-crossing) to the next place where this point occurs. So one period of a simple (sine) wave contains one upwards-and-over excursion, and one downwards-and-up-again excursion, returning to the zero line. The length of one period is the periodic time, T.

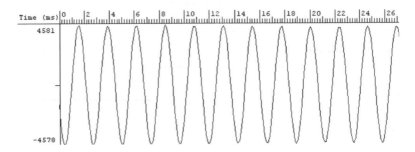

FIGURE 2.5
Part of a periodic wave obtained by sounding a tuning fork close to a microphone.

The source of periodic waveforms in speech is voicing. So whenever we see a speech waveform with a regularly repeating pattern, we know it must have been produced with vocal fold vibration.

The number of repetitions (or cycles) per second is termed the frequency. This was formerly expressed in cycles per second (c.p.s or c/s), but the unit now used is the Hertz (Hz): 1 Hz = 1 c.p.s.

Frequency and period are clearly related. The shorter the period, the more periods will be completed in one second. The relationship is $f = 1/T$, where f is in Hz and T in seconds. Similarly, $T = 1/f$.

Human hearing covers a range of about 20 Hz to 20,000 Hz. Frequency is related to the auditory sensation of pitch: the higher the frequency, the higher the pitch. The A which is sounded as the orchestra tunes up has a frequency of 440 Hz; middle C has a frequency of 264 Hz. An octave corresponds to a doubling of frequency. So the C below middle C has a frequency of 132 Hz, the one above it 528 Hz. Alternating current mains supply in the UK has a frequency of 50 Hz; when this is heard over a loud-speaker, the effect is of a deep hum. The normal speaking voice of an adult male has an average fundamental frequency of about 120 Hz.

One thousand Hertz = 1 kilohertz (kHz). The frequencies corresponding to the pitch of the voice are of the order of a few hundred Hz. A soprano may be able to reach the second C above middle C, which has a frequency a little over 1 kHz. But everyone's speech contains energy at frequencies higher than this. Speech is intelligible (though it doesn't sound very natural) if only frequencies up to about 2.5 kHz are reproduced (as they are in a communications radio link); the telephone passes frequencies up to about 3 kHz. A 'hi-fi' system will typically pass frequencies up to 20 kHz.

## Digitising speech

Nowadays sound waveforms are mainly handled in digitised form. The tracks on a CD, or wav files in a computer, are simply long strings of numbers representing waveforms sampled at regular intervals. The sampling rate controls what frequencies will be preserved when the wave is reconstructed. Basically you have to sample at a rate that is at least twice the highest frequency you need to show. A CD works at a sample rate of more than 40 kHz, enabling it to provide 'hi-fi' sound to 20 kHz or so. For many of the waves shown in this book we were able to use slower sampling rates of 16 kHz or even 10 kHz, giving us much smaller wav files.

Music files in computers and on the Internet aren't usually wav files, but MP3s. This is a clever way of compressing the information in a wav file, so that it takes up less storage. The compressed version can then be expanded again, with little loss of quality. It works for speech too (but isn't necessarily the best way to process speech). Actually, methods of data compression and expansion were originally developed for speech – and the need to fit more and more telephone conversations into a channel with limited capacity was a spur to the development of speech technology.

## Aperiodic waves – voiceless

Not all sounds have periodic waveforms. A waveform that does not repeat along the time axis is termed aperiodic; sounds with aperiodic waveforms strike us as 'noises' rather than tones. Hisses, rumbles and roars are examples. An aperiodic sound results from random, irregular vibration. Voiceless sounds in speech have aperiodic waveforms; the source of random energy is the turbulent flow of air through the articulatory constriction. Aperiodic waves can be sampled and digitised just like periodic ones, of course.

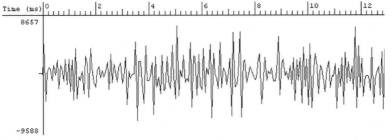

FIGURE 2.6
A section about 13 ms in duration cut from an aperiodic wave (actually a sustained [s] sound).

Certain speech sounds (for example, voiced fricatives such as [v]) employ voice and noise together. The waveforms of such sounds are correspondingly a mixture of periodic and aperiodic. The waveform for a fully voiced [v] shows a basically periodic appearance, with added noise.

One type of periodic waveform has a very simple wavelike appearance. They are sine waves, such as are produced by the simplest vibrating systems (e.g. a tuning fork, or the electronic tone generator used

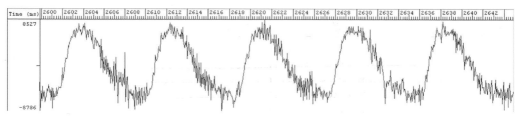

FIGURE 2.7
The waveform for a sustained [v] sound, showing a mixture of periodic and aperiodic energy.

when a person's hearing is being tested). This waveshape is of great mathematical and physical importance, as any more complex wave can be regarded as being composed of a number of sine waves of different frequencies and amplitudes added together. Human speakers don't and can't produce sine waves (but the wave produced by whistling is fairly sine-like).

In practice, however, the periodic tones encountered either in speech or music are not sine waves (or pure tones), but complex periodic tones. The waveform of a complex tone is periodic, and the period and corresponding frequency can be calculated. But the waveshape within each period shows a pattern – sometimes very complicated – which results from the simultaneous presence of many component frequencies.

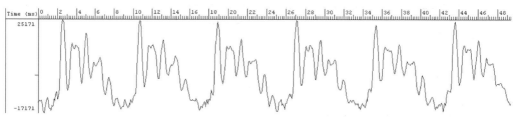

FIGURE 2.8
A sustained [a] vowel, showing a complex periodic wave.

## Chapter summary

We normally speak while breathing out. Air passing out of the lungs must go through the larynx, where its flow is controlled by the vocal folds. They may be open (as for breathing, and for voiceless sounds), closed ( for a glottal stop) or vibrating (producing voice). Voicing makes a distinction between consonants such as [v] (voiced) and [f] (voiceless), and this is utilised in many languages of the world. Voiced sounds have complex periodic waveforms, and voicing is the only source of periodic energy in speech.

M – V⁺   F – V⁻   J – V⁺   M – V⁺
T – V⁻   S – V⁻   F – V⁻   J – V⁺
W – V⁺   S – V⁻   M – V⁺   J – V⁺
T – V⁻            A – Vowel   A – Vowel
                     V⁺          V⁺

S – V⁻
ð – Vowel V⁺
N – V⁺
D – V⁺
1 – ...     7 – V⁻
2 – V⁻      8 – vowel
3 – V⁻      9 – V⁺
4 – V⁻      10 – ...
5 – V⁻
6 – V⁺

# Exercises

## Exercise 2.1

Take the days of the week (*Monday, Tuesday* . . .) and the months of the year (*January, February* . . .). Identify the first segment of each as a voiced consonant, a voiceless consonant or a vowel. Do the same for the initial segments of the names of the digits *one* to *nine*.

## Exercise 2.2

Decide whether the final sound of the following words is voiced or voiceless:

1  bus  V⁻
2  use (noun)  V⁻
3  as  V⁺
4  breathe  V⁺
5  has  V⁺
6  off  V⁻
7  buzz  V⁺
8  use (verb)  V⁺
9  teeth  V⁻
10  rule  V⁺
11  of  V⁺
12  booth  V⁺

## Exercise 2.3

Every English word contains at least one voiced segment, but not every word contains a voiceless segment. In fact, whole phrases and sentences can be concocted that do not contain any voiceless segments (e.g. *I'm worried by Lilian's wandering around Venezuela alone*). What is the longest all-voiced sequence you can devise?

## Exercise 2.4

At a certain stage of development, many children acquiring English have a rule of **context-sensitive voicing.** In one form of this, the consonants [b d g v ð z ʒ dʒ] may only occur in the child's speech when followed directly by a vowel; in all other positions they are replaced by their voiceless counterparts. Similarly, all voiceless consonants must be replaced with their voiced counterparts when followed directly by a vowel. Consonants other than those listed are not affected. So for example *pad* is pronounced [bæt] *pan* becomes [bæn] and so on. A number of words are given below with a transcription of the normal adult pronunciation. Give the pronunciation expected from a child with context-sensitive voicing. Assume that the child's speech has no other differences from the adult target.

V  V⁻
V⁺  V

|        | adult pronunciation | Child |
|--------|---------------------|-------|
| bag    | [bæg]               | bæk ✓ |
| boot   | [buːt]              | buːt ✓ |
| beaker | [biːkə]             | biːgə ✓ |
| can    | [kæn]               | gæn ✓ |
| coach  | [kəʊtʃ]             | gəʊtʃ ✓ |
| pad    | [pæd]               | bæt ✓ |
| Paddy  | [pædi]              | bædi ✓ |
| jug    | [dʒʌg]              | dʒʌk ✓ |

Adult.                                    child

V V⁻

V⁺V

| father | [fɑːðə] | vɑːð ə ✓ |
| footpath | [fʊtpɑːθ] | vʊtbɑːθ ✓ |
| Jack | [dʒæk] | dʒæk ✓ |
| motor | [məʊtə] | məʊdə ✓ |
| rabbit | [ræbɪt] | ræbit ✓ |
| song | [sɒŋ] | sɒŋ ✓ |
| shop | [ʃɒp] | ʃɒp ✓ |
| teatime | [tiːtaɪm] | diːdaɪm ✓ |

..................................................................................................................................

**Further reading**

For more on sound waves, and on periodic and aperiodic sounds in speech, see Dennis B. Fry, *The physics of speech*, Cambridge: Cambridge University Press, 1978. Detailed information on the functioning and use of the laryngograph can be found in E. R. M. Abberton, D. M. Howard and A. J. Fourcin, Laryngographic assessment of normal voice: A tutorial, *Clinical Linguistics & Phonetics*, 3 (1989), 281–96.

# 3 Place of articulation

## CHAPTER OUTLINE

### KEY TERMS

*Active articulator*

*Articulation*

*Double articulation*

*Passive articulator*

*Place of articulation*

*Vocal tract*

In this chapter you will learn about: active and passive articulators; complex articulation; instrumental techniques for investigating place of articulation; the anatomy of the vocal tract; the concept of articulation; the main places of articulation for consonant sounds.

## Introduction

In this chapter we shall look at one of the features used to describe the production of consonant sounds. In Chapter 2 we saw that consonants can differ in voicing. So, for example, [p] is voiceless and [b] is voiced, [s] is voiceless and [z] is voiced, and so on. However, it is fairly easy to see that [p] and [b], for instance, have quite a lot in common. If you say the English words *pat* and *bat* while looking in a mirror you will see that the first thing you do for each word is close your lips. It isn't so easy with [s] and [z], but you may be able to feel that for both these sounds the tip of your tongue gets very close to the roof of your mouth not far behind your upper front teeth. Try saying *Sue* and *zoo*, making the first consonant very long. The topic of this chapter is where in the vocal tract consonants are produced.

Before we look at the details, a word of warning. Speech is really a matter of movement. Try saying the first sentence of this paragraph out loud and concentrate on the movements you are making with your lips, tongue and jaw. You should notice that there are no pauses between sounds. Things are moving all the time. However, it is impossible to capture this continual movement on paper and we need to have some points of reference, some way of categorising the similarities and differences between speech sounds. So our warning is: when we say, for example, that the consonant at the beginning of the English word *thing* is made by the tip of the tongue and the back of the upper front teeth, we may seem to be saying that the consonant is produced by the vocal tract taking up a static position, but this leaves out a lot of the story. How did it get there? How long does it stay there? How does it move away again? Some of these aspects of speech production form the topic for Chapter 6, where we will see that the precise articulation of a sound is influenced by the sounds around it. First, we need to establish the basic terminology and concepts for the classification of speech sounds before we consider these more detailed aspects of the production of speech. This chapter and the next will introduce the basics. We start with the places in the vocal tract where speech sounds can be made.

*This is the sort of advice one receives: 'Press your tonsils against the underside of your larynx. Try, with the convex part of the septum curved upwards so as almost – but not quite – to touch the uvula, try with the tip of your tongue to reach your thyroid. Take a deep breath, and compress your glottis. Now, without moving your lips, say 'Garoo'.' And when you have done it they are still not satisfied.' From* Three Men on the Bummel *by Jerome K. Jerome.*

## A brief tour of the vocal tract

We will now begin a brief guided tour of the vocal tract. It might be helpful if you have a small pocket mirror and a small torch. We will start at the front of the vocal tract and work our way inside. You can use the vocal tract outline in Figure 3.1 to check where we are at any stage.

We begin with the lips. Notice that you can move both your upper and your lower lip. You can also round your lips and protrude them. Try looking in the mirror and saying a long [u] sound as in the English word *boot*. Your lower lip can also quite easily contact your upper front teeth. Try saying the English word *four* while looking in the mirror. Some people can also make the top lip contact the bottom front teeth, but this is a lot trickier and this position is not normally used to produce speech sounds.

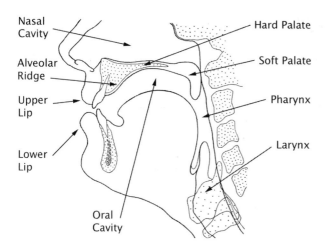

Nasal Cavity

Alveolar Ridge

Upper Lip

Lower Lip

Oral Cavity

Hard Palate

Soft Palate

Pharynx

Larynx

FIGURE 3.1
The vocal tract.

For the next stage of our tour we will be concerned with the roof of the oral cavity. You can get an idea of the shape of this by moving the tip of your tongue slowly back. Start with the tongue tip on the edge of your upper front teeth. As you move it backwards, it will travel along a bony ridge called the alveolar ridge. Then the roof of the mouth domes upwards. The roof is still hard at this point because there is bone under-lying the surface. As you move your tongue tip further back, you may be able to feel that the roof of the mouth becomes soft. Not everyone can curl the tongue far enough back to feel this, so don't try too hard. This area is called the soft palate or velum. That's about as far as we can go with the tongue tip.

For the next bit you really need a mirror and a torch. If you open your mouth as wide as you can and shine the torch into it, you should be able to adjust the angle of your mirror so that you can see to the very back of your oral cavity. In the centre, there is a small fleshy part hanging from the end of the soft palate. This is called the uvula (the name means 'little grape' in Latin).

Beyond the uvula there is a cavity leading down to the larynx and the lungs. This cavity is known as the pharynx.

We dealt with the structure of the larynx in Chapter 2, where we were concerned with its function in producing voice. As we will see, the larynx is also important for the production of consonant sounds. Finally, we must not forget that above the roof of the mouth is a large space – the nasal cavity. There are no moveable parts in this, so it is not possible to perform an articulation here. The nasal cavity is important for speech sound production, however, as we shall see in Chapter 4.

Next we shall turn our attention to the tongue. For the purposes of describing speech sounds we need to recognise five areas of the tongue. These are:

- the tip at the very front end
- the blade, which is the part which lies below the alveolar ridge when the tongue is at rest

- the front, which lies below the hard palate when the tongue is at rest
- the back, which lies below the soft palate when the tongue is at rest
- the root, which faces backwards towards the rear wall of the pharynx.

You can see all of the above marked on the vocal tract outline in Figure 3.2.

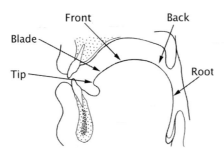

FIGURE 3.2
Areas of the tongue.

*This picture comes from a book published in 1667. The author wanted to prove that the letters of the Hebrew alphabet reflect the tongue shape for the relevant sound. The right-hand symbol in the picture looks like the tongue in the figure. Unfortunately, the sound is [p] and the tongue is not involved in the production of bilabial sounds!*

## Articulation

The term articulation is used to refer to the narrowing or constriction of the vocal tract during the production of a speech sound. Two articulators are involved, a passive articulator, which does not move, and an active articulator, which moves toward the passive articulator. The passive articulator is usually some part of the upper surface of the vocal tract and the active articulator is most often some part of the tongue. For some speech sounds both articulators move, so the distinction between passive and active cannot be maintained.

There are many different kinds of articulation. For example, in producing the sound [p] the vocal tract is completely closed because the two articulators are in firm contact. In a sound like [w], on the other hand, the articulators do not actually touch each other. For all of the descriptions of articulations below, we must remember that the lungs are pushing a stream of air out of the vocal tract and that the articulation interferes with this airstream in some way. If the two articulators are in firm contact, then the airflow will be blocked. If there is a gap between the articulators, then air will escape. This aspect of an articulation is one of the topics for Chapter 4. In this chapter we shall concentrate on where in the vocal tract articulations take place when we are producing consonant sounds.

## Place

The location in the vocal tract where an articulation occurs is called the place of articulation. For most articulations the term used to describe the place of articulation is based on the name of the passive articulator concerned. Here is a list of places of articulation:

*Lips*

Bilabial: both the upper and lower lips are active articulators for this place. Sounds like [p b m] are bilabial. For all of these, the two lips are in contact and the vocal tract is completely closed. For a sound like [ɸ] the lips are close together and air is pushed between them. This sound occurs in Japanese. If you know a Japanese speaker, ask them to pronounce the word *Fuji* and watch their lips closely.

*Teeth + low Lip* Labiodental: the active articulator is the lower lip and the passive articulator is the edge of the upper front teeth. [f v] are labiodental sounds. For these sounds, the lip does not contact the teeth firmly and air can escape between the two articulators. Another labiodental sound which is used sometimes in English is [ɱ]. Here the contact is firm and there is no escape of air. This sound is found for the *m* in words like *comfort* and *triumph*.

*Back teeth + tip tongue* Dental: the active articulator is the tongue tip and the passive articulator is the back or the edge of the upper front teeth. The sounds at the beginning of the words *think* and *though* are dental in our pronunciation. The symbols are [θ] and [ð] respectively. Another example of a dental sound is the *t* sound in *eighth*. The symbol for this is [t̪]. (Not all kinds of English use [θ] and [ð].)

*Al ridge + tongue* Alveolar: the active articulator is the tip or the blade of the tongue and the passive articulator is the alveolar ridge. [t d n l s z] are all alveolar sounds used in English. For the first four of these there is firm contact between the articulators, but for the last two there is a gap through which air can escape.

Postalveolar: there are two sorts of postalveolar sound. Both have the rear part of the alveolar ridge as the passive articulator. One type has the tip of the tongue as the active articulator. An example is the sound at the beginning of the word *red* in most varieties of English. Here the tongue tip is curled back slightly and gets close to, but does not actually touch, the back of the alveolar ridge. The symbol is [ɹ]. This type of sound is sometimes called apical postalveolar. The second type has the tongue blade as the active articulator. The sound at the end of the word *fish* is an example. The symbol is for this is [ʃ]. The tongue blade is raised so that it approaches the back part of the alveolar ridge. This type of sound is sometimes called laminal postalveolar.

*① Al ridge back + tip tongue* *② Al ridge back + blade tongue*

Retroflex: the active articulator is the tongue tip and the passive articulator is the hard palate. The tongue is curled back so that it approaches the roof of the mouth behind the alveolar ridge. This type of sound does not occur in most accents of English, but does occur in many languages of India and in the English of speakers from those areas, as well as many other languages. [ʈ ɖ ɳ] are examples of retroflex sounds. The Tamil (Southern India and Sri Lanka) word [maɳɖe] 'skull' contains two retroflex consonants. Notice that the symbols all have a descending hook to the right.

*hard palate + tongue tip.*

Palatal: the active articulator is the front of the tongue and the passive articulator is the hard palate. An example of a palatal sound regularly used in English is the consonant at the beginning of the word *yes*. The

*Hard palate + front tongue*

symbol for this is [j]. Another example, from French this time, is the consonant at the end of the word *montagne* ('mountain'). The symbol for this is [ɲ]. This sound also occurs in Spanish, for example the second consonant in *mañana* [maɲana] ('tomorrow') and in Italian, for example the third consonant in *lasagna* [lasaɲa].

*Soft palate + back tongue*

Velar: the active articulator is the back of the tongue and the passive articulator is the soft palate. [k], as at the beginning of *cow* and [g] as a the end of *dog* are examples of velar consonants used in English.

*Back of soft palate - velum + back tongue*

Uvular: the active articulator is the back of the tongue and the passive articulator is the very back part of the velum, where the uvula is located. Uvular sounds do not occur in English, but can be found in some varieties of Arabic. They sound like very far back velar sounds. For example, [q] is the uvular equivalent of [k] and [ɢ] is the uvular equivalent of [g].

*Pharynx + root of tongue*

Pharyngeal: the active articulator is the root of the tongue and the passive articulator is the rear wall of the pharynx. Again we do not use this place of articulation for English, but Arabic has pharyngeal sounds. For instance, [ħ] sounds like a very intense and noisy *h* sound.

*Vocal folds ↓ together*

Glottal: the articulators are the vocal folds, both of which are active. For [ʔ], known as glottal stop, the vocal folds are in firm contact, blocking the airflow from the lungs. Glottal stop is well known as a feature of the accent of English spoken in London (and in many other places too). Listen to a Londoner saying *butter* or *water*. It is very likely that the [t] in the middle will be replaced by [ʔ].

Here is a table listing the active and passive articulators for each place of articulation:

| Table 3.1 Summary of place of articulation labels. | | |
|---|---|---|
| Place of articulation | Active articulator | Passive articulator |
| Bilabial | upper and lower lips | *none* |
| Labiodental | lower lip | upper front teeth |
| Dental | tongue tip | upper front teeth |
| Alveolar | tongue tip or blade | alveolar ridge |
| Postalveolar | tongue tip or blade | rear of alveolar ridge |
| Retroflex | tongue tip | hard palate |
| Palatal | tongue front | hard palate |
| Velar | tongue back | soft palate |
| Uvular | tongue back | uvula |
| Pharyngeal | tongue root | rear wall of pharynx |
| Glottal | vocal folds | *none* |

We will now have a look at some examples of vocal tract outlines illustrating different articulations. There are four of these in Figure 3.3. Before reading the rest of this section, have a look at them and see if you can decide what the place of articulation is in each case.

In outline (a), we can see that the lips are open and that the tongue tip is touching the alveolar ridge. Notice also that the rear surface of the soft palate is in contact with the rear wall of the upper part of the pharynx. The airways through the oral and nasal cavities are completely blocked. This is an alveolar articulation of the kind used for [t] or [d].

In outline (b), again the lips are open and the soft palate is in more or less the same position as before. This time, however, the back of the tongue is bunched up and is in contact with the soft palate. This is a velar articulation of the kind used for [k] or [g].

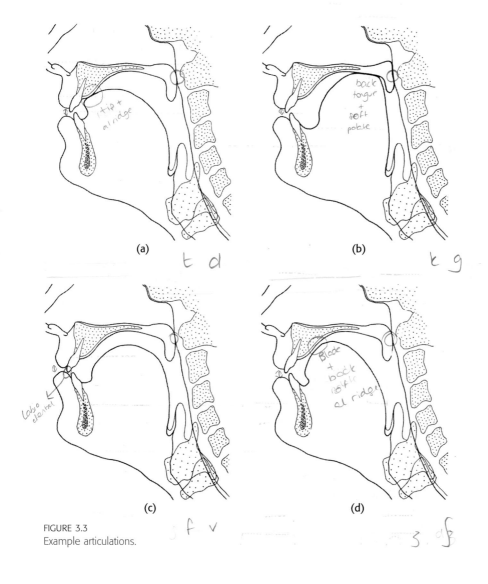

FIGURE 3.3
Example articulations.

In outline (c), the tongue does not seem to be doing anything interesting. The soft palate is in the same position as for the previous two outlines. Notice that the lower lip is very close to the upper front teeth and
that the lips are open. This is a labiodental articulation. [f] and [v] are
produced like this.

Finally, in outline (d) the tongue is bunched up so that the blade is very
close to the rear part of the alveolar ridge, although it does not actually
touch it. The lips are open and the soft palate is as before. This is a (laminal)
postalveolar articulation, as for [ʃ] or [ʒ].

## Complex articulations

So far, the articulations we have met have been simple, in the sense that
they have only one constriction in the vocal tract and involve only one pair
of articulators. However, some speech sounds are more complex than this.
As an illustration, let's look at what happens in a sound like [w], as at the
beginning of the English word *well*. If you look in a mirror while saying this
sound, you should see that your lips are rounded and protruded. So there
is a bilabial articulation going on. What you won't be able to see and what
is very difficult to feel, is that at the same time the back of the tongue is
raised towards the soft palate. It doesn't actually touch the soft palate, but
it gets reasonably close. So there is a velar articulation going on. Sounds
like this are called double articulations and [w] is known as a labial-velar.
Other labial-velar articulations include simultaneous [k] and [p], which
occurs in a number of West African languages, such as Yoruba (Nigeria).

Another example of a double articulation is the first sound in the French
word *huit* (= 'eight'). The symbol for this is [ɥ]. Again there is lip rounding
and protrusion, but this time it is the front of the tongue which is raised
towards the hard palate. This sound has a labial-palatal articulation.

Double articulations all have in common the fact that the two constrictions are of the same type. So in [w], for example, both constrictions
are fairly wide. In the West African simultaneous [kp] sound, both articulations are complete closure. But there is a second type of complex
articulation where this is not the case. Let's take the first sound in the
English word *twin* as an example of this. Again, if you look in a mirror
while saying this sound, you should see that your lips are rounded –
again we have a bilabial articulation. At the same time, your tongue tip
or blade forms a complete closure by contacting the alveolar ridge. But
this is not a double articulation, because one of the constrictions (the
alveolar one in this case) is narrower than the other one. This is a case of
a primary articulation, accompanied by a secondary articulation and
the sound at the beginning of *twin* is called a labialised alveolar and is
symbolised [tʷ].

## Homorganic sounds

Sounds that have the same active and passive articulators are said to be
homorganic. For example [t d n l s z] are homorganic since they all have the

tip of the tongue as the active articulator and the alveolar ridge as the passive articulator. But [t] and [t̪] are not homorganic, even though they both use the tongue tip, because the passive articulator is different (alveolar ridge in one case, hard palate in the other). Similarly [n] and [ɲ] are not homorganic either, because although both are formed on the hard palate the active articulator is different (tongue tip versus tongue front). Languages quite often make use of homorganic sequences of consonants. For example the English words *hand, cold, best, jump, think* all end with homorganic sequences.

## Instrumental techniques

You may be wondering how we know what articulations are used for speech sounds. Most of what goes on in speech is very difficult to see and takes place very rapidly. For a long time phoneticians had to rely mostly on their own intuitions and feelings. Some more objective techniques were available, but these tended to be very laborious and time-consuming. More recently, especially since computer technology became widely available, it has been possible to record the movements and positions of a speaker's articulators with a fair degree of accuracy.

### Electropalatography

One technique for doing this is electropalatography. This involves the speaker wearing a specially made false palate in which a number of electrodes are embedded. The electrodes are sensitive to the contact by the speaker's tongue. The outputs of the electrodes are continuously monitored by computer while the speaker is talking and the resulting analysis is displayed as a series of figures known as palatograms.

A number of different electropalatography schemes are in use, but one common one involves a false palate with 62 electrodes. These are arranged in groups to cover the alveolar ridge and hard palate. The conventional way of displaying the output is in a grid of cells like that in Figure 3.4 A. The alveolar area is at the top and the border with the soft palate area at the bottom. If a cell is empty, then no tongue contact was recorded there. Contact is shown as a filled cell, as in B–E in the figure.

The examples shown represent static positions of the articulators, but usually electropalatography is used to record the changing state of tongue contact during the production of a sequence of speech sounds.

Before we look at the palatograms in more detail, we must remember that this technique can give us useful information about *some*, but *not all*, speech sounds. It cannot tell us about the articulation of sounds that do not involve some part of the tongue as an articulator – bilabial or glottal sounds for instance – or sounds where the articulation does not take place in the oral cavity, such as pharyngeal sounds.

If we look at palatogram B in the figure, we can see that all the blackened cells are at the back of the oral cavity. We can also see that the vocal tract is completely blocked at this point, and presumably further back too, beyond the area covered by the palate. This is what one might

*The earliest known artificial palate for speech research was used in America in 1880. It was made of a sheet of thin black rubber painted with a mixture of chalk dust and alcohol. Tongue contact wiped away the coating and then the palate was removed and photographed.*

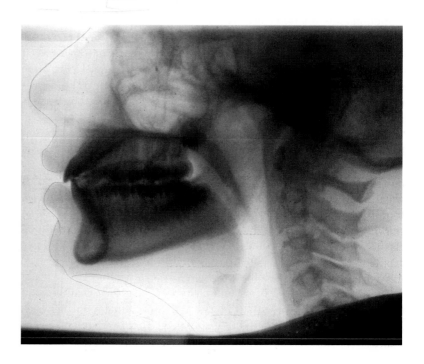

velar

A

velar

B

velar

C

dental

D

alveolar

E

FIGURE 3.4
Example palatograms.

FIGURE 3.5
An x-ray photograph of
the vocal tract at rest.

expect to see for a velar sound such as [k]. In palatogram C the same kind of blockage is seen, but seems to be even further back.

Palatograms D and E are reasonably similar. They both show active contacts at the front of the oral cavity. D is a dental sound and E an alveolar. Again there is a complete blockage in both. Notice also that there are active contacts all the way down both sides of the oral cavity. We will deal with this aspect of articulation in greater detail in Chapter 4. For now we will just point out that if the rims of the tongue do not contact the sides of the roof of the mouth, then air can escape that way. The [d] sound at the beginning of *dog* would produce a palatogram like D, whereas the [l] sound at the beginning of *log* would produce a palatogram without the active contacts at one or both sides.

## X-rays

Another way of investigating the articulation of speech sounds is to use x-ray photography or even x-ray cinematography. An x-ray photograph showing the vocal tract appears as Figure 3.5.

The subject is an adolescent female, and her vocal tract is in a relaxed breathing position. Her teeth are lightly together, her lips parted slightly, and the velum down to permit breathing through the nose. The outline of the alveolar ridge and hard palate can be seen clearly, as well as soft tissues such as the tongue outline.

Figure 3.6 shows an x-ray photograph of an adult male subject in the position for a close central vowel in Russian. The superimposed numbers on the picture show (1) the centre of the tongue and (2) the nasal cavity just above the hard palate, and (3) the end of the velum, which is in a raised position, closed against the rear wall of the pharynx. You can see

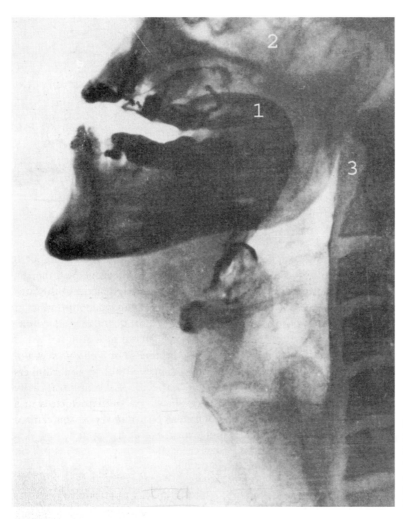

FIGURE 3.6
X-ray view of the vocal
tract in the position for a
vowel (from G. Fant,
*Acoustic Theory of Speech
Production,* The Hague:
Mouton, 1960).

that the tongue is domed upwards towards the rear of hard palate, but
that it is not very close to it. In fact the speaker is producing a vowel sound
rather like the [i] in *beat*, though somewhat further back on the palate.
This articulation is quite similar to that for the consonant sound [j] at the
beginning of *yacht*.

It is often quite difficult to see the details of articulation on x-rays and
one needs quite a lot of experience to make sense of the pictures. It is
usual to present the results of x-ray investigations by showing tracings
from the original photographs. There are a couple of examples of these,
showing consonant articulations, in Figure 3.7. They are from the same
classic study as Figure 3.6 and show the same adult male subject. You
should be able to work out what places of articulation are involved. Trace
A is a dental sound. In fact it is [t̪]. Trace B is a velar [k].

## Magnetic resonance imaging

Apart from the difficulty of interpretation of x-ray pictures, the main
drawback of the technique is the radiation risk to the speaker. A much

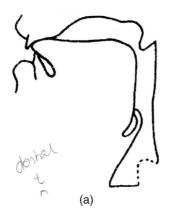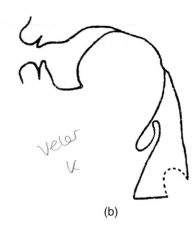

dental
t
n

(a)

velar
k

(b)

FIGURE 3.7
Tracings from X-ray images.

more recent and, as far is known, completely safe technique is magnetic resonance imaging (MRI). Put very simply, this involves placing the subject in an imager which applies a very strong magnetic field to the body. The field causes the vast majority of protons of hydrogen atoms to line up in the direction of the subject's head or feet. Most of the magnetic fields created by these hydrogen protons are cancelled out by a proton lined up in the opposite direction. However, a few protons (2 or 3 out of every million) do not have their magnetic fields cancelled out in this way. The machine applies a radio frequency pulse specific to hydrogen and this causes the uncancelled protons to resonate at a particular frequency. When the pulse is turned off, these protons return to their natural alignment within the magnetic field and give off excess energy as a result. The imager detects this energy and turns the signal into an image. As you can see from the two MRI scans in Figure 3.8, the resulting images are very much clearer and easier to interpret.

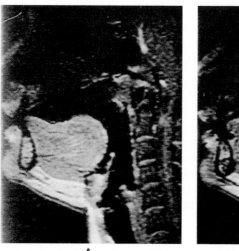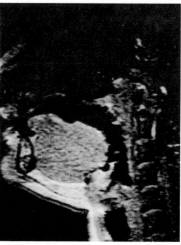

FIGURE 3.8
MRI scans (from
S. Narayanan, A. Alwan
and K. Haker, 'An
Articulatory Study of
Fricative Consonants
using MRI,' *JASA* (1995),
1325–64).

A

B

alveolar s

post alveolar ʃ

Unfortunately, MRI is a much slower technique, at least at present, and it is not easy to get moving pictures of the vocal tract using MRI. Scan A shows an alveolar [s]. Notice that the tip of the tongue is quite far forward and the blade is not very close to the alveolar ridge. Scan B is a postalveolar [ʃ]. This time the tip is a little further back and it is the blade of the tongue which is articulating with the rear part of the alveolar ridge.

## Places of articulation used in languages of the world

In this section we will take a brief look at how place of articulation is used in the world's languages. This is quite a big subject and a complete account at this stage would involve using many terms we have not yet introduced. So to keep things simple we will confine our account to oral stops – sounds like [p] or [tʃ] where there is a complete closure in the vocal tract. There is more detail on this sound-type in Chapter 4.

Quite a few languages use only three places of articulation for stops and the most popular places are bilabial, alveolar (or alternatively dental) and velar. Examples are: Finnish and Maori. English uses four places of articulation for stops: bilabial, alveolar, postalveolar and velar. Other four-place stop systems may use palatal stops instead of postalveolar. Examples are Malay and Gugu-Yulanji (Australia) with bilabial, dental, palatal and velar. Hindi is an example of a language with stops at five places (bilabial, dental, postalveolar, retroflex and velar).

Only a few of the world's languages use as many as 6 places of articulation for stops. These are almost all Australian languages like Aranda, which has bilabial, dental, alveolar, postalveolar, retroflex and velar stops and Diyari with bilabial, dental, alveolar, retroflex, palatal and velar stops.

Places of articulation can be ranked according to their occurrence in stop systems of the world's languages. The ranking looks like this:

Alveolar/dental > velar > bilabial >> palatal > uvular > retroflex > others

Where > means 'occurs more frequently than' and >> means 'much more frequently than'. In fact, the first three places in the ranking are almost equal in frequency of occurrence.

## Chapter summary

In this chapter we have introduced the concept of place of articulation. The main areas of articulation for consonants are the lips, upper front teeth, alveolar ridge, hard palate, soft palate, uvula, the pharynx and the larynx. The tongue can be viewed as consisting of five main areas: the tip, blade, front, back and root. An articulation is a narrowing or constriction of the vocal tract caused by an active articulator approaching a passive articulator, or by two active articulators approaching one another. Articulations may be simple and consist of only one constriction, or they may be complex and consist of two equal constrictions (a double articulation) or of a primary and a secondary articulation.

The chapter includes a brief overview of instrumental techniques for investigating place of articulation: electropalatography, x-ray photography and magnetic resonance imaging and concludes with a look at how places of articulation for oral stop consonants are used by the world's languages.

## Exercises

### Exercise 3.1

In each of the groups of sounds below there is one that is not produced at the same place of articulation as the others. Try to identify this odd one out. You will probably need to look at the IPA chart on page 3 to help you.

(a) [t d s ʃ l]     (b) [ɸ p f b m]     (c) [k ɢ g ŋ x]

*alveolar · postal* — *bilabial · dental ✓*

### Exercise 3.2

Below are some English words. Each has a suggested change associated with it. What English words could result if you perform the change in each case?

Example: *cap*:       change any velar consonant into any bilabial consonant.

Answer:          *pap bap map*

(a) *fight*:        change any labiodental consonant into any velar consonant    *kite gite*

(b) *take*:         change any alveolar consonant into any postalveolar consonant    *shoke joke rake*

(c) *bathe*:        change any dental consonant into any alveolar consonant

*based bane bate    bade ban bazed*
*bate*

### Exercise 3.3

For which of the following English words is the place of articulation the same for all of the consonant sounds in the word? (Hint: watch out for silent letters!)

(a) kind    (b) sent    (c) palm    (d) align    (e) lazy

*all alv    all bilabial    all alv    all alv*

### Exercise 3.4

For each of the English words listed below we have provided two pronunciations. Those in the Adult column are what you might expect from an adult speaker, though they may not be the same as your pronunciation. In the Child column are pronunciations which could be produced by a young child.

| Word | Adult | Child |
|------|-------|-------|
| thumb | [θʌm] *dental/bilabial* | [vʌm] *labiodental/bilabial* |
| push | [pʊʃ] *bilabial/post alv* | [bʊç] *bilabial* |
| talk | [tɔːk] *alveolar/velar* | [dɔːt] *alveolar/alveolar* |
| other | [ʌðə] *dental* | [ʌvə] *labiodental* |
| bag | [bæg] *bilabial/velar* | [bæt] *bilabial/alveolar* |
| measure | [meʒə] *bilabial/post alv* | [mejə] *bilabial* |
| thing | [θɪŋ] *dental/velar* | [vɪn] *labiodental/alveolar* |
| both | [bəʊθ] *bilabial/dental* | [bəʊf] *bilabial/labiodental* |
| good | [gʊd] *velar/alveolar* | [dʊt] *alveolar/alveolar* |
| shoe | [ʃuː] *post alveolar* | [juː] |

(a) List all the places of articulation for consonants used by the adult speaker for these words.

(b) List the corresponding places of articulation used by the child.

(c) Sometimes the child uses a voiceless sound in place of the adult's voiced sound. Try to work out when this happens.

(d) Conversely, the child also sometimes uses a voiced sound where the adult uses a voiceless one. When?

## Exercise 3.5
Below there are some unlabelled vocal tract outlines. Try to work out what the place of articulation is in each case.

## Exercise 3.6
The vocal tract diagrams below have had the outline of the tongue removed. Photocopy or trace the outlines and then try to fill in the tongue outline for the articulations indicated. In each case draw the relevant part of the tongue in contact with the passive articulator.

## Exercise 3.7
On page 3 we mentioned that an articulation involving the upper lip and the lower front teeth is possible, but that it is not normally used for the production of speech sounds. Can you think of any other possible articulations that we have not mentioned?

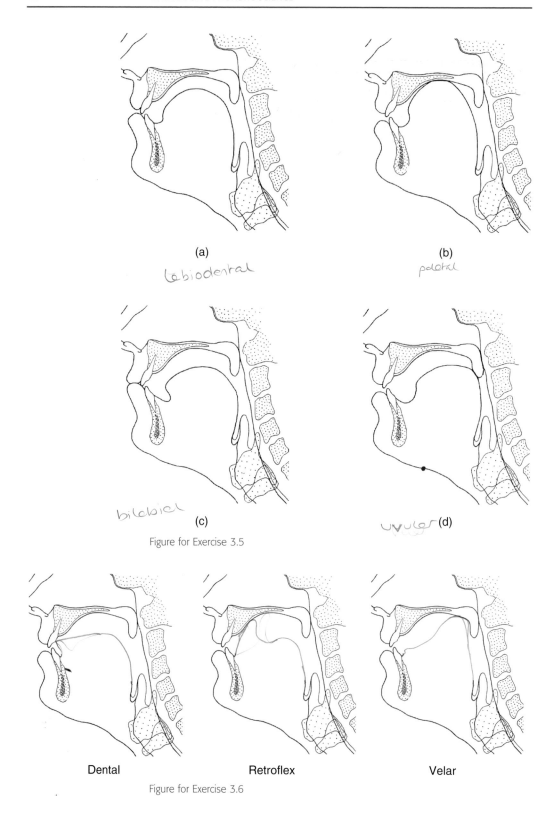

(a)

labiodental

(b)

palatal

bilabial

(c)

Figure for Exercise 3.5

uvular (d)

Dental

Retroflex

Velar

Figure for Exercise 3.6

**Further reading**

An excellent account of place of articulation with many examples from languages around the world can be found in chapter 2 of Peter Ladefoged and Ian Maddieson, *The sounds of the world's languages*, Oxford: Blackwell, 1996. Another very detailed account you might like to look at is chapter 8 of J. C. Catford, *Fundamental problems in phonetics*, Edinburgh: Edinburgh University Press, 1977. There is a survey of the sound systems of over 300 languages in Ian Maddieson, *Patterns of sounds*, Cambridge: Cambridge University Press,1984.

# 4 Manner of articulation

## CHAPTER OUTLINE

In this chapter you will learn: how the articulators may constrict the airstream in different ways for the production of consonant sounds; how sounds may be classified according to manner of articulation; how sounds may be classed as obstruent or sonorant; how manners of articulation are used in the world's languages.

**KEY TERMS**

*Affricate*

*Approximant*

*Degree of stricture*

*Flap*

*Fricative*

*Lateral*

*Manner of articulation*

*Median*

*Nasal*

*Obstruent*

*Plosive*

*Sonorant*

*Stop*

*Tap*

*Trill*

## Introduction

We have now seen that consonant sounds may differ in voicing and in place of articulation. The final basic distinction between consonants is known as manner of articulation and that is the subject of this chapter. A manner of articulation label, such as 'plosive' or 'fricative', refers to the way in which the airstream used for a speech sound is modified by the primary and secondary articulators. Is the airstream completely blocked? Can the air escape through the nasal cavity? Does the air pressure inside the vocal tract rise? These are the sorts of questions we will be investigating below.

Once we have learnt to apply manner labels correctly we shall be in a position to give a three-term label to a consonant, specifying its Voice, Place, Manner, usually abbreviated VPM. VPM labels are useful shorthand for identifying most consonants of the world's languages, although they are not the complete story by any means.

'The breath, circulating in the lungs, is forced upwards and impinges on the head, reaches the speech organs and gives rise to speech sounds. These are classified in five ways – by tone, by length, by place of articulation, by process of articulation and by secondary features. Thus the phoneticians have spoken: take careful heed.' This quote is taken from an Indian work thought to have been written sometime between 500 and 150 BC.

## Airflow, pressure, turbulence

In order to describe some aspects of the way air flows through the vocal tract during the production of a consonant, it is useful to simplify things a little and view the tract as a straight tube rather like a bicycle pump. In the case of the vocal tract air is usually set in motion by the lungs, but in our simpler model we'll use a piston that fits tightly into the tube as in Figure 4.1.

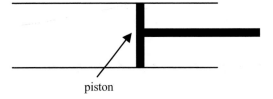

piston

FIGURE 4.1
Simple tube and piston model of the vocal tract.

If we were to push the piston to the left, the air in the tube would be displaced and pushed out of the tube. As the tube is open and without any obstruction, the air would flow out without making any appreciable noise. The air particles would all move parallel to one another in what is known as laminar flow.

FIGURE 4.2
A blocked tube.

In Figure 4.2 we have blocked the end of the tube. Now when we try to push the piston, the air particles to the left of it cannot escape and they become more and more crowded together as the space between the piston and the blockage gets smaller. The air pressure inside the tube rises. Eventually of course the piston will become very difficult to move and if we continue with some mechanical means to push the piston, the tube will burst apart. If we were suddenly to remove the blockage, air would burst out of the tube with a loud pop.

*Plosive?*

FIGURE 4.3
A constricted tube.

In Figure 4.3 we have introduced a narrowing into the tube. The air can escape, but not as freely as in the unconstricted tube. The air pressure between the piston and the constriction will rise and the air flowing through the constriction will become turbulent, that is, the air particles will no longer flow in parallel paths but will collide into one another and make a noise.

*Fricative?*

Try this simple experiment. First purse your lips as though you were going to whistle. Now breathe out as gently as you can. You should not hear any noise at all. The air is flowing through the constriction too slowly to become turbulent. Now, with exactly the same lip position, imagine you are trying to blow out all the candles on a birthday cake. This time you should hear quite a strong hissing noise caused by the turbulent airstream. From this we can see that the airflow must be rapid enough and the constriction narrow enough if there is to be any turbulence and any noise.

## Degree of stricture: obstruent and sonorant

We will now leave our simple tube model behind and examine what happens in the vocal tract itself. First, it is fairly obvious that the two articulators for a consonant sound may take up a variety of different positions with respect to one another. For our purposes it is adequate to recognise three distinct positions or degrees of stricture.

1. Closure: the articulators are in firm contact    → *Obstruent*

*Obstruent* ← 2. Narrowing: the articulators are close together but not touching
*Sonorant* ← 3. Approximation: there is a reasonably wide gap between the articulators

Degrees 1 and 2 cause a rise in air pressure inside the vocal tract (unless the air can escape by another route) and sounds produced like this are called obstruents. Degree 3 does not cause a pressure rise and sounds produced in this way are called sonorants.

This obstruent/sonorant distinction is a very important one both phonetically and phonologically and we will come across it again and again. Just to give a very simple example: the rise in air pressure during an obstruent makes it difficult to maintain vocal fold vibration for a long period. Obstruent sounds quite often lose their voicing in unfavourable environments – they become devoiced. Sonorants tend not to be affected in the same way. We will look at devoicing in more detail in a later chapter.

## Stops: oral and nasal, plosive and affricate

The narrowest sort of constriction one can produce in the vocal tract is of course a complete blockage of the airstream. For this the two articulators are in firm contact for an appreciable amount of time. Try saying a long [n] sound. You should be able to feel that the tip and/or blade of your tongue is pressing firmly against your alveolar ridge and the sides of your tongue are pressed against your upper side teeth and gums. The same is true for a sound like [t] or [d], but these sounds usually do not last long enough for us to get a clear impression of what the articulators are doing. Such sounds, where the vocal tract is completely blocked for a time are called stops, and they can be produced at many places of articulation, bilabial, labiodental, dental, alveolar and so on. The diagrams in Figure 4.4 show the position of the articulators for the two alveolar stops: (a) [t] (or [d]) and (b) [n].

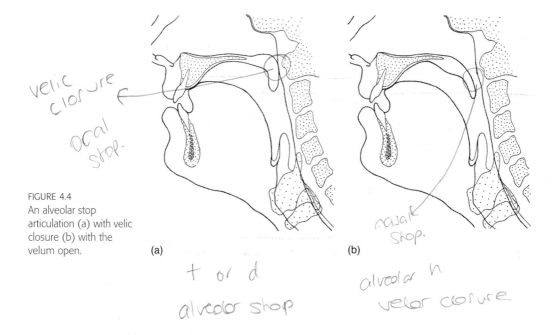

*velic closure* ←
*ocal stop.*

FIGURE 4.4
An alveolar stop articulation (a) with velic closure (b) with the velum open.

(a)            (b)

*nasal stop.*

*t or d*
*alveolar stop*

*alveolar n*
*velar closure*

| Table 4.1. Places of articulation and symbols for nasals. | | | | | | |
|---|---|---|---|---|---|---|
| Bilabial | labiodental | alveolar | palatal | retroflex | velar | uvular |
| m | ɱ | n | ɲ | ɳ | ŋ | ɴ |

Although diagrams (a) and (b) in Figure 4.4 are both of alveolar stops, there is of course a difference between them. Look at the position of the soft palate. In diagram (a) it is raised and is in contact with the rear wall of the pharynx. This is called a velic closure or a velopharyngeal closure. This closure prevents air escaping through the nasal cavity. Stops made with a velic closure are called oral stops. Oral stops belong to the obstruent class, as there is an appreciable rise in air pressure in the vocal tract. In diagram (b) there is no velic closure and air can escape freely through the nasal cavity, although it is prevented from escaping through the oral cavity by the alveolar stop articulation. Stop articulations without a velic closure and with nasal airflow are called nasal stops or, more simply, nasals. Nasals are sonorant sounds, because the airstream produced by the lungs can escape via the nasal cavity and there is no rise in air pressure inside the vocal tract.

Try this experiment. Say the word *ado* and repeat it over and over. After the first two or three repetitions pinch your nostrils firmly and keep repeating the word. Then release your nostrils again and repeat the word some more. You should have had no difficulty saying the word with your nostrils blocked and the sound of the word should have been exactly the same when your nostrils were blocked and when they were free. Now follow the same procedure with the word *unknown*. No problem with it when your nostrils were free, was there? But very probably you will have found that this word is impossible to say normally when pinching your nostrils. The air cannot flow out of your nose as it should for the nasal stops in this word and so the vocal tract quickly fills with air. The air pressure rises, the vocal folds stop vibrating and you get to feel a little uncomfortable.

Nasals in most languages of the world are voiced and can occur at many places of articulation. Table 4.1 shows the voiced nasals from the IPA consonant chart. However, voiceless nasals are perfectly possible and a small number of languages do use them. In order to symbolise a voiceless nasal, the voiced nasal symbol is used, but it is accompanied (above or below) by a small circle. So a voiceless bilabial nasal is represented as [m̥]. This sound is used in Burmese, for example in a word like [m̥a] meaning *notice*. It may also be used in English at the beginning of the interjection usually written *hmm!* (= [m̥m]).

We now turn to look at oral stops in more detail. Let us take the voiceless bilabial oral stop [p] as an example. For this, the lips are completely closed, blocking the airstream through the oral cavity. There is also a velic closure, so the air cannot escape via the nose. This configuration of the articulators is maintained for a short time, around 120 ms. During this phase the air pressure inside the vocal tract rises rapidly. When the bilabial closure is released, the compressed air bursts out of the vocal tract with a small explosive noise. Such sounds are called plosives. They can be viewed as consisting of three phases (1) The approach phase, when the articulators are forming the oral closure , (2) the hold or compression phase, when the air pressure rises and (3) the release or plosion phase when the articulators part and the compressed air is released. This is sometimes represented as in Figure 4.5.

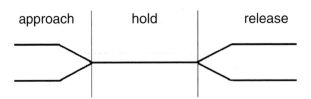

FIGURE 4.5
Phases of plosive
production.

Plosives are one kind of oral stop. Another kind involves the same approach of the articulators, the same kind of hold phase, but a much slower parting of the articulators during the release phase. During the slower release, the air rushing between the two articulators makes a hissing sound. Such consonants are known as affricates. English has two affricate consonants: a voiceless postalveolar affricate [tʃ], as at the beginning and end of church, and its voiced counterpart [dʒ], as the beginning and end of judge. There are many other possibilities, however. German, for instance, has a voiceless alveolar affricate [ts], as at the beginning of the word Ziel [tsiːl], meaning 'aim, goal'.

The phases of production of an affricate can be represented as in Figure 4.6.

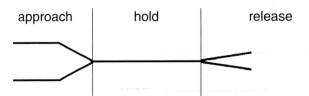

FIGURE 4.6
Phases of affricate
production.

## Fricatives: median and lateral

Fricatives are consonant sounds that are produced with a very narrow opening between the active and passive articulators. As we saw above on pp. 105–6, when air is forced through a narrow gap, the flow becomes turbulent. It is this turbulence that creates the acoustic energy for fricative sounds.

Fricatives may be produced at many different places of articulation and may have all kinds of modifications. The first distinction between fricative types we will discuss is that of median vs lateral fricatives.

As a good example of a median fricative, let us take [s] – voiceless alveolar median fricative. If you produce an [s] sound and then, without changing the position of the articulators, breathe in forcefully, you should feel cold air on the middle of your alveolar ridge. You should not feel anything at the sides of your oral cavity. This is because the articulators are arranged so that air flows only through a narrow channel in the centre of the cavity. This is why an articulation of this type is termed median. The sides of the tongue are in firm contact with the upper side teeth and gums, preventing airflow passing that way. A palatogram for [s] might be as in Figure 4.7.

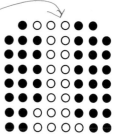

FIGURE 4.7
Palatogram of [s].

A lateral fricative has the articulators in a position where airflow is blocked on the midline of the oral cavity, but there is a narrow space between the sides of the tongue and the upper side teeth and gums, so the airstream can escape laterally. In order to get an impression of what this sounds like, first produce a long [l] sound. Then, keeping the articulators in the same position, turn off the vocal fold vibration and blow hard. The sound involved is [ɬ], a voiceless alveolar lateral fricative. The tongue tip contacts the alveolar ridge firmly, preventing air escape. One or both sides of the tongue are close to, but not actually touching the upper side teeth. The pattern of palate contact would be something like that in Figure 4.8.

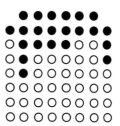

FIGURE 4.8
Palatogram of [ɬ].

Table 4.2 shows the symbols for the median fricative consonants from the IPA chart.

The consonants above come in voiceless (left) and voiced (right) pairs. The voiced fricatives have two simultaneous sound sources: the friction noise of the turbulent air produced at the place of articulation and the sound made by the vibrating vocal folds. We can see the difference between the voiceless and voiced fricative sounds in the two speech pressure waveforms in Figure 4.9. The sounds involved are [s] and [z].

The two lateral fricatives on the IPA chart are both alveolar – the voiceless one we have already met and the voiced one is symbolised [ɮ]. An example of the voiceless alveolar lateral fricative in use is the Welsh word *cyllell* ('knife') [kəɬeɬ]. An example of the voiced alveolar lateral fricative is the first sound in the Zulu word [ɮaːla] ('play').

## Approximants: median and lateral

Approximants, like fricatives, have no complete closure in the vocal tract and also come in two main varieties, median and lateral. Unlike fricatives, however, approximants are sonorants and do not have a stricture narrow enough to cause a rise in air pressure and turbulence, at least at the rates of airflow found in normal speech.

| Table 4.2. Median fricative consonants of the IPA. | | | |
|---|---|---|---|
| bilabial | ɸ β | palatal | ç ʝ |
| labiodental | f v | velar | x ɣ |
| dental | θ ð | uvular | χ ʁ |
| alveolar | s z | pharyngeal | ħ ʕ |
| postalveolar | ʃ ʒ | glottal | h ɦ |
| retroflex | ʂ ʐ | | |

(a)

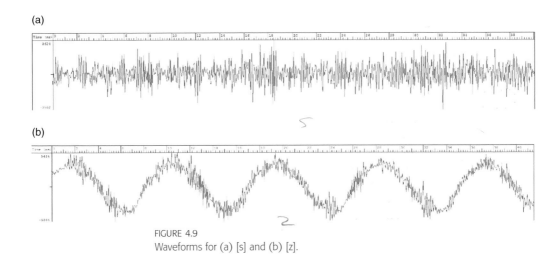

(b)

FIGURE 4.9
Waveforms for (a) [s] and (b) [z].

Lateral approximants have a complete closure between the articulators on the midline of the vocal tract, but one or both sides of the tongue are not very close to the upper side teeth and gums. When air escapes over the tongue rims and out of the oral cavity, it does so without becoming turbulent. Essentially, the position of the articulators is the same as that for the lateral fricative depicted in Figure 4.8.

Lateral approximants may occur at a number of places of articulation and are usually voiced. Here are some examples:

voiced alveolar    [l]
voiced retroflex   [ɭ]
voiced palatal     [ʎ]

Lateral approximants are often simply called laterals. We are familiar with the voiced alveolar lateral in English. An example of a retroflex lateral in use is the word [aɭtə] meaning 'day' in Aranda, an Australian language. The palatal lateral occurs in Italian, for instance. The word *aglio* ('garlic') [aʎʎo] contains a long version of this sound.

Median approximants have no complete closure anywhere on the midline of the vocal tract. Air can pass freely over the centre of the tongue and exit without turbulence. You may come across two older terms for median approximants: glide and frictionless continuant.

Some median approximants are very like vowels. They are produced in the same area of the oral cavity as vowel sounds. They are sometimes called semivowels. Examples are [w] voiced labial-velar median approximant, as at the beginning of *well* and [j] voiced palatal median approximant, as at the beginning of *yes*.

Other median approximants are not so vowel-like. These include sounds such as [ɹ], which is a voiced postalveolar median approximant (shown in Figure 4.10), [ʋ] a voiced labiodental median approximant, [ɰ] a voiced velar median approximant, and [ʁ] a voiced uvular median approximant. Essentially, at any place where a fricative is possible you can also

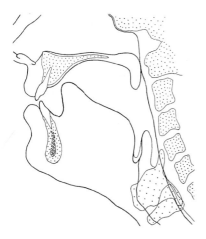

FIGURE 4.10
The articulation of [ɹ].

make a median approximant. 'Median approximant' is usually abbreviated to just approximant.

## Taps, flaps and trills

The final aspect of manner of articulation that we shall examine has to do with the timing rather than the nature of the events involved. We will start by looking at the difference between a plosive and a tap and take as our examples the two consonants [d], voiced alveolar plosive, and [ɾ], voiced alveolar tap. The latter sound is quite familiar to speakers of English and is used in many varieties of US English for the consonant in the middle of words like *atom*. The sequence of events for both of these sounds is essentially the same, but everything happens much more quickly for the tap. Crucially, the amount of time the two articulators stay in contact is very short for the tap (around 20 ms), much shorter than for the plosive. This means that there is no time for an appreciable increase in air pressure in the case of the tap and therefore this sound type belongs to the sonorant class. The timing of a plosive and a tap is compared in the schematic diagrams in Figure 4.11.

The lower diagram in Figure 4.11 shows what happens during the production of a trill (sometimes called a roll). This sound type consists of a series of very rapid tap-like closures between the active and the passive articulator. The mechanism by which this is achieved is very similar to the way in which the vocal folds vibrate. The rate of vibration is, however, much slower because the structures involved have a much greater mass. Figure 4.12 shows the speech pressure waveform for [r] voiced alveolar trill pronounced between two vowels. The effects of the individual closures of the tongue tip show up as very brief troughs in the waveform. There are five such troughs and the trill lasts approximately 370 ms, so the rate of vibration of the tongue tip is about 23 Hz.

Spanish is an example of a language that uses both an alveolar tap and an alveolar trill, for instance *pero* [peɾo] means 'but' and *perro* [pero]

> *r sounds and laterals taken together are sometimes called 'liquids'. Contrary to what you might think, this doesn't describe their sound or the way they are produced. It results from an inappropriate translation of the Greek word hygros which means 'variable' or 'inconstant' when applied to the changeable behaviour of these sounds in the detailed analysis of Ancient Greek versification.*

tap                      trill

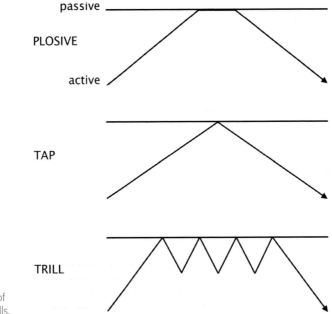

passive

PLOSIVE

active

TAP

TRILL

FIGURE 4.11
Timing comparison of
plosives, taps and trills.

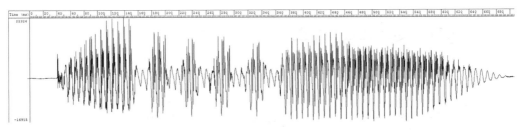

FIGURE 4.12
Speech pressure waveform for [r].

means 'dog'. Trills at other places of articulation are found in the world's languages. A voiced uvular trill [ʀ] is reasonably common. It sounds a little like a gargle. The uvula itself trills against the back of the tongue. A much rarer trill, found in only one or two languages, is [ʙ] voiced bilabial trill. This is the sort of noise that is often represented as *Brrr* and is used to indicate that you are feeling cold.

The final manner of articulation we shall discuss is the flap. This is very similar to a tap in that there is a single extremely brief closure between the articulators. It is difficult to diagram the sequence of events for a flap in the same manner as that used in Figure 4.11. The diagram would be identical to that for a tap. However, there is an important difference between the two articulations. For the tap, the active articulator moves rapidly towards the passive articulator and rapidly away again, as we have seen. For a flap, the active articulator strikes the passive articulator as it passes by. The only flap symbol on the IPA chart is [ɽ] voiced

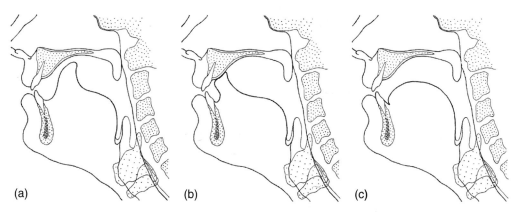

FIGURE 4.13
The sequence of events in a retroflex flap.

retroflex flap. Figure 4.13 shows the articulation of this sound. First, the tongue tip curls back behind the alveolar ridge, and then flaps forwards and downwards, striking the rear part of the alveolar ridge as it does so. An example of a voiced retroflex flap in use in a word is [saɽi], which means 'burnt' in Punjabi.

## Voice, place, manner labels

The manner of articulation labels that we have introduced are: plosive, affricate, nasal, fricative (lateral and median), approximant (lateral and median), tap, flap and trill. These labels complete a very frequently used method of specifying consonants known as Voice, Place, Manner (VPM) labels. To give a simple example, let us consider the sound [s]. First we need to determine if the vocal folds are vibrating or not during the production of the sound. As they are not, we label the sound voiceless. Next we need to consider which articulators are concerned in the production of the sound. For [s], the tongue tip or blade articulates with the alveolar ridge, so the place of articulation is alveolar. Finally we need to specify exactly what kind of articulation is formed for this sound. The active articulator, the tongue tip/blade, approaches close to the alveolar ridge and touches at the sides, but does not form a complete closure. Furthermore, the airstream produced by the lungs is made turbulent when it passes through the narrow constriction. The manner of articulation is therefore fricative. Putting all this together, [s] has the VPM label 'voiceless alveolar fricative'.

*S = V - Alveolar fricative.*

## Use of manners of articulation in the world's languages

In Chapter 3 we had a brief look at the use of place of articulation in the world's languages by concentrating on oral stops, that is, plosives and affricates. Here we will look at how the world's languages use manner of articulation.

All known languages have plosives, but that is not true for the other manners we have described above. The vast majority of languages have median fricatives, and typically languages have a fricative system that is as large or larger than the oral stop system of the language. English is typical in this respect with oral stops at four places: bilabial, alveolar, postalveolar and velar, and fricatives also at four places: labiodental, dental, alveolar and postalveolar. Welsh is a language where the fricatives outnumber the oral stops. The language has labiodental, dental, alveolar median, alveolar lateral, postalveolar and velar fricatives, but only bilabial, alveolar and velar plosives, and no affricates. A few languages lack fricatives completely. Most of these are Australian languages.

Most languages have nasals, usually at two or three places of articulation. Again English is typical with bilabial, alveolar and velar nasals. French is an example of a language with nasals at four places: bilabial, dental, palatal and velar. Languages without nasals are very rare. An example is Rotokas, spoken on the Pacific island of Bougainville, which has the smallest number of consonants of any known language. It has only six, three voiceless plosives, one voiced plosive, one voiced fricative and a tap.

Median approximants of the 'semivowel' type occur in most languages, though it is quite rare to find a language with more than two or three of them. The commonest are [w] and [j] and English is again typical in having just those two. French is an example of a language with three, adding [ɥ] to those found in English. Nama (Namibia and South Africa) is an example of a language lacking this sound type, although it has a fairly large consonant system.

Most languages have some sort of r sound. This may be a median approximant like the postalveolar [ɹ] in English or the uvular median approximant [ʁ] found in some varieties of French. Other languages use a tap or trill and some, as we have already seen for Spanish, use both. An example of a language with none of these sound types is Hawaiian.

Finally we will look at lateral approximants. Again, most languages have this type of sound, usually at the alveolar or dental place of articulation. If a language has two lateral approximants, they are likely to be dental/alveolar plus palatal, as in Italian and some varieties of Spanish, or plus retroflex as in Norwegian and Malayalam (Southern India). A velar lateral approximant, made by forming a closure between the centre of the back of the tongue with one or both sides of the tongue lowered, was at one time thought not to occur in any language, but relatively recently a number of languages using this sound have been reported, mostly from New Guinea. In response to this, the IPA adopted the symbol [ʟ] to represent the sound. A few languages, including Japanese and Maori (New Zealand), have no lateral approximants.

## Chapter summary

In this chapter we continued our survey of articulation and have looked at some of the details of how the articulators constrict the airstream in various ways. We have seen that manner of articulation is not a simple feature, but comprises a number of different and largely independent dimensions. First the articulators may constrict the airstream to different degrees: either blocking it completely, or constricting it enough to cause air turbulence, or leaving a considerable gap for the air to pass without turbulence. Secondly, the soft palate may be raised, preventing nasal airflow, or lowered, allowing such flow. Thirdly, a closure may be made on the midline of the oral cavity with or without a lateral opening allowing air to escape over the rims of the tongue. The rate of release of a closure is the fourth factor distinguishing speech sounds. A further aspect of manner of articulation concerns the speed of the whole gesture for the articulation; for taps, the articulators are in contact for only a very brief period.

A very important distinction among manners of articulation has also been introduced: the sonorant-obstruent distinction will be referred to again and again in the coming chapters. Plosives, fricatives and affricates, the obstruents, are articulated with a constriction that causes air pressure to rise inside the vocal tract. Other consonants, together with all vowels, are sonorants and are made with a configuration of the articulators which allows the pressure inside the vocal tract to be approximately equal to the pressure outside.

## Exercises

**Exercise 4.1**
In the sentence *Susie saw five of the shows, she says* all of the consonant sounds have the same manner of articulation. Which? See if you can think of some similar English sentences.

**Exercise 4.2**
Which of the following English words contain no sonorant consonants?

*soon, clasp, talked, beauty, sky, cows, thorough, quick, captive, chalk*

**Exercise 4.3**
In Welsh words often undergo a process called initial mutation. Each word has a number of mutated forms, which are used in different contexts. Here are some examples of two of the mutations.

| Basic Form | Mutation I | Mutation II | Meaning |
|---|---|---|---|
| [pen] | [ben] | [fen] | *head* |
| [tad] | [dad] | [θad] | *father* |
| [karjad] | [garjad] | [xarjad] | *love* |

| [basged] | [vasged] | not applicable | *basket* |
| [damwain] | [ðamwain] | not applicable | *accident* |
| [garð] | [arð] | not applicable | *garden* |

(a) What have the initial consonants of the Basic Forms in the first block of words got in common? *plosives* V⁻

(b) What change does Mutation I cause to these consonants? V⁻ → V⁺

(c) What change occurs with Mutation II? *plosives → affricatives/*

(d) Consider the same three questions for the second block of words.

### Exercise 4.4

Look at the following speech pressure waveforms and try to decide the manner of articulation of the consonant sound between the two vertical lines.

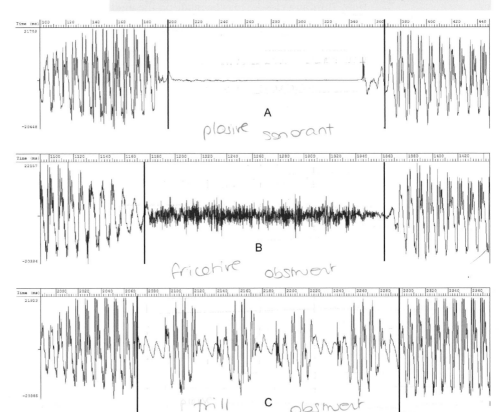

A — *plosive  sonorant*

B — *fricative  obstruent*

C — *trill  obstruent*

### Exercise 4.5

D, a young English child, exhibits the following features in her speech.

(a) if a word contains an alveolar lateral approximant, then any other approximants in the same word will also be alveolar lateral

(b) all alveolar and postalveolar fricatives are produced as alveolar plosives of the appropriate voicing.

How would D pronounce the following words?

*lorry, shoes, yellow, woolly, silly, puzzle, swallow, umbrella*

loli, tuːd, lelaʊ, wʊli, tili, pʊdl, twɒlaʊ, ɪmblelə

### Exercise 4.6

Some speakers have difficulty with alveolar fricatives and produce alveolar lateral fricatives instead. Explain the articulatory difference between the two sound types. How would an English speaker with this problem pronounce the following words?

*sixty, amusing, results, cousins, sensible*

### Exercise 4.7

A language X has three kinds of *r* sound : a voiced alveolar tap, a voiced alveolar trill and a voiced uvular fricative. The tap is used between vowels, the trill at the beginning of a word or immediately following a consonant and the fricative at the end of a word or immediately before a consonant. Here are some words in X in their spelling form, where all three *r* sounds are represented by the letter *r*. How would these words be pronounced?

*dramar    taran    garsat    rakra    aramard*

### Exercise 4.8

In a language Y, all words of the form $C_1C_2VC_3C_4$, conform to the following restrictions

(a) $C_1$ must be an obstruent
(b) $C_2$ must be a sonorant
(c) If $C_3$ is a sonorant, $C_4$ must be an obstruent
(d) If $C_3$ is a nasal, $C_4$ must be a homorganic plosive
(e) If $C_3$ is an obstruent, it must be a plosive and $C_4$ must be a fricative

Say whether each of the words below is a possible word of Y and if not, why not.

[slamb]   [flant]    [gwalm]  [spats]   [twalf]
[kjaŋg]   [blams]   [ljalʃ]    [zjalt]    [kramd]
[dlaps]   [snand]

### Exercise 4.9

A language Z has a voiceless plosive, a voiced plosive and a voiced nasal at each of the following places of articulation: bilabial, alveolar, palatal, velar and uvular.

(a) Show the stop system of this language as a table with place of articulation horizontally and stop type vertically.
(b) Z also has voiceless and voiced fricatives at all of the same places of articulation. Add the fricative system to your table.
(c) Here are some words of Z. Based on these, say whether the statements (i–v) about Z are true or false. If you think a statement is false, quote a word from the data set which proves this.

Data set

[quχaɴ]   [cuçi]    [saza]    [ɟuju]    [guɣi]
[dasa]    [zaβa]   [gaʁuɲ]  [baɸam]  [tazas]
[nusaɸ]   [ɲiɣax]  [ceʁaç]  [ɢajuχ]  [sasan]

Statements:

(i) All consonants in a word are homorganic.
(ii) Stops may not occur between vowels.
(iii) The only obstruent consonants permitted word-finally are voiceless fricatives.

(iv) Front consonants (articulated on the alveolar ridge or further forward) may not occur in the same word as back consonants.

(v) Voiced fricatives may not occur word-initially.

## Exercise 4.10

The IPA consonant chart has some shaded cells representing combinations of place and manner that are 'judged impossible'. One of these combinations is 'pharyngeal nasal'. Explain why this sound type is impossible.

## Exercise 4.11

Here is a list of all the consonant sounds used in one variety of English. Each is accompanied by a keyword in orthography. Complete the table below. See how far you can get with this without looking anything up.

| | Keyword | Voice | Place | Manner |
|---|---|---|---|---|
| p | pie | voiceless | bilabial | plosive |
| t | tie | v − | alveolar | plosive |
| k | key | v − | velar | plosive |
| b | buy | v + | bilabial | plosive |
| d | die | v + | alveolar | plosive |
| g | guy | v + | velar | plosive |
| m | my | voiced | bilabial | nasal |
| n | no | v + | alveolar | nasal |
| ŋ | sing | v + | velar | nasal |
| f | fee | v − | labiodental | fricative |
| v | van | v + | labiodental | fricative |
| θ | thigh | v − | dental | fricative |
| ð | though | v + | dental | fricative |
| s | so | v − | alveolar | fricative |
| z | zoo | v + | alveolar | fricative |
| ʃ | she | v − | post alveolar | fricative |
| ʒ | measure | v + | post alveolar | fricative |
| tʃ | chip | v − | post alveolar | affricate |
| dʒ | jam | v + | post alveolar | affricate |
| w | wet | v + | labial-velar | median approximant |
| ɹ | red | v + | post alveolar | median approximant |
| l | let | v + | alveolar | median approximant |
| j | yes | v + | palatal | median approximant |
| h | hat | v − | glottal | fricative |

In Chapter 1 we used [r] for the English sound. Now that we have learned about several r types, we are using the more specific symbol [ɹ].

## Exercise 4.12

Hyponasal and hypernasal:

(a) In hyponasal speech, when the nasal cavity is blocked as it is when you have a heavy cold, nasal stops are replaced by the corresponding oral stops. Give hyponasal versions of:

singing [sɪŋɪŋ]    onion [ʌnjən]    murmur [mɜːmə]

(b) In hypernasal speech, where a velic closure is impossible because the velum is paralysed or has a hole or split in it, air flows through the nasal cavity the whole time. Oral stops become nasal stops and all sonorant sounds have accompanying nasal airflow (they are nasalised). These are hypernasal versions of English words. Try and work out what they are. The marks over the vowels indicate nasalisation.

[n̥ĩːŋãĩm]   [m̥ẽĩm̥ə̃]   [mẽĩɲ̥ĩŋ]

## Further reading

For a good, but fairly technical account of the aerodynamics of speech production, see chapter 3 of J. C. Catford, *Fundamental problems in phonetics*, Edinburgh: Edinburgh University Press, 1977. For this chapter, as for chapter 3, an excellent source of examples from many languages is Peter Ladefoged and Ian Maddieson, *The sounds of the world's languages*, Oxford: Blackwell, 1966.

4.9.

|  | BILABIAL | ALVEOLAR | PALATAL | VELAR | UVULAR |
|---|---|---|---|---|---|
| VOICELESS PLOSIVE | p | t | c | k | q |
| VOICED PLOSIVE | b | d | ɟ | g | ɢ |
| VOICED NASAL | m | n | ɲ | ŋ | ɴ |

# 5 Vowels

## CHAPTER OUTLINE

In this chapter you will learn about the basic concepts necessary for the description and classification of vowels, including: acoustic resonance, excitation spectrum and filtering by resonances, vowel spectra and formants, articulation of vowels, the relationship between vowel articulation and acoustic properties, the differences between monophthongs and diphthongs, oral and nasalised vowels, long and short vowels. The chapter also deals with: vowel systems in the world's languages, vowel instability and variability.

## Introduction

In the vast majority of languages, nearly all syllables include a vowel as their central portion or nucleus. Vowels are sonorant sounds and are produced with a relatively open vocal tract. Vowels are nearly always voiced sounds. This chapter will introduce the basic concepts necessary for the description and classification of vowels, and will begin with a brief description of the main acoustic properties of vowels, including the concepts resonance, spectrum and formant. Also covered are the vowel quadrilateral, cardinal vowels, vowel symbols and diacritics and the distinctions between long and short vowels and between monophthongs and diphthongs. The chapter ends with a brief survey of the types of vowel system found in languages around the world.

## Spectrum and resonance

As water is poured into a glass, you can hear a note that gradually rises in apparent pitch as the liquid approaches the top. Why is this? The volume of air above the surface of the liquid in the glass has a resonant frequency. This is the frequency at which it naturally vibrates. As the glass fills, this volume gets smaller and the resonant frequency rises. We hear this rise in frequency as a rise in pitch. Any enclosed body of air has a resonant frequency which depends on both its volume and on the size of the opening to the outside. Try this experiment for yourself: tap on the bottom of an empty mug and then half cover the top with your other hand and tap again. You should be able to hear a difference in the notes that are produced with the two different sizes of opening.

The mouth cavity is an enclosed volume of air. Its size and the size of the opening at the lips can be altered, changing the resonant frequency of the mouth. The equivalent of tapping on the bottom of the mug is the vibration of the vocal folds in the larynx. No cavity will produce a sound unless it is supplied with acoustic energy from an external source. This energy constitutes the input or excitation. The excitation produced by the larynx has many component frequencies. Only some of these will be picked out and reinforced by the resonant characteristics of the vocal tract.

You may be unfamiliar with the notion of a sound in which several different components are present at the same time. Think of this example. If you pluck a single string on a guitar, a single note is produced. However, if you pluck two or more strings at the same time, the notes produced are added together. Moreover, you can pluck one string forcefully and others more gently, so that the loudness of the individual notes varies. We don't generally hear the individual components of complex sounds, but the components can be separated if such a sound is analysed on a computer. The usual way of presenting such an analysis is called a spectrum.

Figure 5.1 shows a typical spectrum of larynx excitation. The horizontal axis shows frequency and the vertical axis shows amplitude. Each of the

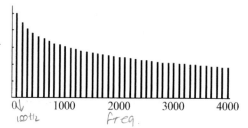

FIGURE 5.1
Schematic representation
of larynx spectrum.

vertical bars represents one of the components of the larynx tone before
it has been filtered by the vocal tract.

Notice that the components are at equal steps along the frequency
scale. So the lowest frequency component is at 100 Hz, then next at 200
Hz, the third at 300 Hz and so on. Notice also that the lowest frequency
component has the highest amplitude and that the spectrum shows an
overall downwards slope. These two features, the equal spacing of components and the sloping spectrum, are important properties of the acoustic
energy produced by the human larynx. This energy is the input to the
vocal tract for vowels and other voiced speech sounds. The spacing of the
components may be wider or narrower and depends on the rate of vibration of the vocal folds. This affects our perception of the pitch of the
sounds we hear. The constant downward slope of the larynx spectrum is
modified by the vocal tract above the larynx to shape the spectrum in various ways and to produce the sounds we recognise as human speech.

There are many familiar examples in everyday life where resonance is
used to pick components from a complex spectrum and suppress unwanted
components. A radio or TV antenna brings in a vast spectrum of signals
and the tuner, which has a variable resonant frequency, works as a filter
to select the wanted signal. A filter need not pick out only one frequency
but can simultaneously alter the shape of the spectrum in a number of
different regions. The graphic equaliser on a sound system is an example
of this. You can boost certain frequencies and reduce others.

The vocal tract is a complex filter rather like a graphic equaliser. The
various resonances of the vocal tract filter out the energy in some frequency regions of the input spectrum and leave other frequency regions
unaffected. This produces an output spectrum which has peaks and
troughs of energy. The peaks are called formants. Because of the sloping
shape of the input spectrum the lowest frequency formant has the highest amplitude and the amplitude of the higher frequency formants gradually decreases as can be seen in the examples in Figure 5.2. The most
important property of a formant is its frequency and, as we shall see, the
formant frequencies of the output spectrum are crucial in distinguishing
vowels from one another. In principle there are many formants extending
up through the frequency range. In practice only the lowest two or three
are of importance for speech and they are labelled F1 (lowest), F2 and F3.

Figure 5.2 (a) shows the spectrum of the vowel sound [i] as in keep;
Figure 5.2 (b) shows the spectrum of the vowel [ɑ] as in calm.

For the vowel [i], F1 is low in frequency. In the figure shown, the peak is
at 250 Hz. Then there is a wide trough in the spectrum, indicating that in

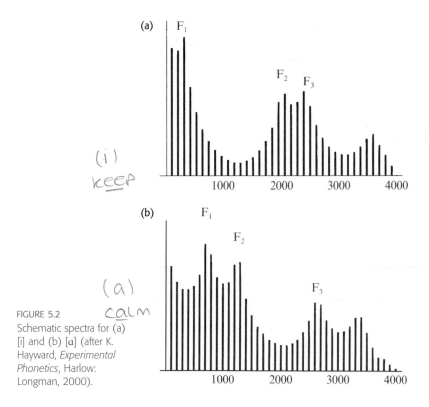

(i)

keep

(a)

calm

FIGURE 5.2
Schematic spectra for (a)
[i] and (b) [ɑ] (after K.
Hayward, *Experimental
Phonetics*, Harlow:
Longman, 2000).

this frequency region the energy of the excitation has not been reinforced by the resonances of the vocal tract. F2 is quite high in frequency – the peak is around 2 kHz and F3 400 Hz higher.

Compare this with the spectrum for the vowel [ɑ]. The peak for F1 is around 800 Hz. For F2, it is at 1100 Hz and F3 is at 2.6 kHz.

The precise formant frequencies for any vowel are determined by the overall size of the speaker's vocal tract – lower for males than females and higher for children than for adults. This is because smaller cavities have higher resonant frequencies than larger cavities. However, any speaker's [i] vowel will have a low F1 and a high F2 and any speaker's [ɑ] vowel will have F1 high and fairly close to F2. It is the pattern of formant frequencies and their relationship to one another that is important rather than the absolute values.

The location of formant peaks in the frequency range does not occur arbitrarily, but is determined in an orderly way by the shape of the mouth when forming a vowel.

## Vowel articulation

Vowels are articulated by raising some part of the tongue body (that is the front or the back of the tongue, not the tip or blade, see Figure 3.2) towards the roof of the oral cavity. The shape of the opening formed by the lips is also important.

## Vowel height

The height of a vowel refers to the relationship between the highest point of the tongue and the roof of the oral cavity. If the tongue is raised so as to be close to the roof, then a close or high vowel such as [i] is produced. If the tongue is only slightly raised, so that there is a wide gap between its highest point and the roof of the oral cavity, then an open or low vowel, such as [ɑ], results. Vowels produced with tongue positions between high and low are sometimes called mid, such as the vowel in the English word *dress*. Vowels between close and mid are called half-close (or high mid, or close mid – the terms are interchangeable); vowels between open and mid are half-open (or low mid, or open mid).

   There is a direct connection between the height of a vowel and the frequency of F1. High vowels have a low F1 and low vowels have a high F1.

## Vowel location

The location of a vowel refers to the part of the tongue which is highest in the production of the vowel. Front vowels, such as [i], are produced by raising the front of the tongue towards the hard palate. Back vowels, such

*[handwritten margin notes:]*
*High – close = [i]*
*Low – open = [a]*

*High = low F1*
*Low = high F1*

*front vowels – [i] raise front tongue to hard palate*

(a)

(b)

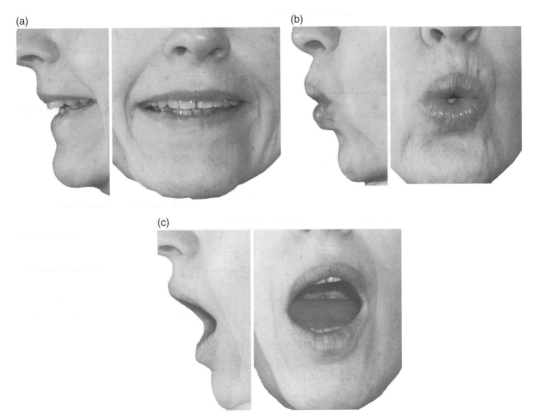

(c)

FIGURE 5.3
Lip position: (a) unrounded (spread) in a close vowel, [i]; (b) rounded in [u]; (c) unrounded (neutrally open) vowel [ɑ].

*[handwritten: Back vowel [u]*
*raise back tongue*
*to soft palate]*

as [u], are produced by raising the back of the tongue towards the soft palate. Central vowels, such as the vowel in the Southern British pronunciation of the English word *first*, are produced by raising the centre part of the tongue towards the junction of the hard and soft palates. A short mid-central vowel, termed *schwa* and symbolised [ə] is in fact the most frequent vowel in English speech. It is heard, for example, in the first syllable of *about*, the middle syllable of *photograph*, and at the end of *soda*.

*[handwritten: Centre vowel [ɜ:]*
*raise centre tongue*
*in between hard +*
*soft palate [ə]]*

Again this aspect of the articulation of a vowel is reflected in the spectrum. The frequency of F2 is high for front vowels and low for back vowels.

*[handwritten: freq F2 - high - front vowels*
*- low - back vowels]*

## Lip position

The position of the lips is the third factor which controls vowel quality. For most purposes a two-way classification of rounded vs unrounded is adequate. Figure 5.3 illustrates lip position.

Rounding the lips makes the mouth opening smaller and this, as we saw with the experiment with the mug, has an effect on the resonant frequencies. Rounding the lips lowers all formant frequencies, the most important effect being on F2. In Figure 5.4 there are two spectra. (a) is for the high front unrounded vowel [i] and (b) is for the high front rounded vowel [y], as in the French word *lune* [lyn] 'moon'.

The two spectra are quite similar, except for the position of F2.

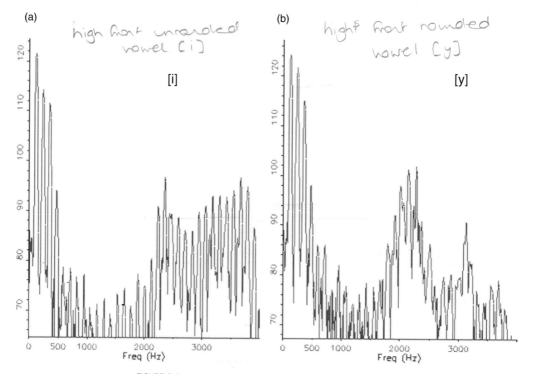

*[handwritten above figure (a): high front unrounded vowel [i]]*

*[handwritten above figure (b): high front rounded vowel [y]]*

FIGURE 5.4
Spectra of real utterances of [i] and [y]. In the rounded vowel F2 is about 375 Hz lower. F3 is also lowered, so that it is only about 250 Hz above F2.

# Long and short vowels

Compared with many consonants, vowels are loud and long. But vowels can be sustained for shorter or longer times, and many languages make use of a distinction between long and short vowels. A long vowel in such languages can be symbolised with a following length mark, thus [ɑ] is a short unrounded back open vowel and [ɑː] is its long counterpart. Maori (New Zealand) is a language that has long and short versions of each of its five vowel qualities, and some examples are given below:

| Long | Meaning | Short | Meaning |
|------|---------|-------|---------|
| [kiː] | to say | [ki] | at |
| [hokoː] | to buy | [hoko] | 20 times |
| [tahaː] | calabash | [taha] | side |

Most accents of English have vowel-length distinctions, but usually the long and short members of a pair are also distinguished by clear quality differences as well, for example the two vowels of the words *beat* and *bit*.

# Oral and nasalised vowels

A further distinction that is utilised by many languages is between oral vowels and nasalised vowels. An oral vowel is produced with the soft palate in a raised position, so that there is no airflow through the nasal cavity. A nasalised vowel on the other hand is produced with a lowered soft palate, allowing airflow through both oral and nasal cavities simultaneously. The resonances of the nasal cavity are added to those of the rest of the vocal tract and the vowel has a characteristic nasal quality. Nasalisation is indicated by a diacritic [˜] over the relevant vowel symbol. Table 5.1 shows pairs of French words that are distinguished by the absence or presence of nasalisation of the vowel.

| Table 5.1 Oral and nasalised vowels in French | | | | | |
|------|------|--------|------|------|-----------|
| *fait* | [fɛ] | 'fact' | *fin* | [fɛ̃] | 'end' |
| *faux* | [fo] | 'false' | *font* | [fõ] | '(they) do' |

# Monophthong vs diphthong

In some languages (English is one) the quality of a vowel can change within a single syllable. Such vowel-glides are known as **diphthongs**. Examples of English words containing diphthongs are *tie*, *toy*, *town*. Vowels whose quality remains relatively constant are known as monophthongs.

If the vowel is changing then the formant frequencies will be changing. This can be seen in a display known as a spectrogram. Figure 5.5 shows the

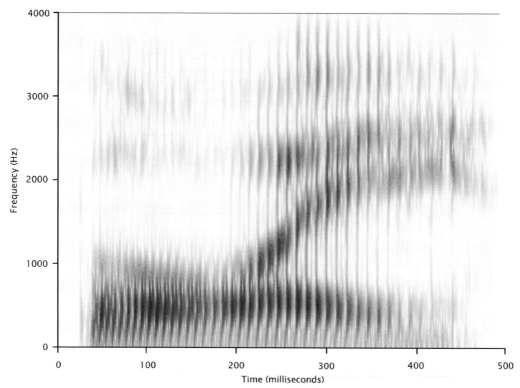

FIGURE 5.5
Spectrogram of an utterance of the word 'boy'.

spectrogram for the English word *boy*, which contains the diphthong [ɔɪ]. The horizontal axis shows time. The vertical axis shows frequency. The darkness of the trace shows the amount of energy present at a given time and frequency.

The formants show up as dark bands running horizontally. At the very beginning the formants show brief movements (transitions) connected with the production of the consonant sound. For the vowel, F1 starts high and then descends. This is because the diphthong is moving from a low quality to a high one. F2 starts low and rises, because the tongue is moving from a back position to a front one and at the same time the lips are changing from a rounded posture to an unrounded one.

## The vowel quadrilateral

The area in the oral cavity within which the highest point of the tongue must occur for the articulation of a vowel is roughly like the quadrilateral shown in Figure 5.6. The quality of a particular vowel can be indicated by placing a dot on the diagram. The meaning of this dot is something like: the vowel x sounds as if it is produced with the highest part of the tongue in this position. The dot in the quadrilateral in the figure indicates the usual quality of the vowel [ɪ] in the English word *sit*. The quality indicated

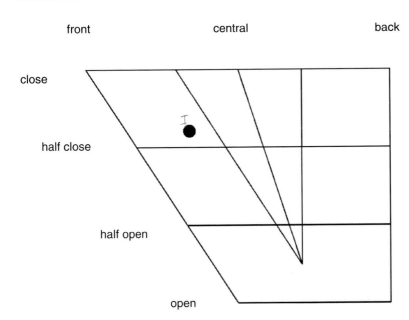

front                    central                    back

FIGURE 5.6
The vowel quadrilateral,
and position of English [ɪ].

is around half close, front but not as front as possible. Lip position is not indicated on the diagram. It used to be thought that the position of the tongue within the mouth, together with lip position, fully determined the quality of a vowel. It is now known that the configuration of the entire vocal tract needs to be taken into account. The vowel quadrilateral has been retained as a useful tool, but it should be thought of as representing an auditory space, rather than an accurate articulatory one.

## Cardinal vowels

As an alternative to specifying the location, height and lip-posture for a vowel, the vowel quality can be related to one of a set of language-independent, reference vowel qualities known as the cardinal vowels. These can be thought of as landmarks in the auditory space provided by the vowel quadrilateral. There are in fact two subsets of cardinal vowels: the primary set [i e ɛ a ɑ ɔ o u], numbered 1–8, 1–5 being unrounded and 6–8 rounded and the secondary set [y ø œ Œ ɒ ʌ ɤ ɯ], numbered 9–16. The secondary cardinal vowels are related to the primary ones by reversing the lip-posture, so for example vowel 1 is close, front, unrounded and vowel 9 is close, front, rounded and vowel 8 is close, back, rounded, so vowel 16 is close, back, unrounded. The cardinal vowels are auditorily agreed qualities and must be learnt from a teacher who knows how they sound, or from a recording. However, vowels 1 and 5 can be given an articulatory specification. Number 1 is produced with the frontest, closest position of the tongue that does not produce audible friction and number 5 is produced with the backest, openest possible tongue position, again without audible friction. Figure 5.7 shows the primary and secondary cardinal vowels on the vowel quadrilateral.

*[handwritten annotations in right margin:]*

— = unrounded
O = rounded

1. i – unrounded
2. e – unrounded
3. ɛ – unrounded
4. a – unrounded
5. ɑ – unrounded
6. ɔ – rounded
7. o – rounded
8. u – rounded

1. i = —      9. y = O
2. e = —      10. ø = O
3. ɛ = —      11. œ = O
4. a = —      12. Œ = O
5. ɑ = —      13. ɒ = O
6. ɔ = O      14. ʌ = —
7. o = O      15. ɤ = —
8. u = O      16. ɯ = —

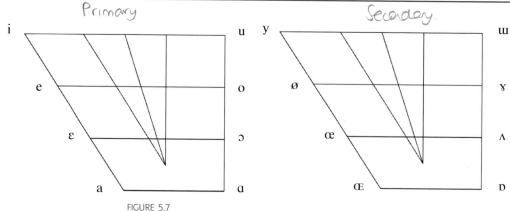

FIGURE 5.7

The primary cardinal vowels (left) and the secondary cardinal vowels (right).

Although some vowels in certain languages may be very like cardinal vowels (for instance the [i] in French is very like cardinal vowel number 1), the cardinal vowels are independent of particular languages and must be learnt.

## Vowel diacritics

A reasonably accurate specification of vowel quality can be symbolised by using diacritics attached to an appropriate cardinal vowel symbol. The three diacritics used are shown attached to cardinal vowel number 2: [ë] meaning centralised, that is closer to the centre of the quadrilateral, but still not in the central triangle, [e̞] meaning closer and [e̞] meaning more open. There are a number of vowel symbols in common use that do not represent cardinal qualities, but that have fairly well-defined positions on the quadrilateral. These are shown in Table 5.2.

*The cardinal vowel system was invented and developed by Daniel Jones (1881–1967) who was Professor of Phonetics at University College London from 1921–1947. The system was first used in print in the first edition of Jones's English Pronouncing Dictionary in 1917.*

| Table 5.2 Commonly used vowel symbols and their cardinal vowel equivalents | | |
|---|---|---|
| ɪ | = | ë |
| æ | = | ɛ̞ |
| ʊ | = | ö |

Most of the phonetic symbols conventionally used to represent the vowels of a particular language are also used as cardinal vowel symbols, but this does not of course mean that the vowels of that language have exactly cardinal qualities. For example the vowel in Southern British *cup* is generally represented [ʌ] for instance in a pronouncing dictionary or textbook on English pronunciation. This symbol represents an open-mid back unrounded cardinal vowel, but the English vowel in question is actually a fairly open central unrounded vowel. In the same accent, the vowel of *dress* is usually represented [e], but is noticeably lower than the cardinal quality represented by this symbol. For certain applications, it is obviously more convenient to be able to use a simple vowel symbol, without having to resort to diacritics.

## Vowel systems

The vowel systems of the world's languages differ widely in terms of size and also in terms of the phonetic features used to differentiate vowels. We have already seen that languages may make use of length distinctions and that some languages use both oral and nasalised vowels. In this section we will confine ourselves to languages that have only monopththongs and that use only the basic features of height, location and lip position.

Figure 5.8 shows an estimate of the number of languages with systems of a particular size. The information used to compile this figure was taken from a database of 317 phonological systems known as UPSID (UCLA Phonological Segment Inventory Database).

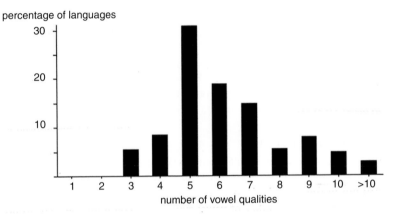

FIGURE 5.8
Size of vowel system in UPSID languages.

The simplest system contains only three vowels – [i a u]. Many languages of Australia, such as Aranda and Nunggubuyu, have a vowel system of this type, but it is also found in other parts of the world.

The most frequently occurring vowel system has five vowels [i e/ɛ a o/ɔ u]. Some five-vowel system languages use close-mid vowels and some use open-mid vowels. Table 5.3 lists some languages with this type of system. As we can see, there are five-vowel languages in all parts of the world.

Taking the five-vowel system as a starting point, there are a number of different ways in which languages may increase the number of vowel qualities in the system. Some languages use both close-mid and open-mid vowels, giving a seven-vowel system [i e ɛ a ɔ o u]. Efik (West Africa) is a language with this system. Another way to augment a vowel system is to add central or centralised vowels. Catalan, for instance, has a seven-vowel system plus [ə]. Kpelle (West Africa) has a system containing [i e a o u] plus the two centralised vowels [ɪ ʊ].

All the systems we have mentioned so far have had front unrounded vowels and back rounded ones. While this is the commonest type of system, there are many languages that add front rounded vowels. French, with the oral vowel system [i y e ø ɛ œ a ɔ o u], is one example. However there are no known languages that use front rounded vowels and that do

| Table 5.3 Some five-vowel languages | |
|---|---|
| Language | Region |
| Batak | Indonesia |
| Greek | Greece, Cyprus |
| Japanese | Japan |
| Kewa | New Guinea |
| Maidu | California |
| Maori | New Zealand |
| Maung | Australia |
| Spanish | Spain, South and Central America |
| Yulu | Sudan |
| Zulu | South Africa |

not use front unrounded ones. Back unrounded vowels also occur in quite a number of languages. Modern Standard Chinese has an unrounded close mid vowel [ɤ], as well as a rounded back vowel [o] at this height.

## Vowel dispersion

We can view the vowel quadrilateral as a perceptual space in which vowels are located. The vast majority of vowel systems conform to the so-called Vowel Dispersion Principle. This is that vowels tend to be evenly distributed in the perceptual space and or at least that they are widely distributed within the limitations of a particular system. This means, for instance, that a three-vowel system containing [i e u] is very unlikely. Some known systems appear not to conform to the above principle and these are known as defective vowel systems. A defective system is one where either (a) there is no open vowel and/or (b) for mid and high regions there is at least one vowel that is not matched by a vowel on the opposite side of the space. The [i e u] system qualifies as defective on both counts, but a system containing [e o a] only would not count as defective. Approximately 14 per cent of UPSID's languages have vowel systems that count as defective. Missing vowels in defective systems are almost always [e], [o] or [u], the last being the most frequently missing. Another way of looking at this is to set up a hierarchy:

$$i / a > e / o > u,$$

where > means is 'more likely to occur in a language than'.

## Vowel instability and variability

Try this simple experiment. Think of a short English sentence and transcribe it, but replace every vowel symbol with [ɜː]. If you were to do this with the sentence *Mary had a little lamb*, the transcription would be [mɜːrɜː hɜːd ɜː lɜːtl lɜːm]. Now practise saying this sentence until you are sure you have it right and see if your friends can understand the sentence when you say it to them. You will very probably find that most of them can. If you do a similar thing with the consonants, replacing them all with [d] say, but keeping the correct vowel qualities, the sentence will be unintelligible.

It seems then that, at least in some languages, vowels carry less information than consonants. It is perhaps because of this that vowels tend to be more variable and unstable than consonants. One consequence is that vowels change over time more rapidly than consonants do. If we look at the system of sounds used in two forms of the same language separated in time by a few hundred years, it is a good bet that there will have been more changes in the vowel system than in the consonant system.

We will illustrate the way a vowel system can change by looking briefly at what is known as the Great Vowel Shift in English. This took place in the fifteenth century and affected the long vowels of Middle English (c. 1100–1450, the language Geoffrey Chaucer spoke) and was complete by the time of Shakespeare, who spoke Early Modern English (c. 1450–1600). Table 5.4 shows the changes that took place.

| Table 5.4 Effects of the Great Vowel Shift in English | | |
|---|---|---|
| Middle English | Early Modern English | Present-day English |
| [iː] | [ei] | [ai] |
| [eː] | [iː] | [iː] |
| [ɛː] | [eː] | [iː] |
| [aː] | [ɛː] | [ei] |
| [ɔː] | [oː] | [əʊ] |
| [oː] | [uː] | [uː] |
| [uː] | [oʊ] | [aʊ] |

So, for example, *house* was [huːs] for Chaucer, [hoʊs] for Shakespeare, and is [haʊs] today and *moon* in Chaucer's day was pronounced [moːn], but was [muːn] by Shakespeare's time and still is.

Vowel changes such as this do not necessarily affect language as a whole in the same way. They may take place in some geographical areas but not in others. This brings us to the second aspect of vowel variability. Two accents of the same language are likely to differ much more in the vowels and diphthongs they use than in their consonant systems. For instance, Southern British English is usually analysed as having eight diphthongs [eɪ aɪ ɔɪ aʊ əʊ ɪə eə ʊə], whereas one form of Jamaican English as only two [aɪ ɔʊ]. So the two varieties agree in having a diphthong in a word such as *time*, but in a word like *day*, Jamaican English has a long monophthong [eː] where Southern British has a diphthong [eɪ].

Here is a reconstruction in Elizabethan pronunciation of the beginning of a famous speech from Shakespeare. Can you read it?

'frɛndz,
'roːmənz,
'kʏntrimɛn,
'lɛnd miː juːɹ
'iːɹz
əi 'kʏm tu 'bɛri
'seːzər, 'nɔt tu
'prɛːz him
ði 'iːvil ðat mɛn
'duː 'lɪvz 'aftəɹ
ðɛm
ðə 'guːd iz 'ɔft
in 'taːrid wið
ðɛːɹ 'boːnz

It is not only the vowel systems that may be different in two accents of a language. Accents may also differ in the lexical incidence of vowels – that is, two accents may use a different vowel quality in some words, even though the two accents have both of the vowels concerned. For instance, both southern and some northern British English accents have [ɑː] and both use it in words like *palm, father, car.* Both accents have [æ] in words like *cat, stand, gas.* However for some words, *path, dance, blast* are examples, southern accents have [ɑː] and northern accents have [æ].

A final point about the difference between the vowels of different accents concerns the exact phonetic quality used to signal a particular vowel. A good example of this is the difference in sound between the vowel used in words like *cow, town, out* in southern British English and in Northern Irish English. Both accents use a diphthong in these words and there are no lexical incidence differences. However, the two diphthongs sound quite different as is shown in Figure 5.9.

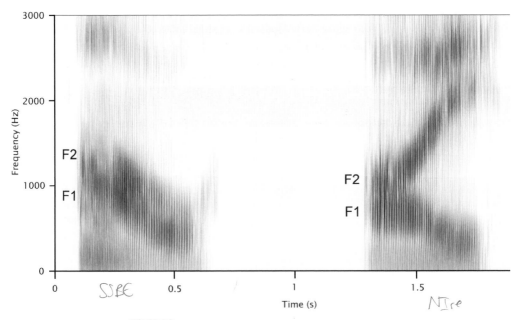

FIGURE 5.9
The diphthong of *cow* or *mouth* as spoken (left) in Southern British and (right) in Northern Irish English. Notice how F2 falls in one but rises in the other.

## Chapter summary

rise =
formant

Vowels are produced when vocal fold vibration excites the resonances of the vocal tract. The excitation spectrum is filtered by the vocal tract, giving rise to peaks in the output spectrum which are known as formants. The patterning of three lowest frequency formants essentially determines vowel quality. This patterning can be related to the articulatory features of vowels (height, location, lip position). Vowels may be long or short, and may be monophthongs or diphthongs. The auditory properties of vowels can be related to a diagram known as the vowel quadrilateral, and fixed landmark qualities in the quadrilateral are known as cardinal vowels. Symbols for these, together with additional symbols and diacritics permit the transcription of vowel qualities.

Languages make use of the basic vowel features in a wide variety of ways. Vowel systems range from the very small with only three vowels to the quite large with 10 or more vowels. Some languages increase the size of their vowel inventory by the use of modifications such as nasalisation, length distinctions and the addition of diphthongs.

Vowels change over time more rapidly than consonants do and vowels can differ quite significantly from one accent of a language to another. Two accents my have different vowel systems. They may differ in the lexical incidence of vowels and the precise phonetic qualities of equivalent vowels may differ.

# Exercises

## Exercise 5.1

Each of the following sets of cardinal vowels has an 'odd one out'. Try to identify this and say why it is unlike the others.

(a) [a ɑ i ɔ e ɛ]
(b) [e i a ø y u]
(c) [ɯ i y u œ]

## Exercise 5.2

In the speech of many New Zealanders, certain vowels appear to have shifted in quality when compared to vowels used in other accents of English. Here are some correspondences, represented in terms of the cardinal vowel system with diacritics.

| | British English | NZ English |
|---|---|---|
| pat | [pɛ̞t] | [pet] |
| pet | [pe̝t] | [pë̝t] |
| pit | [pë̝t] | [pə̝t] |

(a) Describe all the vowel qualities in these words in terms of height, location and lip position.
(b) Plot the approximate position of the vowels on a vowel quadrilateral.

## Exercise 5.3

Here are some words from Kirghiz, a Turkic language.

| Meaning | Pronunciation |
|---|---|
| *apple* | [ɑlmɑ] |
| *forest* | [tokoj] |
| *house* | [yj] |
| *lake* | [køl] |
| *meat* | [et] |
| *salt* | [tuz] |
| *work* | [iʃ] |
| *year* | [ʒɯl] |

Kirghiz has a suffix, meaning *with* or *by*, which is pronounced in eight different ways: [ten], [tøn], [den], [døn], [ton], [don], [tɑn], [dɑn]

When the suffix is added to the end of a word, the pronunciation is chosen as follows:

(a) the first consonant of the suffix must agree in voicing with the last sound of the word to which it is added
(b) the suffix vowel must agree in rounding with the vowels in the word
(c) the suffix vowel must agree in frontness or backness with the vowels in the word

Which form of the suffix should be added to each of the words above?

**Spectrograms for questions 5.4 and 5.5**

The spectrograms and waveforms which follow are for questions 5.4 and 5.5. To assist you, the first is the English word 'shout' with lines added to show division into three segments.

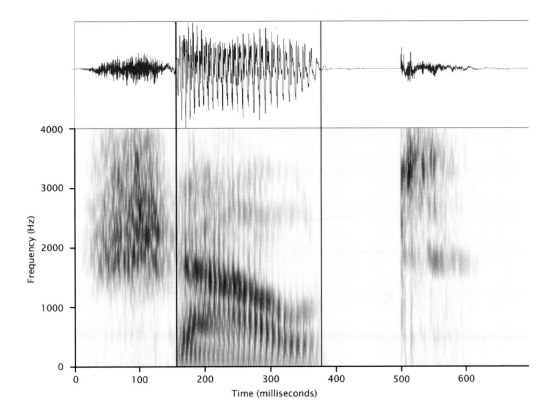

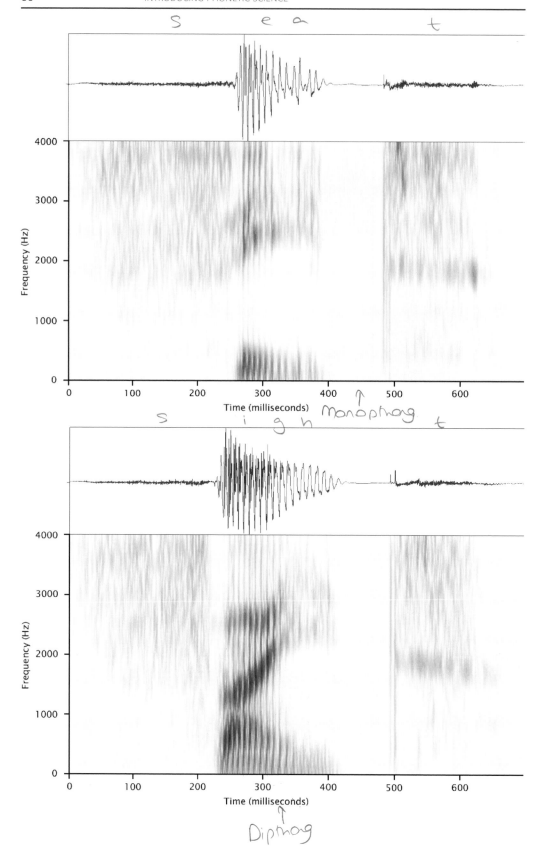

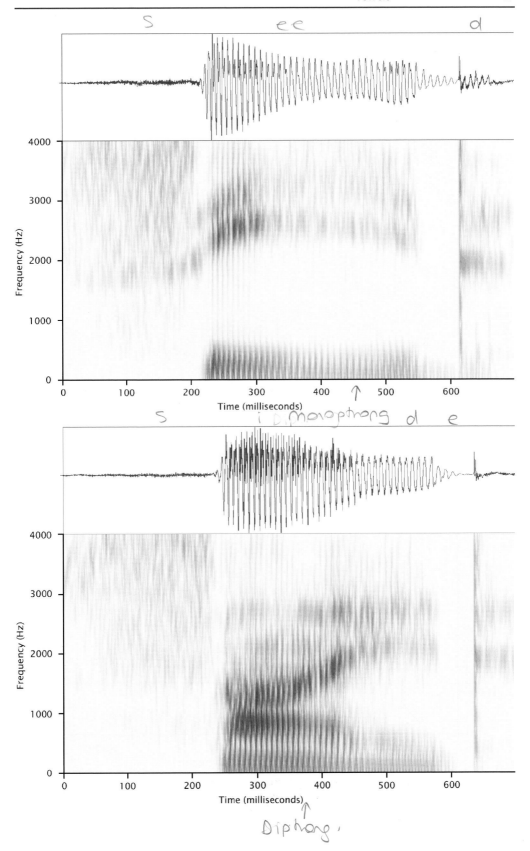

**Exercise 5.4**
Look at the spectrograms (a)–(d) which represent English words of one syllable. Decide which words contain a monophthong and which a diphthong and explain the reasons for your decisions.

**Exercise 5.5**
Words (a) and (b) end in a voiceless consonant and (c) and (d) end in a voiced consonant. Measure the duration of the vowel in each word. For each pair of words (a)–(c) and (b)–(d) calculate the ratio of the longer vowel to the shorter.

**Exercise 5.6**
The spectrograms below are of the Turkish words [**kil**] 'clay' and [**kyl**] 'ashes'. Decide which is which and explain how you have reached this conclusion.

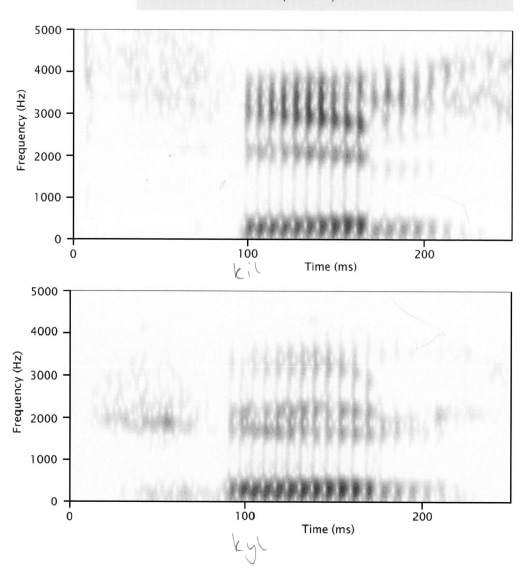

Exercise 5.7
The vowel quadrilaterals (a–d) below show the vowel systems of four real
languages.

(a) Which of the four languages has a mid central vowel [ə]?  C
(b) Which of the four languages has a fully open back vowel?  D
(c) Which languages have a vowel that could be symbolised [ɪ]?  C
(d) Which language does not have a fully back close vowel?  A
(e) Which language has a vowel very similar to primary cardinal vowel
    number 3? B

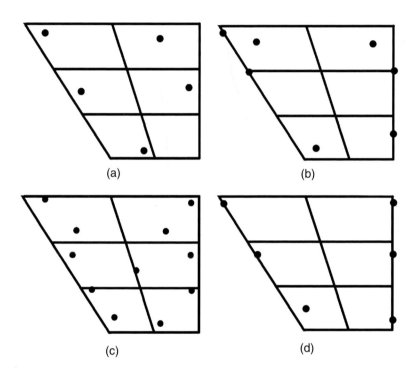

(a)        (b)

(c)        (d)

---

**Further reading**
On vowel systems and vowel dispersion, see Ian Maddieson, *Patterns of sounds*, Cambridge: Cambridge
University Press, 1984, chapters 8 and 9.
   A wide-ranging account of the varieties of English pronunciation found around the world, very useful for
comparing the vowel systems of different varieties of English, is J. C. Wells, *Accents of English*, 3 vols.
Cambridge: Cambridge University Press, 1982.

# 6 Voice II

## CHAPTER OUTLINE

In this chapter you will learn about: aspiration; aspiration and devoicing in English; the use of aspiration in languages of the world; larynx waveforms for normal voice and other phonation types; voice onset time and how to measure it.

## Introduction

As we saw in Chapter 2, one important way in which consonant sounds may differ from one another is by voicing. However, it is important to be aware that the terms 'voiced' and 'voiceless' do not simply refer to the presence or absence of vocal fold vibration. The articulatory and acoustic events that give rise to the perception of voicing and voicelessness are somewhat more complex than the simple story we told in Chapter 2. What counts as voiced in one language may, in some instances, be perceived as voiceless in another language. In this chapter we look at the topic of voicing in more detail and consider the importance of the timing of the onset of vocal fold vibration in relation to other articulatory events. We also look in more detail at vocal fold vibration itself, and distinguish normal voice from other phonation types.

## Voice Onset Time

For voiceless plosive consonants, vocal fold vibration is stopped for a period that is a little longer than the hold phase (the time when the mouth is blocked, see Chapter 4), so that there is still no vocal fold vibration around the moment of release (when the articulators part and the plosion is heard) and possibly for a further brief time afterwards. This delay, measured from the start of the explosion to the point where vocal fold vibration begins, is called the Voice Onset Time (VOT). Though so short that it is best expressed in milliseconds (1 ms = one thousandth of a second) it is very important to the listener. We know from experiments on speech perception that listeners are very sensitive to VOT and use it to categorise the plosive they are hearing as voiceless or voiced. In Figure 6.1 below there is a schematic representation of the three phases of the production of a voiceless velar plosive [k]. Also included in the figure are the waveform and spectrogram of a real utterance of [aka].

## Aspiration

If the VOT is longer than about 30 ms, a plosive doesn't just sound voiceless; the VOT can actually be heard as a brief [h]-like segment following the explosion and the plosive is said to be aspirated. Not all languages have voiceless plosives of this type, but English does, and the initial [p] [t] [k] sounds of words such as *pound*, *time*, *keen* are all aspirated. The symbol for aspiration is a superscript [ʰ] following the sound affected – so [pʰ tʰ kʰ] and so on.

### Aspiration in languages
The commonest pattern in languages around the world is for the voiceless plosives to have a short VOT (something like 10 ms on average); they are therefore voiceless unaspirated plosives. The voiced plosives with which they contrast tend to be fully voiced – that is, to have vocal fold vibration started well before the explosion, and possibly running right through the hold phase of the articulation. Among languages which do this are

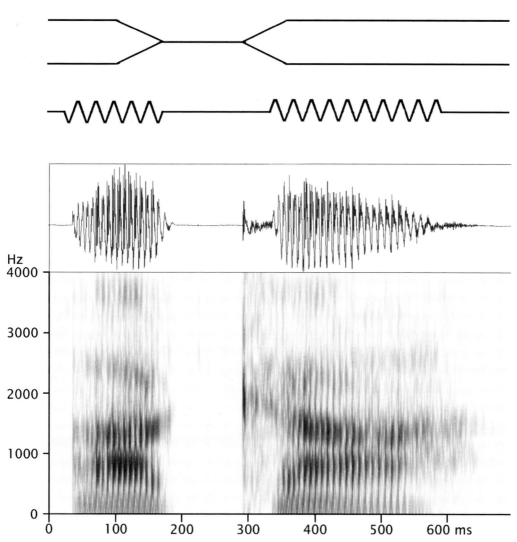

FIGURE 6.1
Schematic parametric representation of the three phases of an intervocalic plosive, and diagrammatic representation of larynx activity, with aligned waveform and spectrogram of a real utterance.

French, Spanish, Italian, Greek, Dutch, Russian, Arabic. There are hundreds more.

English does it a different way. The voiceless plosives have a longer VOT and are thus aspirated. The voiced plosives do not need to be fully voiced, and, depending on the context in which they appear, they may lack vocal fold vibration for some or all of the hold. It is enough if vocal fold vibration begins at about the time of the release – in fact initial plosives with vocal fold vibration beginning much before this do not sound quite right for English. Other languages that do it much the same way as English include German, Japanese and Chinese (both Modern Standard and Cantonese).

Figure 6.2 shows the waveforms for voiced and voiceless plosives in French (a, b) and for English (c, d). The waveforms are aligned at the moment of release of the plosive.

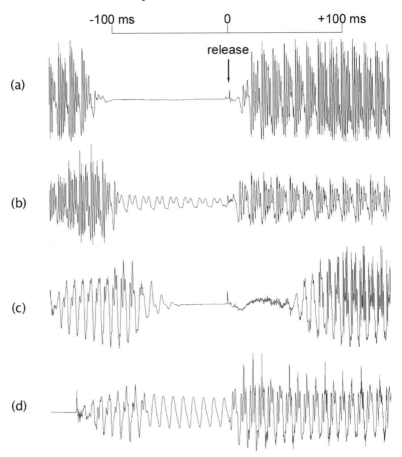

FIGURE 6.2
Waveforms showing intervocalic plosives in French and English, aligned by moment of release. The words are French (a) *apart*, (b) *abeille*, and English (c) *apart*, (d) *obey*. In this context the voiced plosives show voicing throughout the hold phase in both languages.

Aspiration is a matter of degree, and plosives can easily be given more aspiration (i.e. longer VOT) than they customarily get in English. For instance, the aspirated plosives of Modern Standard Chinese sound somewhat more aspirated than English ones. Figure 6.3 is a schematic representation of the full range of possibilities for VOT.

Some languages (an example is Thai) actually distinguish three sets of plosives by VOT. These are likely to be (1) fully voiced (2) short VOT (10 ms or so – i.e. voiceless unaspirated) (3) very long VOT (50 ms or more – i.e. strongly aspirated). The examples in Table 6.1 illustrate this three-way contrast.

The remarks so far apply to plosive consonants in initial position directly before a vowel. If a language distinguishes voiced and voiceless plosives at all it will do so in that position; in other positions, the sounds may be modified. For instance, voiced plosives may become fricatives or approximants when flanked by voiced sounds, as they do in Spanish. An example is the word *beber* ('to drink'), which is pronounced [beβer]. In final position, it is common for the voiced/voiceless contrast not to operate (it is said to be neutralised). This is the case in German, for instance, so while

| Table 6.1 Voicing and aspiration in Thai plosives | | | | | | |
|---|---|---|---|---|---|---|
| voiced | | voiceless unaspirated | | voiceless aspirated | | |
| [ba] | crazy | [pa] | aunt | [pʰa] | cloth |
| [d̪a] | to curse | [t̪a] | eye | [t̪ʰa] | landing place |

the word *Bundes* ('of the union') is [bʊndəs], *Bund* ('union') is [bʊnt]. In English the contrast is maintained in all positions except directly after [s]. The plosives in words such as *spin*, *stop*, *school* have approximately zero VOT and are more-or-less ambiguous between voiced and voiceless categories for speakers of English. Children often invent spellings such as *sdop*, *sgool*, showing their accurate perception of the neutralisation.

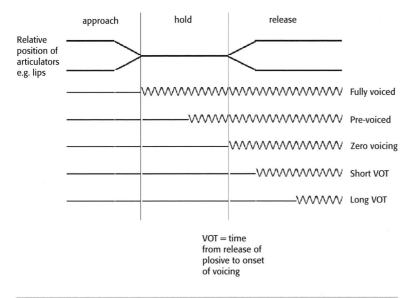

VOT = time from release of plosive to onset of voicing

FIGURE 6.3
Schematic parametric representation of the three phases of plosive production, with five different VOT possibilities.

## Devoicing

English [p t k] are aspirated when at the beginning of a stressed syllable. If an approximant rather than a vowel follows (e.g. *price*, *play*, *twin*, *cute*) the aspiration takes the form of devoicing the approximant, so: [pɹ̥aɪs pl̥eɪ tw̥ɪn kju̥ːt]. If [s] precedes, there is no aspiration and, correspondingly, little or no devoicing of any approximant, so for example, *sprain* [spɹeɪn], *splash* [splæʃ], *squeak* [skwiːk], *studio* [stjuːdiəʊ].

Just as the 'voiced' plosives of English are not necessarily voiced all the way through, so the other 'voiced' obstruents (fricatives and affricates) don't always have vocal fold vibration throughout. The contrast is maintained for the listener by a number of other factors (duration is the most important). To avoid the awkwardness of talking about 'voiced' sounds that are not voiced, English consonants are sometimes called lenis ( = weak i.e. short, quiet, unaspirated, sometimes voiced) and fortis ( = strong i.e. long, loud, aspirated, always voiceless).

Figure 6.4 shows spectrograms of the English words *ice* [aɪs] and *eyes* [aɪz]. While we conventionally represent the difference between these words as a difference in the voicing of the final consonant, vocal fold

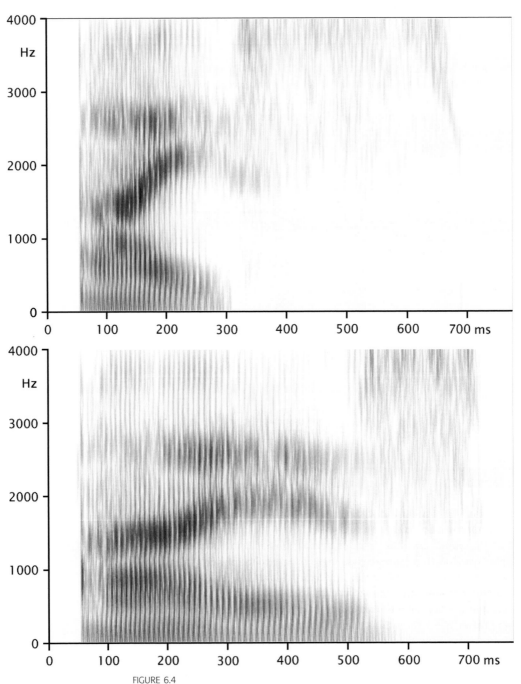

FIGURE 6.4

Spectrograms of the English words *ice* (top) and *eyes*. The diphthong of *ice* is shortened by pre-fortis clipping, while the fortis fricative is considerably longer than the lenis fricative of *eyes*.

vibration is not present throughout the fricative [z]. The most important difference for the listener is in the duration of the [aɪ] diphthong. You can see that the [aɪ] in *ice* is considerably shorter than that in *eyes*. The vowel has been shortened by the presence of a following fortis consonant and this is a regular feature of many accents of English and also of other languages. It is known as pre-fortis clipping.

## Phonation type

The switching on and off of vocal fold vibration, and the timing of these events, are not the only ways in which the larynx contributes to sound distinctions in languages. The nature or type of vibration may also be significant. Sound generation in the larynx is termed **phonation**, and phonation types (sometimes called voice qualities) are recognisably different kinds of vocal fold vibration. All languages use a phonation type called normal or **modal voice** as the basis for all speech. Many languages (for example English) make no systematic deviations from modal voice. In modal voice, the vocal folds vibrate regularly with a rapid closure in each cycle as shown in the laryngograph waveform in Figure 6.5. Remember that the output of the laryngograph shows vocal fold contact as a function of time.

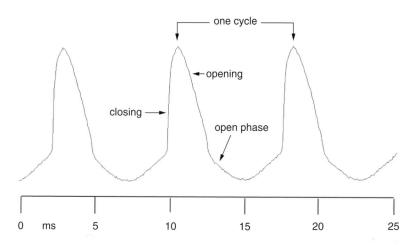

FIGURE 6.5
Laryngograph waveform for modal voice.

In the figure, the main events in one cycle are labelled. The rapid closure of the vocal folds causes a very efficient excitation of vocal tract resonances. Modal voice is a tone in which the individual cycles of vibration are not separately audible and in which there is little or no noise (aperiodic energy) from breath flow, and it can be produced at a wide range of frequencies.

Departure from the laryngeal adjustments required for normal voice may result in such phonation types as **creaky voice** and **breathy voice**. Most widely used in languages is breathy voice, sometimes called murmur, where audible breath noise is heard at the same time as vibration. A laryngograph waveform for one type of breathy voice is shown in Figure 6.6(a). The closed phase in each cycle is short, leaving a long open

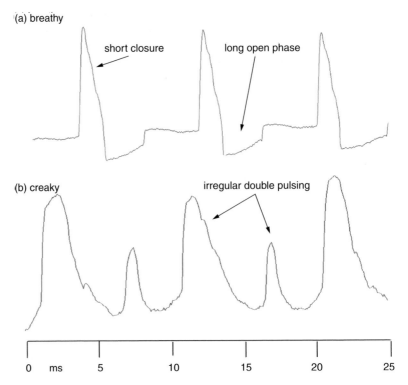

(a) breathy

short closure        long open phase

(b) creaky        irregular double pulsing

FIGURE 6.6
Laryngograph waveform
for (a) one type of
breathy voice, and
(b) one type of creaky
voice.

0    ms      5           10          15          20          25

phase during which breath escapes. In creaky voice the vocal folds
vibrate in a less regular manner with alternate cycles of vibration differing in duration. This can be seen in the laryngograph waveform in
Figure 6.6(b).

An example of a language that makes use of the distinction between
normal voice and breathy voice is Gujarati. Some pairs of Gujarati words
are given in Table 6.2. The mark .. below the vowel symbol indicates breathy
voice.

A language that makes use of the distinction between normal voice and
creaky voice is Jalapa Mazatec, spoken in Mexico. In the examples in Table 6.3
the mark ~ is used to indicate creaky voice.

### Table 6.2 Modal and breathy voiced vowels in Gujarati

| modal voice | | breathy voice | |
|---|---|---|---|
| [baɾ] | *twelve* | [ba̤ɾ] | *outside* |
| [poɾ] | *last year* | [po̤ɾ] | *early morning* |

### Table 6.3 Modal and creaky voiced vowels in Jalapa Mazatec

| modal voice | | creaky voice | |
|---|---|---|---|
| [ja] | *tree* | [ja̰] | *he wears* |
| [ntʰæ] | *seed* | [ndæ̰] | *buttocks* |

We may also convey attitude or mood by altering the way our vocal folds vibrate. Breathy voice is often associated with passionate, intimate utterances. It may be more convincing to say *I love you* with breathy voice than with modal voice. This sort of phonation also is associated with gushing overenthusiasm. Creaky voice is often used when the speaker wishes to signal boredom and is also found in exasperated utterances like *Oh no, not again!*

## Chapter summary

In this chapter we have looked at aspects of the timing of vocal fold vibration. VOT is the interval between the release of a plosive and the onset of vocal vibration and is an important cue for the listener in determining whether the plosive belongs in the voiced or voiceless category. Most languages make use of a two-way distinction according to VOT. The chapter also introduced the notion of aspiration, a feature of plosives that have a long VOT. Looking more closely at the details of voicing in English we considered the topic of devoicing and looked at the conditions under which so-called voiced consonants may be without vocal fold vibration for at least part of their duration. This led to the introduction of the terms fortis and lenis as possible alternatives to the terms voiceless and voiced. Finally, we looked at phonation types, identifying modal (normal) voice and a number of audibly different kinds of vocal fold vibration which may be used distinctively by certain languages and in many languages as signals of the attitude of the speaker. The most important conclusion to be drawn from this chapter is that the voicing of consonants is not simply a matter of the presence or absence of vocal vibration.

## Exercises

### Exercise 6.1
Sketch a schematic diagram showing vocal fold activity for an aspirated voiceless plosive between two vowels, and indicate the following events: hold phase, moment of release, onset of voicing.

### Exercise 6.2
In most accents of English, voiced obstruents are only fully voiced when they are in between two voiced sonorant sounds (for example the [b] in *abbey* [ˈæbi]). Elsewhere they are devoiced – that is, the vocal folds do not vibrate for the whole duration of the sound . For example *this book* will contain a devoiced bilabial plosive [b̥]. Add the devoicing diacritic to the relevant symbols in the transcriptions below:

(a) [jɔː njuː kredɪt kɑːd ʃʊd əraɪv suːn]
(b) [ʃɒpɪŋ ɪn seɪlz ɪz ə gʊd weɪ tə get bɑːgɪnz]

**Exercise 6.3**

Shown below are the waveform and spectrogram of an utterance of the English word *apart*. Measure the VOT of the intervocalic plosive (in milliseconds, to the nearest 5 milliseconds).

**Exercise 6.4**

Consider the voiceless velar plosives in your pronunciation of the following words: *kite sky occur baker basket*. Which do you think have a long VOT, and which a short one? If possible, use computer software to display waveforms of recordings of your versions, and measure VOT for each velar plosive.

**Exercise 6.5**

Shown below are short specimens of the larynx waveform (obtained from a laryngograph). Which of the examples (a) to (f) look as if they are likely to be examples of normal or modal voice?

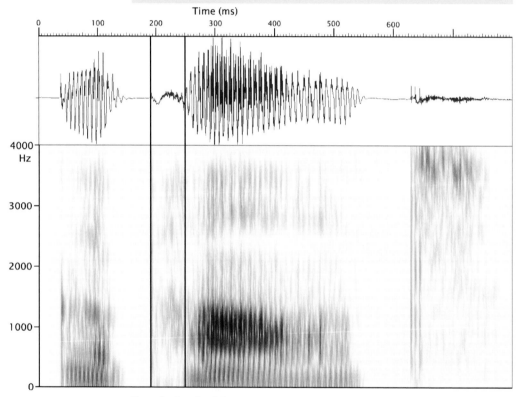

Figure for Exercise 6.3

**Exercise 6.6**

Remember that pre-fortis clipping is a reduction in the duration of a vowel or diphthong when it is in a syllable that has one or more fortis consonants at the end. In which of the following monosyllabic English words are the vowels or diphthongs clipped?

(a) fee    (b) feet    (c) feast    (d) fade    (e) fail    (f) felt

**Exercise 6.7**
Which of the following English words are likely to contain a devoiced approximant?

| | | | | |
|---|---|---|---|---|
| (a) please | (b) blow | (c) quick | (d) crown | (e) grow |
| (f) pure | (g) yours | (h) cool | (i) string | (j) what |

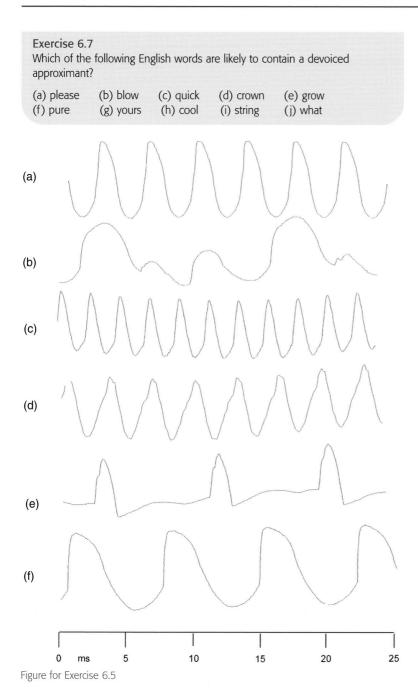

(a)

(b)

(c)

(d)

(e)

(f)

0    ms    5           10          15          20          25

Figure for Exercise 6.5

**Further reading**
John Laver, *The phonetic description of voice quality*, Cambridge: Cambridge University Press, 1980, contains an account of many different phonation types. For more detail on how languages differ in using VOT and aspiration you could look at L. Lisker and A.S. Abramson, A cross-language study of voicing in initial stops: Acoustical measurements, *Word*, 20 (1964), 384–442.

# 7 Airstream mechanisms

## CHAPTER OUTLINE

In this chapter you will learn about: airstream generation; egressive and ingressive flow; ejectives; implosives; clicks; non-pulmonic sounds in the world's languages.

### KEY TERMS

*Click*

*Compression*

*Ejective*

*Egressive*

*Glottalic*

*Implosive*

*Ingressive*

*Pressure*

*Pulmonic/non-pulmonic*

*Rarefaction*

*Velaric*

## Introduction

We have seen how consonant sounds can be described in terms of voice, place and manner of articulation. We now have to consider a further important way in which consonant sounds can differ from one another: the use of different airstream mechanisms. All the sounds we have dealt with up to now have used the same airstream mechanism, known as the pulmonic airstream mechanism because it uses air expelled from the lungs. In the pulmonic airstream, the lungs supply a large volume of air under pressure, enough to power the production of one or more phrase-length stretches of speech between pauses for breath. This is the basis of all normal speech in all languages, and many languages (e.g. English) make no systematic use of any other airstream. But some languages additionally make use of other airstream mechanisms for a proportion of their consonant sounds. Small volumes of air can be pushed or pulled by muscular action in the mouth or pharynx independently of the lungs, and the resulting short-term pressure differences and airflows are enough to power the production of single consonant segments, which sound recognisably different from pulmonic sounds. There are three types of consonants produced this way, known as ejectives, implosives and clicks. Because they are not driven by air pressure from the lungs they are termed non-pulmonic sounds.

This chapter first looks more closely at the generation of air-pressure differences and airflows, first introduced in Chapter 4. It then describes the way in which the various non-pulmonic sounds are produced, how they are symbolised, and gives some examples of how they are used in the consonant systems of the world's languages.

## Airstream generation

In order to make any speech sound, there must be a flow of air through the relevant part of the vocal tract. Flow through the larynx is needed whenever we require to vibrate the vocal folds; flow though a narrow articulatory constriction is needed to generate the noise typical of fricatives; and an interrupted flow, which is suddenly re-started, gives us the transient sound of plosives.

Air movement within the vocal tract depends on the creation of pressure differences. Air always flows from a region of high pressure towards a region of lower pressure. Air is a gas, or more accurately a mixture of gases. A gas may be thought of as particles spread out in space. Pressure is a measure of how many particles there are in a given volume of space. If there are few particles, the gas is at low pressure. Making the space smaller without letting any of the particles escape is called compression, and raises the pressure of the gas. The opposite of this, rarefaction, is obtained when the space is enlarged without letting any more particles in. The concentration of particles is thus lowered and the pressure is reduced. In speech, the necessary compressions and rarefactions are achieved by using muscles to move some part of the vocal tract or respiratory system.

The moving part acts rather like the piston in a pump, and is called the initiator of the airstream. For example, in the pulmonic airstream the initiator is the lungs, moved by the respiratory muscles.

When the pulmonic airstream mechanism is in action, there is a supply of air at high pressure in the lungs and it flows through the vocal tract towards the lower atmospheric pressure in the air around the speaker. Much of the muscular work to power the airstream is actually done when we pause to breathe in. We use our inspiratory muscles to inflate the lungs, which then tend to recoil back, compressing the air within them. The air doesn't come out all at once, of course, because its flow is regulated by the adjustment at the glottis, and the resistance of the various articulatory constrictions we are employing as we speak. As we continue speaking, and the lungs begin to empty, we begin to use expiratory muscles to squeeze more air out of the lungs before we finally have to pause for breath.

## Egressive and ingressive flow

The flow of air we have just described is outwards from the body, a direction of flow that is called egressive. So the full name for the airstream mechanism that forms the basis of all normal speech is the egressive pulmonic airstream mechanism. You will find that it is also possible to reverse this airstream and speak while breathing in, using the ingressive pulmonic mechanism. Try saying a short sentence such as 'Good morning, how are you?' this way. You will probably find that you can make a recognisable attempt at this, but the speech is likely to sound strange, and is difficult for most people to control. Notice that both voiceless and voiced sounds can be made this way, proving that the vocal folds can be made to vibrate when air passes between them in a reversed direction. So far, no language has been found that makes any use of the ingressive pulmonic airstream. But the distinction between egressive and ingressive is important in understanding the non-pulmonic mechanism we are going to consider next.

## Ejectives

The first of the non-pulmonic airstream mechanisms we will look at is the one that is used to produce ejectives, which are the commonest non-pulmonic consonants among the languages of the world. Remember that languages that make use of ejectives will still make use of the pulmonic egressive airstream as the ordinary basis of speech. Each time an ejective consonant occurs, the non-pulmonic mechanism is powered-up briefly, but there will generally be a return to the pulmonic mechanism for the following segment.

In the production of an ejective, the glottis is closed, and the air that is compressed (and eventually pushed out) is that between the closed glottis and the articulation in the oral cavity. For this reason, the name of the airstream is egressive glottalic. Ejectives are symbolised by adding an apostrophe to the symbol for any voiceless obstruent. This gives symbols such as [p' t' k' tʃ'].

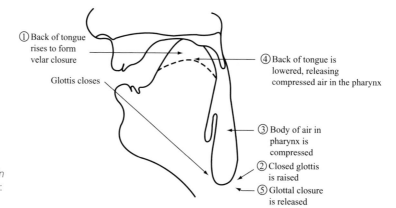

FIGURE 7.1
The sequence of events
in the production of an
ejective velar stop (after
P. Ladefoged, *A Course in
Phonetics*, Fort Worth, Tx:
Harcourt, 2001).

The sequence of events in the production of a typical ejective [k'] is as follows. As shown in Figure 7.1, (1) the back of the tongue rises to form a closure on the velum, just as for any velar stop. At about the same time, the glottis closes. The velum is also in its raised position, closed against the rear wall of the pharynx, so that no air can escape through the nose. (2) The closed glottis is raised (the whole larynx moves up) reducing the volume of the pharynx cavity and thus (3) increasing the pressure of the air in the pharynx. (4) The back of the tongue is lowered, just as for the release of an ordinary velar stop, thus releasing the compressed pharynx air and producing an audible explosion. The glottis remains closed during the release and for a short time afterwards. Finally (5) the glottal closure is released – for instance, the vocal folds may begin to vibrate for a following vowel. This description is of an unaffricated ejective stop, and this is the commonest type of ejective found in languages. Other types are possible, however, and both ejective affricates and less commonly ejective fricatives are found in languages.

## Acoustic and auditory properties of ejectives

Ejectives sound different from pulmonic egressive consonants. One of the most noticeable differences is that the burst for an ejective stop tends to be much more intense. This is because a higher pressure difference can be produced with the glottalic airstream mechanism. During the burst of an ejective and for a short time afterwards, the glottis remains closed. This means that the burst is followed by a period of silence rather than by aspiration or the immediate onset of voicing. Languages differ in the length of time for which the glottis remains closed, and if the time is very short the ejective auditorily resembles an unaspirated pulmonic egressive plosive quite closely. You can see the differences between a typical ejective and the corresponding pulmonic consonant in Figure 7.2.

## Ejectives in languages

Ejectives are the commonest type of non-pulmonic sound. They occur in many languages of America and Africa and in languages of the Caucasus. They occur alongside the corresponding pulmonic sounds, and the

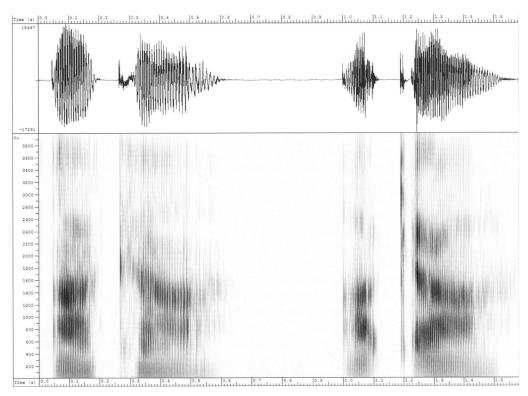

FIGURE 7.2
Waveforms and spectrograms for [akʰa] (left) and [ak'a] (right).

difference in airstream mechanism can be the only difference between contrasting words. For example in Hausa, which is spoken in Nigeria, [kaːɽaː] means 'to screen off', whereas [k'aːɽaː] means 'to increase'. In Chechen, one of the Caucasian languages, [tsa] means 'not', but [ts'a] with an ejective affricate means 'house'.

Here are examples showing a range of contrasting ejectives and pulmonic sounds from Chontal (Mexico):

| [p'os] | 'sweepings' | [pos] | 'pale' |
| [t'ub] | 'gourd' | [tub] | 'spittle' |
| [k'uʃ] | 'it hurts' | [kuʃ] | 'go' |
| [ts'ilen] | 'split' | [tsilen] | 'rip' |
| [tʃ'uju] | 'lift it up' | [tʃuju] | 'sew it' |

## Other uses of ejectives

Even in languages where the difference between ejectives and pulmonic consonants is not used to signal a difference between words, speakers may occasionally use ejectives. For example the English phrase *Definitely not* may be said with an ejective at the end, giving the impression that the speaker is being decisive or insistent. Most speakers of English use ejectives only occasionally, and only when a silent pause follows. We don't hear normal speakers of English using ejectives in initial position before a vowel.

Ejectives may sometimes be used in place of pulmonic consonants in certain types of disordered speech, so that those who are training to be speech and language therapists must learn to recognise them.

## Implosives

Implosives use the ingressive glottalic airstream; instead of moving up to compress the air as in ejectives, the glottis is moved down so as to enlarge the pharynx and produce suction. So implosives are essentially reverse ejectives, but straightforward voiceless implosives are actually very rare in languages. The implosives that are commonly encountered have a further small complication in that they are voiced. Instead of being completely closed as it is pulled down, the glottis is vibrating to produce voice. Obviously, to produce voice, air from the lungs must be flowing up through the glottis. Voiced implosives thus employ two airstream mechanisms simultaneously. The symbols for implosives are based on those for voiced plosives, and always have a hook attached to the top right: [ɓ ɗ ɠ].

The sequence of events in a typical voiced implosive, [ɓ] is shown in Figure 7.3. (1) The lips close, as for any bilabial stop. (2) As the vocal folds continue vibrating in a flow of lung air, the whole larynx is moved down, thus enlarging the pharynx and tending to reduce the pressure of air inside it. (3) The reduction in air pressure may not be very great, because it is offset by further air from the lungs flowing through the glottis to keep vocal fold vibration going. When (4) the lips are opened, air pressure in the mouth is still a little below atmospheric pressure, so airflow (briefly) is inwards.

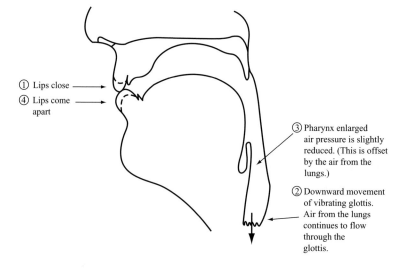

FIGURE 7.3
The sequence of events in the production of a bilabial implosive (after P. Ladefoged, *A Course in Phonetics*, Fort Worth, Tx: Harcourt, 2001).

① Lips close
④ Lips come apart

③ Pharynx enlarged air pressure is slightly reduced. (This is offset by the air from the lungs.)

② Downward movement of vibrating glottis. Air from the lungs continues to flow through the glottis.

## Auditory and acoustic characteristics of implosives

Implosives sound like rather peculiar fully voiced plosives. From the listener's point of view, an implosive is not recognised from the ingressive airflow itself, but from the characteristic sound which results from the complex change of shape during the production of the consonant. There are probably also cues for the listener in the type and frequency of vocal fold vibration that occurs during the implosive manoeuvre.

Figure 7.4 contains spectrograms to illustrate the difference between a typical voiced pulmonic egressive plosive and a typical implosive.

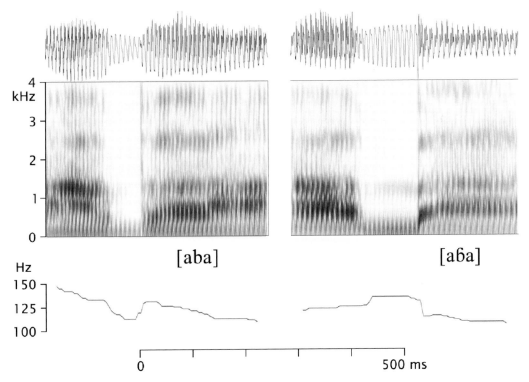

FIGURE 7.4
Waveforms and spectrograms for a voiced pulmonic plosive (left) and a voiced implosive (right). The fundamental frequency curve (bottom) shows that the two manoeuvres can have different effects on the rate of vocal fold vibration.

## Implosives in languages

Implosives are the next most common type of non-pulmonic sound after ejectives. They occur in numerous languages of America, Africa and Asia. In certain languages, implosives contrast with voiced pulmonic egressive plosives. In others (Swahili is an example) implosives occur, but as variants of voiced plosives.

Sindhi, a language of Pakistan, has both voiced pulmonic egressive plosives and implosives at various places of articulation. Some of these are illustrated below.

|            | bilabial        | alveolar           | velar             |
|------------|-----------------|--------------------|-------------------|
| pulmonic   | [buʈʊ] 'shoes'  | [dʊnʊ] 'navel'     | [ɡano] 'song'     |
| implosive  | [ɓarʊ] 'child'  | [ɗarʊ] 'crevice'   | [ʄərʊ] 'heavy'    |

Unlike ejectives, implosives are not used in English as stylistic variants of pulmonic plosives. They are, however, sometimes heard in disordered speech, especially from speakers with severe hearing impairment.

There seem to be universal tendencies in the places of articulation that are favoured for ejective and implosive consonants. Looking at cross-language generalisations, for languages that do not have complete sets of implosives and ejectives, the commonest ejective is [k'] while the commonest implosive is [ɓ]. Hausa, for example, makes use of both implosives and ejectives, but the implosives are found only at front places of articulation, and there is no ejective at the bilabial place. There may be a natural explanation of these preferences in the way that the airstreams are generated. For example [k'] has a back place of articulation, and thus a small initial volume of air trapped above the glottis. A fixed amount of larynx-raising will therefore produce a greater increase in pressure than would be available with a more forward place of articulation.

## Clicks

Clicks use the ingressive velaric airstream. Figure 7.5 shows the sequence of events in a dental click. (1) The tongue tip forms a dental closure, just as it would for a dental plosive. At the same time, the back of the tongue is raised to touch the velum, and the sides of the tongue are in contact

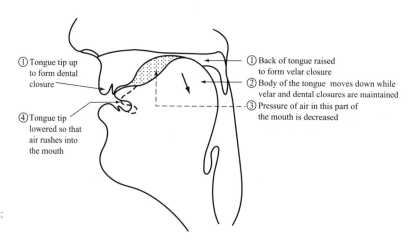

① Tongue tip up to form dental closure

④ Tongue tip lowered so that air rushes into the mouth

① Back of tongue raised to form velar closure
② Body of the tongue moves down while velar and dental closures are maintained
③ Pressure of air in this part of the mouth is decreased

FIGURE 7.5
The sequence of events in the production of a dental click (after P. Ladefoged, *A Course in Phonetics*, Fort Worth, Tx: Harcourt, 2001).

with the palate and teeth, so that a small volume of air is trapped between the tongue and the upper surface of the mouth. (2) While the two closures are maintained, the body of the tongue moves down so as to enlarge the volume and (3) the pressure of the enclosed air decreases. (4) The dental closure is released and a characteristic click sound is heard as air rushes in. The action of the tongue against the upper surface of the oral cavity is rather like that of a rubber suction cup being pressed against a surface and then pulled away.

For all clicks the back of the tongue is making a closure against the velum, but the forward closure may occur at various places of articulation. Those included in the IPA are shown in the table below. Notice that the IPA symbols for clicks are not based on letters of the Roman alphabet.

| bilabial | dental | alveolar | palatoalveolar | alveolar lateral |
|----------|--------|----------|----------------|------------------|
| [ʘ] | [ǀ] | [ǃ] | [ǂ] | [ǁ] |

The symbol shown here for an alveolar click is also used to represent clicks made with the tongue tip further back, and whose place of articulation is described as postalveolar or retroflex. The characteristic sounds of the different clicks result not only from differences in place of articulation, but also from the type of release. For example the dental click may characteristically have a noisy, affricated release, while the palatoalveolar click tends to have a quick, sharp release. For the alveolar lateral click, the closure is released at the side of the tongue rather than in the centre.

## Click modifications

Clicks are produced by a manoeuvre that takes place entirely within the mouth, leaving the lungs, larynx, pharynx and nasal cavities free to act independently and so add various modifications to clicks, including voicing and nasality. The basic clicks themselves are of course unvoiced, but if during the production of a click the vocal folds are made to vibrate on a flow of egressive pulmonic air, and if at the same time the velum is down, allowing the voiced airstream to escape via the nose, the click is said to be voiced and nasalised, although it might be more accurate to say that the click is accompanied by voice and nasality. This is symbolised with [ŋ] before the click symbol, because the pulmonic air flowing up through the vibrating larynx and into the nasal cavity encounters a vocal-tract position just like that for a regular velar nasal consonant (recall that clicks have the back of the tongue closed against the velum). So a voiced nasalised dental click is represented as [ŋǀ]. If the vocal folds are made to vibrate, but the velum is held shut, the click will be accompanied by voice, but not by nasality, and the result is described as a voiced click. This is represented with symbol [ɡ] along with the click symbol. So for example [ɡʘ] is the symbol for a voiced bilabial click. It is worth pointing out that when clicks are voiced, or voiced-and-nasalised, they use two airstream mechanisms simultaneously to produce sound, because the egressive pulmonic airstream mechanism is being employed at the same time as the ingressive velaric airstream mechanism.

Strictly, plain voiceless clicks should also be thought of as being always accompanied by [k], an unaspirated voiceless velar plosive, resulting from the closure between the back of the tongue and the velum, which is made for all clicks. So [k|] is another way of symbolising a voiceless dental click. Variations in the way that this accompanying [k] is released give rise to further click modifications. If it is released with aspiration, for example, the whole click is described as being voiceless and aspirated.

## Acoustic and auditory characteristics of clicks

Clicks are very different from all other sounds regularly heard in speech. The noise as a click is released is generally very intense. When we hear an utterance containing a number of clicks, it may seem as if a series of abrupt sounds from a percussion instrument are mingled with a much more familiar sequence of vowels and consonants.

Figure 7.6 shows spectrograms for a dental click and an alveolar lateral click in intervocalic position.

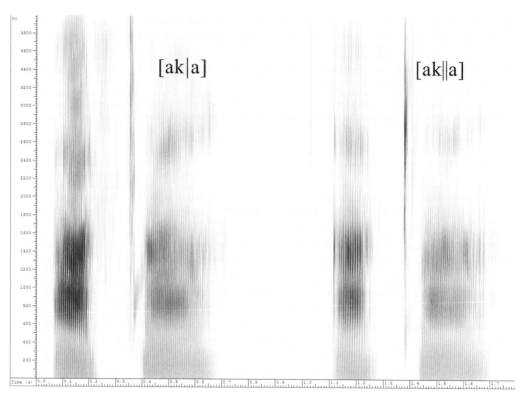

FIGURE 7.6
Spectrograms of a voiceless dental click (left) and voiceless alveolar lateral click (right).

## Clicks in languages

Languages that use clicks as regular speech sounds are found only in the southern part of Africa. They are all of the Khoisan languages (this group includes the various Bushman languages) and also certain neighbouring

Southern Bantu languages (e.g. Zulu and Xhosa). Among languages that have clicks, it is common to find not only several different places of articulation, but also at each place several different series of clicks with different modifications.

Examples of voiceless, voiced and (voiced) nasalised clicks in Zulu are given below. The transcriptions have been simplified to remove some details that are not relevant at this stage.

|  | dental |  | postalveolar |  | alveolar lateral |  |
|---|---|---|---|---|---|---|
| voiceless | [ǀaǀa] | 'be clear' | [ǃaǃa] | 'undo' | [ǁoǁa] | 'relate' |
| voiced | [gǀagǀa] | 'marry' | [gǃagǃa] | 'scatter' | [gǁugǁuma] | 'be nervous' |
| nasalised | [ŋǀeŋǀeza] | 'jingle' | [ŋǃeŋǃeza] | 'ring' | [ŋǁeŋǁeza] | 'urge horse' |

## Other uses of clicks

Although clicks as speech sounds are restricted to relatively few languages, some of the click sounds themselves are in fact familiar to most people, regardless of what language they speak. A bilabial click [ʘ] is a kissing noise, a dental click [ǀ] is the 'tut-tut' of disapproval, the postalveolar or retroflex [ǃ] is made in imitation of horses' hooves, and the alveolar lateral [ǁ] is the 'gee-up' sound used to encourage horses.

*Although the languages that use clicks are all in the southern part of Africa, there are two distinct and unrelated language families involved: the Khoisan languages and the southern Bantu languages. Speakers of the two types of languages are culturally distinct and have different styles of life. As other Bantu languages from elsewhere in Africa do not have clicks, it is reasonable to suppose that the clicks in Zulu and Xhosa must somehow result from the influence of Khoisan. There are other instances of phonetic and phonological properties being shared by languages that are spoken in the same area though not closely related. For example, the languages of the Indian sub-continent belong to two distinct stocks (Indo-European and Dravidian) but the retroflex place of articulation for consonants is a feature of Indian languages from both families.*

## Chapter summary

In this chapter we have looked at the generation of the air pressures and airflows needed for the production of speech sounds, and then at those sound-types made with an airstream that is not supplied by the lungs. These are called non-pulmonic sounds. Sound generation in speech relies either on the compression of air, giving an outward (egressive) flow or the rarefaction of air, resulting in inward (ingressive) flow. Three types of non-pulmonic consonants are used in languages. Two of these types use a glottalic airstream mechanism. Ejectives are produced with an egressive airflow generated by larynx raising. Implosives are made with an ingressive flow generated by lowering the larynx. The third type, clicks, use the velaric ingressive airstream mechanism, produced by rarefying a small volume of air enclosed in the mouth. We have seen that there are sounds that make simultaneous use of pulmonic and non-pulmonic airstreams and have considered various modifications that can be applied to clicks.

## Exercises

### Exercise 7.1

Look at the following descriptions of the production of non-pulmonic consonants. In each case, work out exactly what sound is being described and give the appropriate symbol.

(a) *The back of the tongue rises and makes firm contact with the velum which is in a raised position sealing off the nasal cavity. The tip and blade rise and make contact with the alveolar ridge. The sides of the tongue make a complete seal with the sides of the palate. The vocal folds are open and not vibrating. The centre of the tongue is drawn down, reducing the air pressure in the space enclosed between the tongue and palate. The seal at one side of the palate is broken by lowering the tongue rim. Air rushes in and a brief burst of noise is generated.*

(b) *The back of the tongue rises and makes firm contact with the velum which is in a raised position sealing off the nasal cavity. Air is being expelled by the lungs making the vocal folds vibrate. The whole larynx is lowered, enlarging the space between the velar closure and the vocal folds. The air pressure in this space decreases. The back of the tongue moves away from the velum and a burst of noise is heard as air flows in. The vocal folds continue to vibrate.*

### Exercise 7.2

Look at the following description of the production of [p']. Two important points, essential for the successful generation of the airstream, have been left out of the description. Identify what these are.

*The lips come together and form a complete closure . The glottis is closed. Air pressure inside the vocal tract rises. The lips part and a burst of noise is produced as air rushes out.*

## Exercise 7.3

For each of the following sounds draw a diagram of the vocal tract and write a short paragraph describing the production of the sound between two vowels, paying particular attention to the generation of the airstream:
(a) voiceless alveolar ejective stop (unaffricated)
(b) voiceless bilabial click
(c) voiced nasalised dental click

## Exercise 7.4

The sound system of Zulu uses four airstream mechanisms: pulmonic egressive, glottalic egressive, glottalic ingressive and velaric ingressive. For each of the Zulu consonants listed below, give an appropriate phonetic symbol and say which of the airstream mechanisms are used to produce the sound. Remember that certain sounds make simultaneous use of more than one airstream mechanism.
(a) voiceless alveolar lateral fricative
(b) voiced bilabial implosive
(c) voiceless dental click
(d) voiceless alveolar ejective affricate
(e) voiced nasalised postalveolar click
(f) voiceless velar ejective affricate
(g) voiceless aspirated velar plosive
(h) voiced alveolar lateral click
(i) voiceless velar ejective stop (unaffricated)
(j) voiced bilabial nasal

## Exercise 7.5

The speech of Mr Y, a speaker of English, shows the following abnormal features:

- wherever other speakers have voiceless obstruents Mr Y replaces these with their ejective equivalents
- wherever other speakers have a voiced plosive or a nasal stop Mr Y uses an implosive at the corresponding place of articulation.

Alter the transcriptions of the following sentences to show how they would be pronounced by Mr Y.

(a) Watch what you're doing    [wɒtʃ wɒt jɔː duːɪŋ]
(b) Can I get a glass of milk?    [kæn aɪ get ə glaːs əv mɪlk]
(c) Is it five past nine?    [ɪz ɪt faɪv pɑːst naɪn]

## Further reading

There is a lot of information about non-pulmonic sounds in Peter Ladefoged and Ian Maddieson, *Sounds of the world's languages*, Oxford: Blackwell, 1996. See section 3.2 on airstream mechanisms, and chapter 8 on clicks. For advice on understanding non-pulmonic sounds, and how to make them yourself, see J. C. Catford, *A practical introduction to phonetics*, Oxford: Oxford Uuniversity Press, 2nd edn, 2001.

# 8 Speech sounds and speech movements

## CHAPTER OUTLINE

In this chapter you will learn about: sounds involving more than one articulation; how sounds are influenced by neighbouring sounds; overlapping articulations; variation in segment duration; how to draw diagrams of estimated articulator movements.

## Introduction

In previous chapters we have gradually built up the descriptive framework that enables us to understand most of the ways in which speech sounds can differ from each other. For example, in the case of consonant sounds, we have looked at the airstream mechanism, at the various functions of the larynx, and at places and manners of articulation. There is still more to be done, though, because so far we have been assuming for the sake of simplicity that segments occur one-at-a-time in a sequence, and that within each segment there is one articulation at a time. Both of these assumptions need to be modified, because by themselves they lead to a very static view of what speech is like. The articulators and the places of articulation we have identified, for example, are nothing like as tidy and distinct in reality as our labels suggest. We have only to look inside our own mouths with a mirror, or at an X-ray picture of the vocal tract, to be reminded that the tongue is not divided neatly into the sections we have labelled blade, front and back, or that it is very hard to say where the alveolar ridge ends and the hard palate begins. In the same way, the assumptions that the vocal tract does one thing at a time, and that the resulting sound is effectively determined by that one activity, is immediately called into question if we observe our vocal tract movements in pronouncing a word or a phrase. What we observe is complex, co-ordinated movement. From an acoustic point of view, of course, it will always be the whole configuration of the vocal tract that shapes its response, not just the activities of the articulators we're focusing on when we give simple phonetic labels.

We will turn to speech movements in the later part of this chapter, but we begin by looking at sounds that, even from the static segmental viewpoint, have two simultaneous articulations.

## Primary and secondary articulation

When we were looking at the basic properties of consonants in terms of their place of articulation in Chapter 3, we briefly mentioned the concept of secondary articulation. Apart from a constriction at the primary place of articulation a consonant may have another less extreme constriction at a different place. In Chapter 3 we gave the example of [tʷ] with lip rounding added to an alveolar plosive. This is called labialisation and can be applied to consonants at just about any place of articulation. Figure 8.1 shows the position of the articulators during the hold phase of [tʷ]. The diacritic [ʷ] shows that the sound in question is labialised. Though the diacritic is placed after the relevant symbol, it does not mean that the labialisation follows the sound to which it is added. In this example, the hold phase of the alveolar plosive can be affected just as much as the release. Figure 8.1 actually shows the position that would be expected during the

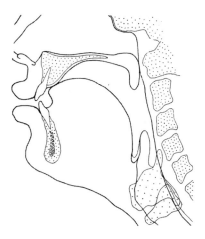

FIGURE 8.1
Position of the articulators
in a labialised alveolar
stop. From the side,
labialisation appears as lip
protrusion.

hold phase. Notice that lip rounding shows up from the side as lip
protrusion.

Labialisation is not the only possible type of secondary articulation. The
additional constriction can alternatively be at the hard palate, at the soft
palate or in the pharynx.

A secondary constriction between the front of the tongue and the hard
palate is known as palatalisation, symbolised by means of the diacritic [ʲ].
Figure 8.2(a) shows the position of the articulators in the hold phase of a
palatalised alveolar plosive [tʲ]. A raising of the back of the tongue towards
the velum gives velarisation, illustrated again on an alveolar plosive in
Figure 8.2(b). The general diacritic for velarisation is [ˠ], but an alternative
symbolisation, a wavy dash through the middle of a symbol, is commonly
used for certain velarised sounds, such as [ɫ] which indicates a voiced
velarised alveolar lateral approximant.

(a)                                    (b)

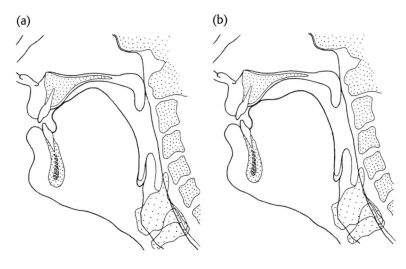

FIGURE 8.2
Position of the articulators
in (a) palatalised, and (b)
velarised alveolar stop.

Pharyngealisation involves a narrowing of the pharynx. One way of achieving this is to pull the root of the tongue backwards into the pharynx. It is symbolised with the diacritic [ˤ]. Figure 8.3 shows a pharyngealised alveolar plosive.

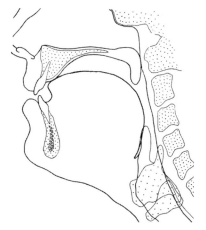

FIGURE 8.3
Estimated position of articulators in the production of a pharyngealised alveolar stop.

## Acoustic effects of secondary articulations

Sounds with secondary articulations are audibly different from plain sounds that lack them. The effects of secondary articulations are quite complex, because they alter the overall shape of the vocal tract, not only during the relatively steady portion at the middle of a consonant articulation, but also in the transitional movements into and away from the combined articulation. For instance, rounding the lips, as in labialisation, has the effect of lowering all the resonant frequencies of the vocal tract. This has an audible effect on the burst of a plosive (try producing [t] and [k] releases with and without rounded lips). Palatalisation, velarisation and pharyngealisation involve movements of the whole body of the tongue, very like those used in vowels. These adjustments take time to set up and remove, and as a result vowels that are next to consonants with secondary articulations are often affected in recognisable ways as the tongue manoeuvres into position. Figure 8.4 shows spectrograms of the English words *bit* and *built*. Comparing the two vowels, which are both supposedly examples of [ɪ], you can see big differences. This is because the vowel in *built* is affected by the tongue getting ready for the velarisation of the lateral consonant. The difference is audible, too, especially if you cut off the remainder of each word and listen only to the two instances of [bɪ-].

## The linguistic use of secondary articulation

There are many languages that use the difference between consonants with secondary articulation and consonants without secondary articulation to distinguish one word from another. Irish is a good example of such

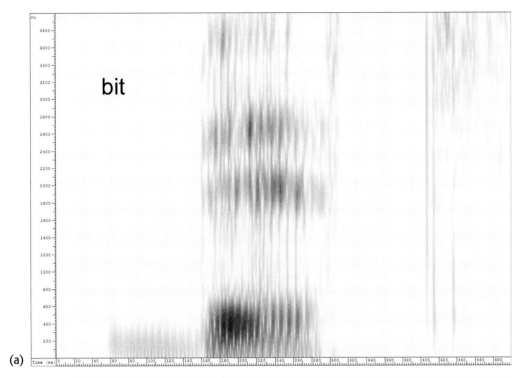

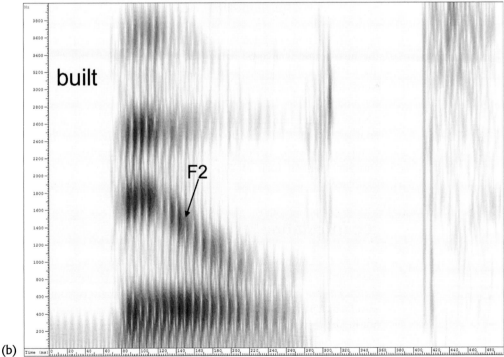

FIGURE 8.4
Spectrograms of *bit* and *built*, showing the effect of the velarised lateral consonant on
F2 of the preceding vowel.

a language and there are examples of pairs of Irish words distinguished in this way in the table below.

| Non-velarised | | Velarised | |
|---|---|---|---|
| [leː] | 'range' | [lˠeː] | 'of the day' |
| [niː] | 'washing' | [nˠiː] | 'nine' |

| Non-palatalised | | Palatalised | |
|---|---|---|---|
| [bɑːd] | 'boat' | [bɑːdʲ] | 'boats' |
| [suːl] | 'of eyes' | [suːlʲ] | 'eye' |

Russian is a language that makes extensive use of the difference between velarised consonants and palatalised consonants. [ugəlˠ] 'corner' and [ugəlʲ] 'coal' is a pair of Russian words exemplifying this. Some languages use labialised and non-labialised consonants in the same way. In Kwakiutl, a language spoken in Canada, [q'asa] means 'sea otter', but [qʷ'asa] means 'crying'. Arabic is well known for having what are usually called 'emphatic' versions of certain consonants in contrast with plain versions. The emphatic sounds are pharyngealised (or velarised, or both). For example, in the Arabic spoken in Qatar [sad] means 'to prevail', whereas [sˤad] is the name of a letter of the alphabet.

### Velarisation in English

In many accents of English (such as standard southern British) there is a pair of sounds distinguished by presence or absence of a secondary articulation. Both are voiced alveolar lateral approximants, one velarised and one not. The non-velarised lateral, informally called 'clear l', occurs when the next sound is a vowel or [j]. The velarised lateral, informally called 'dark l' and usually symbolised [ɫ], occurs elsewhere. So for many accents words like *lead*, *low*, *follow*, *lure* have a non-velarised [l], whereas words like *bell* and *belt* have the velarised version. However, the status of these sounds in English is different from the examples given above for Irish. In English, [l] and [ɫ] are tied to mutually exclusive environments and the difference between them can never be used to distinguish one word from another. We will look at this difference in status in more detail in Chapter 9.

## Coarticulation

We now turn to look at some aspects of speech movements. Look at the spectrogram and waveform of the English sentence *We were away a year* in Figure 8.5. Notice that there are no gaps in either the spectrogram or the waveform. The vowels and consonants that we hear as separate units are not in fact separate at all. If we were to take a moving X-ray film of a vocal tract producing this sentence we would see no pauses between segments. The vocal tract would be in continual motion.

During the production of speech any particular articulator is required to go through a rapid sequence of varied gestures. The position that an

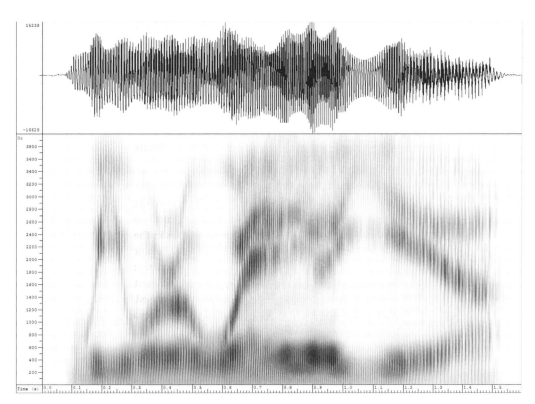

FIGURE 8.5
Spectrogram and waveform of *We were away a year*.

articulator achieves for a sound is likely to be influenced by its position during the previous sound, and the position it will be required to move towards for the following sound. Another way of thinking of this is that properties of one sound tend to spread onto neighbouring sounds. This phenomenon is known as coarticulation. The following sections look at some of the different forms coarticulation may take.

## Fine adjustment of place of articulation

In the English phrase *keep calm*, for example, for the first [k], as the body of the tongue will have to take up a high front position for the following vowel, the point of contact of the tongue with the roof of the mouth is likely to be quite far forward on the velum, whereas the reverse is observed for the second [k], where the following back vowel has the effect of retracting the point of contact. Thus the frontness of the vowel in *keep* spreads onto the first [k], and the backness of the vowel of *calm* onto the second [k]. If you repeat the phrase a number of times you should be able to feel the difference in the two [k] sounds.

A very similar adjustment of point of contact may affect alveolar sounds. As an example from English, consider the two plosive sounds in *daydream*. You should be able to feel that the point of contact for the second is somewhat further back on the alveolar ridge than for the first. This is caused by the post-alveolar position required for the immediately following consonant [ɹ], which like the [d] is formed with the tongue tip and blade.

A sound that is shifted forwards in place of articulation may be described as **advanced** and this is symbolised by means of a subscript plus sign, so the word *keep* can be represented as [k̟ʰiːp]. A backward shift may be termed retraction and **retracted** sounds are very logically shown with a subscript minus sign, so that *calm* may be transcribed [k̠ʰɑːm]. The subscript minus sign applies to alveolar sounds too, so that [d̠] indicates a plosive retracted from the alveolar place so that it is post-alveolar. The subscript plus sign, when applied to an alveolar symbol, essentially indicates a dental articulation and we have already met a diacritic for dental, so that [d̟] is equivalent to [d̪]. A voiced dental plosive may be heard in the phrase *good thing* for example.

## Nasalisation caused by coarticulation

We have already seen that vowels can be produced with a lowered soft palate and that the resulting nasalised vowels function as separate sounds in certain languages. In other languages, such as English, nasalised vowels result from coarticulation. The lowered velum position required for a nasal consonant may spread onto an adjacent vowel. So the vowel in words like *ban* and *bang* is likely to be somewhat nasalised, [bæ̃n, bæ̃ŋ], whereas we have an oral vowel in words like *bad, bat, back, bag* and so on. The examples we have given involve anticipation of the nasality of the following consonant, but it is also possible for nasality to persist into a vowel that follows a nasal consonant: compare the vowels in *mad* and *bad*. If a vowel is both preceded and followed by nasals, it will be affected from both directions: compare the vowels of *moon* and *boot*.

It is not only vowels that can be affected by the spread of nasality, but also sonorant consonants such as English [w ɹ l j]. You may find examples in your pronunciations of words like *film, news, Henry, runway*.

## Diagrams of velum action

A good way of understanding the timing of velum movements relative to other speech events is by means of diagrams of the type shown in Figure 8.6. Diagrams that show the positions of different articulators as a function of time are called **parametric diagrams**. A parameter can be thought of in this context as one of the important time-varying properties that describe relevant aspects of speech production.

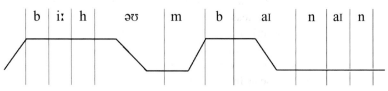

FIGURE 8.6
Parametric diagram of velum action in *Be home by nine*.

The velum is in the down position before the speech starts, to allow the speaker to breathe quietly in and out through the nose. The first segment of the utterance is an obstruent, and so the velum rises to prevent the escape of air through the nose. All obstruent consonants require the velum to take up this closed position. The first sound that requires the velum to be in the down position is the final consonant in the word *home*, but notice that the movement towards this position takes place during the preceding diphthong, which is somewhat nasalised as a result. The velum must be closed for the hold phase of the following plosive, and so the closing movement takes place during the last portion of the [m]. The diphthong of *by* is similarly nasalised, this time by the first consonant of *nine*, and the diphthong of *nine* itself is affected by both preceding and following nasals. At the end of the utterance the velum remains down as the speaker returns to quiet breathing. Notice that there are no silent gaps between words, and that coarticulation of nasality occurs both within words and across word boundaries.

## Drawing velum diagrams

1  transcribe the word or phrase phonetically
2  divide into segments, with one column for each
3  find any obstruent consonants, and indicate that the velum is up for these
4  find any nasal consonants, and indicate that the velum is down for them
5  fill in remaining segments, showing coarticulation where it occurs
6  remember to start and finish with the breathing position (which does not have the effect of nasalising adjacent segments).

## Overlapping articulations

The examples of coarticulation we have looked at so far involve a single moving articulator, but it is also possible for the movements of quite separate articulators to overlap in time, giving new combinations of properties. For example in the word *bread*, it is very likely that during the production of the first consonant, the tongue tip will take up the position required for the second consonant. This is possible because the bilabial plosive has no particular specification for what the tongue tip must do. Because of this coarticulation, the [b] in this context is quite different from the one in *bed* for example.

## Coarticulation of plosives

In Chapter 4 the production of plosive consonants was described in terms of approach, hold and release phases. When plosives occur in sequence, these phases of production can be affected by coarticulation in various ways. Consider the English word *act*, where there is a sequence of a velar and an alveolar plosive. It is very likely that the timing of the production of these plosives will be as in Figure 8.7.

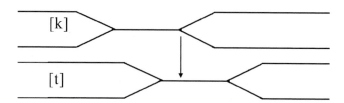

FIGURE 8.7
Overlapping [kt] phases.

Notice that the release phase of the first plosive takes place during the hold phase of the second plosive. This means that although the back of the tongue breaks its contact with the velum, no audible plosion will be heard at this stage, because the air is stopped by the alveolar closure. A transcription of *act* in the pronunciation represented in Figure 8.7 is [æk⌐t] where the diacritic indicates inaudible release. In general in English the release of the first plosive in a sequence is inaudible. The sequence may be within a word, or may result from putting two words together, as in *black tie*. It is worth noticing that languages may handle this situation in different ways. For instance both French and German regularly have audible release for the first of two plosives in a sequence. Examples like this show us that languages can differ in their coarticulatory patterns.

When two successive plosives are at the same place of articulation, coarticulation takes a different form. In a word like *background*, for example, the velar closure is formed for the [k] and retained for the [g]. The first plosive lacks any release phase, and the second lacks an approach phase, as shown in Figure 8.8. The same diacritic is used for this, so that *background* would be transcribed ['bæk⌐graʊnd].

> *Find a native speaker of French or German and explore the differences in pronunciation of plosive sequences, using French* acte *or German* Akt.

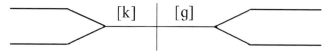

FIGURE 8.8
Phases of [kg] sequence.

## Coarticulation and secondary articulation

One property that commonly spreads onto adjacent sounds is lip rounding. In the word *sweet*, for example, it is very likely that the lip rounding required for the [w] will be anticipated during the [s]. This has an obvious auditory effect, as you can hear by comparing it with the consonant at the beginning of the word *seat*. The [s] of sweet has the secondary articulation of labialisation, symbolised [sʷ]. In this instance the secondary articulation results from coarticulation. You should be careful not to confuse the two concepts. A sound may have an inherent secondary articulation that cannot be explained as resulting from coarticulation. For instance, the English consonant [ʃ] is always somewhat rounded for many speakers, regardless of the context in which it occurs.

## Duration variation

We have pointed out previously that it is not always easy to identify the beginnings and ends of segments in the acoustic signal. Nevertheless, useful segmentations can often be made and the duration of speech sounds can be estimated. Figure 8.9 shows a spectrogram of the English word *sounds*. Plausible segmentation points are indicated, enabling us to determine that the [s] has a duration of approximately 130 milliseconds, the diphthong [aʊ] a duration of about 250 milliseconds, the nasal [n] about 125 milliseconds, the plosive [d] about 80 milliseconds, and the final fricative [z] around 165 milliseconds.

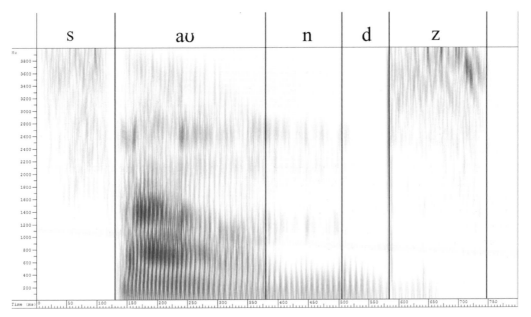

FIGURE 8.9
Spectrogram of *sounds* with segmentation.

Speech sounds measured in this way generally have durations somewhere in a range of about 30 milliseconds to 200 or 300 milliseconds, but the duration of a particular sort of segment is not fixed. It will vary depending on the context in which the segment appears. For instance, the last sound or two at the end of an utterance are generally prolonged, an effect known as pre-pausal lengthening. As another example, a syllable-initial consonant is generally longer when alone but considerably shorter when preceding another consonant in a cluster. This can be seen in Figure 8.10, where we have spectrograms of the two words *sigh* and *sky*.

In Chapter 6 we pointed out that the duration of a vowel may be influenced by whether the following consonant is voiced or voiceless. This effect is very prominent in some accents of English and is known as pre-fortis clipping.

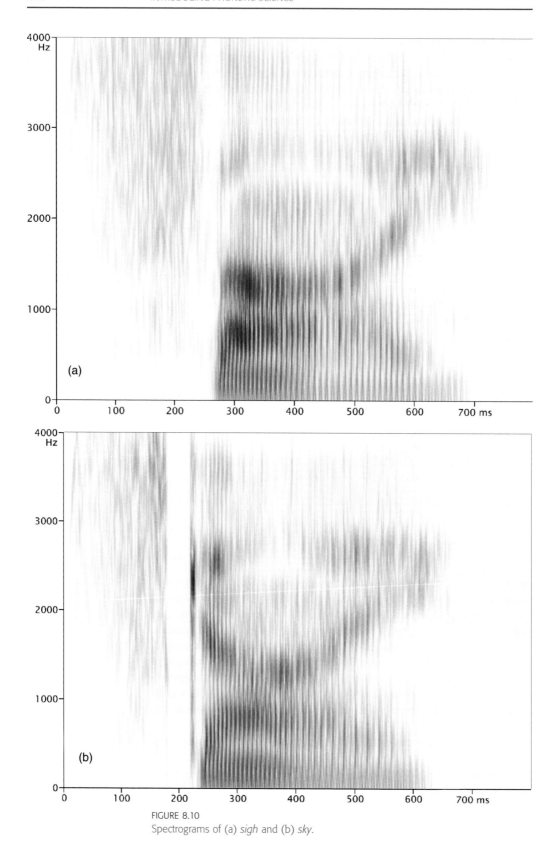

FIGURE 8.10
Spectrograms of (a) *sigh* and (b) *sky*.

Other factors that influence segment duration include overall speech rate, and the degree of stress placed on syllables.

## Acoustic and physiological data

There are a number of different ways of investigating coarticulation and showing how the vocal tract changes shape over time. Spectrograms show the changing acoustic patterns, or direct measurements can be made of articulator positions.

### Spectrograms

A simple illustration of the use of spectrograms to reveal coarticulatory effects is shown in Figure 8.11. Spectrogram (a) is of the word *key* and (b) is of the word *car*. Following the release of the two plosives the formants can be seen moving towards the frequencies characteristic of the two different vowels, but it is clear that the formants do not start at the same frequencies. This difference is a reflection of the coarticulatory variation in precise point of contact between the articulators.

### Electropalatography

The technique of electropalatography is explained in Chapter 3 and is ideal for investigating some aspects of coarticulation. As an illustration of this look at Figure 8.12. Here we have electropalatograms showing the hold phase of [k], produced by a speaker of Catalan, in three different environments. Notice that the closure extends further forward in the oral cavity for the [k] produced in the environment of a high front vowel (the leftmost picture).

### X-ray studies

Although X-ray studies are now very rarely carried out because of the danger of irradiation, some classic studies show coarticulation very clearly. Figure 8.13 consists of tracings from X-ray pictures of the vocal tract. The lefthand column shows the positions for steady vowels [y ɑ u] and the righthand column shows the hold phase of [g] pronounced between vowels of each type. One can clearly see the relationship between the position of the tongue for the vowel and the location of the closure for the plosive.

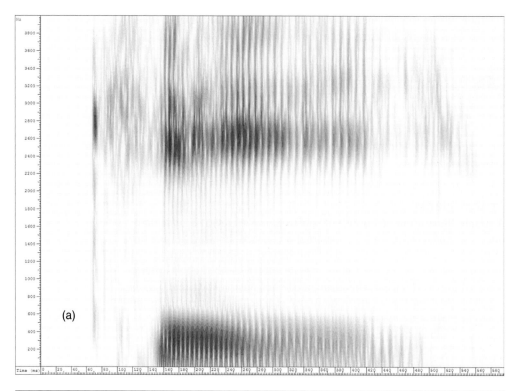

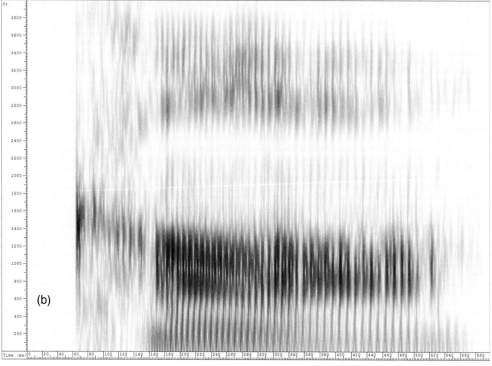

FIGURE 8.11
Spectrograms of (a) *key* and (b) *car*.

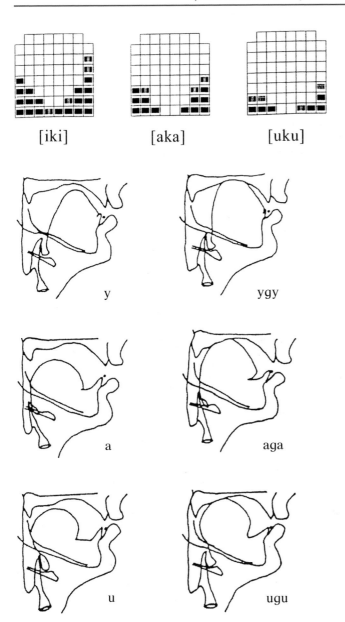

[iki]   [aka]   [uku]

FIGURE 8.12
Electropalatograms of intervocalic [k] in three contexts (after W. J. Hardcastle and N. Hewlett, *Coarticulation*, Cambridge: Cambridge University Press, 1999).

FIGURE 8.13
X-ray tracings showing coarticulatory effects of surrounding vowels on a velar stop (after S. Öhman, 'Numerical Model of Co-articulation', *JASA* 41 (1967)).

## Chapter summary

In this chapter we have looked at the articulation of speech sounds in more detail. We have seen that sounds may have more than one constriction. Common secondary articulations are labialisation, palatalisation, velarisation and pharyngealisation. The articulation of all sounds is likely to be influenced by the context in which they appear. Examples of such influence are: the addition of a secondary articulation to a sound, the fine adjustment of the place of articulation, the addition of nasalisation, or variations in duration. The chapter also introduced diagrams showing the activity of articulators as a good way of indicating the co-ordination of speech movements.

## Exercises

### Exercise 8.1
Give a description of the movements of the articulators during the pronunciation of the word *swim* [sʷɪm]. Pay particular attention to coarticulation.

### Exercise 8.2
Draw parametric diagrams, showing velum activity and vocal fold vibration, for the following words.

(a) time
(b) pounds
(c) training
(d) screen
(e) important

You may need to refresh your memory of the details of aspiration and devoicing as explained in Chapter 6.

### Exercise 8.3

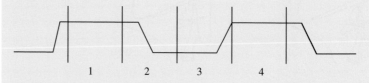

This diagram shows velum movement in a word with four segments labelled 1, 2, 3, 4. Which of the following English words would be produced with velum movement matching the diagram. Explain your decisions and suggest other words that would match.

(a) camp    (b) cold    (c) mission    (d) elms    (e) film

### Exercise 8.4
In the following passage, find all the places where overlapping of plosives may occur. Remember that the two plosives do not have to be in the same word.

The chap grinned. He picked himself up off the floor and rubbed his knee. Up till that moment the atmosphere had been quite relaxed. Everyone started to look tense. Maybe he wouldn't be able to do it.

### Exercise 8.5
Look at the spectrograms of *sigh* and *sky* in Figure 8.10 and estimate in milliseconds the durations of the two examples of [s].

### Further reading
For much more detail on the descriptive framework for segments, see J. Laver, *Principles of phonetics*, Cambridge: Cambridge University Press, 1994. Chapter 11 is concerned with multiple articulations of all kinds, including secondary articulation. For an up-to-date survey of coarticulation, see W. J. Hardcastle and N. Hewlett, *Coarticulation: Theory, data and techniques*, Cambridge: Cambridge University Press, 1999. Part IV of the same book is devoted to ways of measuring and imaging speech.

# 9 Basic phonological concepts

## CHAPTER OUTLINE

In this chapter you will learn: the way that sound differences are used to distinguish words; how similar, non-contrastive sounds can be grouped into phonemes; how sounds form patterns in a language; how to look for patterns in samples of phonetic data; about the grouping of sounds into syllables; differences between languages in permitted sound groupings; about widespread phonological processes in languages; about phonological features and phonological rules.

### KEY TERMS

Allophone
Alternation
Assimilation
Coda
Contrast
Distribution
Elision
Environment
Feature
Lenition
Minimal pair
Onset
Phoneme
Phonological process
Rhyme
Rule

## Contrast

Imagine a language where all word-initial consonants are voiceless and all consonants elsewhere in a word are voiced. This would mean that in this language a word like [pidag] is possible, but one like [bitak] is impossible. The voicing of a consonant in this language is completely determined by some aspect of the environment of the consonant, in this case the position within a word. It is impossible for this language to use the phonetic distinction between voiced consonants and voiceless ones to distinguish one word from another, even though the language has voiced and voiceless pairs of consonants. We can say that in this language there is no voicing contrast or, equivalently, that voicing of consonants is not contrastive in this language.

In English and in many other languages, voicing is contrastive for consonants. We can demonstrate this with a pair of words like *fussy* [fʌsi] and *fuzzy* [fʌzi] in English or a pair in French like *choux* [ʃu] 'cabbage' and *joue* [ʒu] 'play'. In the imaginary language we have just considered such pairs of words could not occur.

Most languages in the world make some use of the voicing contrast, but it is not universal. For example in almost all indigenous languages of Australia, voiced and voiceless plosive consonants are used non-contrastively. The language Dyirbal is very similar to the imaginary example used here. In Dyirbal, plosives are generally voiced when they occur between vowels, and voiceless when they occur at the beginning of a word, as in [tiban] meaning 'stone'. But Dyirbal additionally allows a free variation between voiced and voiceless in initial position, and will also accept the same variation within words (though native speakers don't generally do it). So 'stone' can be any of [diban] [tiban] [tipan] [dipan].

An example of a phonetic distinction that is not contrastive in English is velarisation. Many accents of English have a velarised lateral approximant [ɫ], which appears before a consonant or before a pause, as in *milk* or *cool*, alongside an ordinary non-velarised [l] which appears when there is a vowel or [j] following as in *look* or *familiar*. It is easy to see that if the velarised sound occurs automatically according to differences in the surrounding sounds, then the presence or absence of velarisation can never be found on its own as the only factor that distinguishes one word from another.

## Minimal pair

In order to prove conclusively that a phonetic distinction is contrastive in a particular language it is necessary to find a pair of words in the language that differ in only one segment. The differing segments must be in the same position in the two words, and be different in only their values for the phonetic distinction in question. Finally, the two must mean different

| Table 9.1 Minimal pairs in various languages | | | | |
|---|---|---|---|---|
| LANGUAGE | EXAMPLE OF MINIMAL PAIR | | | |
| Burmese | [ma] | *healthy* | [m̥a] | *order* |
| Ewe | [efa] | *he was cold* | [eɸa] | *he polished* |
| German | [laidn] | *suffer* | [laitn] | *to lead* |
| Italian | [fato] | *fate* | [fatːo] | *done* |
| Korean | [pul] | *fire* | [pʰul] | *grass* |
| Spanish | [pero] | *dog* | [pero] | *but* |
| Welsh | [gwin] | *wine* | [gwiːn] | *white* |

things – that is, they must not simply be alternative pronunciations of the same word. Such a pair of words is called a minimal pair. The words *fussy* and *fuzzy* constitute a minimal pair in English, as do *choux* and *joue* in French. The presence or absence of a segment can also make a minimal pair. For example *tack* and *tax* form a minimal pair in English.

Languages make contrastive use of a wide variety of phonetic differences, and a small number of examples appear in Table 9.1. The sound differences that are contrastive in a language seem obvious and clear to speakers of that language, but may seem strange and difficult to a person who does not speak the language.

## Environment and distribution

The environment of a segment is simply its position relative to other sounds. An environment can be symbolised A__B. The underscore (__) represents the position of the segment in question, while A means the segment(s) occurring before it and B means the segment(s) that follows it. To give an example from English: one of the environments for the segment [t] in English is [s]__[j]. This tells us that [t] can be found in between [s] and [j] in English words, such as *student* and *stew*. An example of an environment where [t] cannot be found in English is #__[g]. The symbol # means 'word boundary', so the environment statement means: at the beginning of a word before a [g]. The environment V__# means: at the end of a word after a vowel. Of course, [t] in English can be found in this environment, but [w], for example, cannot.

If we were to draw up a long list of all the environments in which [t] can be found in English then we would in a sense have completely specified the distribution of [t] in English, but the list would be cumbersome and unrevealing. By searching for patterns in the list, we can hope to summarise it with general statements. For instance, in the imaginary language we introduced above where voicing is not contrastive, a summary of the distribution of [t] in that language would be that it occurs at the beginning of a word regardless of what follows. We can symbolise this as #__.

Remember that distributions only apply in the language for which they are worked out, and any particular type of sound is quite likely to have different distributions in different languages. For instance, the word-final environment __# is part of the distribution of the sound [d] in English, as we can see from words such as *red* and *cold*, but not of the sound [d] in German. No matter how long we search, we will never find an example of a German word ending in the sound [d] because in German all word-final obstruents have to be voiceless.

## Phoneme and allophone

We saw above how [l] and [ɫ] are not contrastive in English. We can find further sounds in this non-contrastive set. For instance, in words like *health*, where an l-sound is followed by a dental fricative, a common pronunciation involves [ɫ̪], which is a voiced velarised dental (rather than alveolar) lateral approximant. A speaker cannot use the difference between dental place and alveolar place for lateral approximants in English to signal a difference in word identity, so the difference between the two laterals is non-contrastive. Another member of this set is [ɫ̃], which is a voiced nasalised and velarised alveolar lateral approximant. This is found immediately before [n] and [m] in words like *film* and *kiln* or in phrases like *all men,* and again cannot contrast with any of the other lateral approximants in English.

The consonant sounds we have identified here are similar phonetically in that they are all voiced lateral approximants. They differ in some aspects of their production and the differences are perfectly audible if one listens carefully. However, these phonetic differences are irrelevant for distinguishing between one word and another in English. We sum this up by saying that the set of lateral sounds we have just identified belong together in one of the **phonemes** of English, a **phoneme** being one of the basic phonological units of which all words in the language are composed.

We represent a phoneme with a symbol placed in slant brackets, as opposed to square brackets. The various sounds that make up a phoneme are known as its **allophones**. The sounds [l] [ɫ] [ɫ̪] [ɫ̃] are allophones of an English phoneme that we can represent as /l/. Using the brackets in the same way, we can say for instance that the aspirated bilabial plosive [pʰ] is one of the allophones of the /p/ phoneme in English (of course, there are other allophones of /p/ too, which are found in different environments).

The grouping of sounds into phonemes is different in different languages, or even in different varieties within one language. The two sounds [d] and [ð] belong to different phonemes in English, but are allophones of a single phoneme in Castilian Spanish, where [ð] is an allophone of the /d/ phoneme. As this example shows, allophones of a phoneme are often sufficiently different that entirely different phonetic symbols are needed for them. To give another example, the two sounds [f] and [v] belong to different phonemes in present-day English, but in Old English, spoken about 1000 years ago, the two sounds were allophones of a single /f/ phoneme. See Table 9.2 for further examples of phonemes and some of their allophones in various languages. We saw earlier that the sound differences that are contrastive in a particular language may seem surprising to an

> *Don't forget the distinction between spellings and sounds. Plenty of German words are written with a final d but the pronunciation is always with [t]. For instance the noun which is written Tod 'death' is pronounced [toːt], identically with the adjective written tot meaning 'dead'.*

## Table 9.2 Phonemes and allophones in various languages

| language | phoneme | allophones |
|---|---|---|
| Burmese | /j/ | [j ȷ̊ . . .] |
| Canadian English | /aɪ/ | [aë̞ əë̈ . . .] |
| British English | /t/ | [tʰ tʷ . . .] |
| | /əʊ/ | [əö̞ ɒö̈ . . .] |
| | /r/ | [ɹ ɹ̊ . . .] |
| Castilian Spanish | /b/ | [b β . . .] |
| French | /r/ | [ʁ χ . . .] |
| General American | /t/ | [tʰ ɾ . . .] |
| German | /x/ | [x ç . . .] |
| Japanese | /t/ | [t ts . . .] |
| Modern Standard Chinese | /i/ | [i ɯ . . .] |
| Old English | /h/ | [h x . . .] |
| South American Spanish | /s/ | [s h . . .] |
| Welsh | /m/ | [m m̥ . . .] |

observer who speaks a different language. In a corresponding way, the extent of the phonetic differences among allophones of one phoneme can seem surprisingly large, yet speakers of the language in question accept the allophones as versions of 'the same sound' and may find it hard to hear the differences even when they are pointed out.

## Complementary distribution

When we compare the distributions of two sounds in a language, we may find that they are partially similar – that is, the two sounds share some environments. For example [pʰ] may appear in much the same environments as [tʰ] in English. However, if we compare the environments of two sounds that are allophones of the same phoneme in the language in question we will often find they can never appear in the same environments – their distributions are completely different from one another. This is called complementary distribution. Consider the Canadian English example in Table 9.2. The phoneme /aɪ/ has amongst its allophones a sound [əë̈], which occurs only before voiceless consonants, in words such as *white* or *rice*. Another allophone is [aë̈], which occurs elsewhere, for example in words such as *why*, *wide* or *rise*. These two sounds are in complementary distribution in this accent of English. However, the fact that two sounds are in complementary distribution is no guarantee that they should be classed as allophones of the same phoneme. Allophones of the same phoneme must also have some shared phonetic characteristics. To take an extreme example, if one were investigating a new language and found that [ʒ] and [m] happen to be in complementary distribution, we would not be tempted to regard the two sounds as being allophones of one and the same phoneme, because they are just too dissimilar phonetically.

## Alternation

Phonology is not only concerned with the establishment of the phonemes of a language and the distribution of sounds. It is concerned with sound patterns in general. Sound patterns are of two basic types:

- alternations, where a word turns up in two or more forms, and there are systematic sound-differences between the forms.
- distributional regularities concerning sounds, such as restrictions on possible sound sequences within words, syllables etc. We deal with this topic later in this chapter.

As an example of an alternation, consider the word *fan*. It is generally pronounced with an alveolar nasal at the end [fæn], but in *fan club* it can be pronounced with a velar nasal [fæŋ], making it indistinguishable from *fang*. In *fan belt*, there is a third alternant [fæm]. The only satisfactory way to account for the fact that many words or components of words have more than one pronunciation is to suppose that some pronunciations are derived by rules from other possible pronunciations, or that all pronunciations are derived by rules from some kind of abstract form.

## Phonological processes

Phonological processes operate upon natural groupings of sounds, and give rise to alternations in the forms of words. Phonological processes belong to a small number of frequently occurring types.

- assimilation, where a sound becomes more like some other sound in its immediate context. Here are some data showing a simple assimilatory process from Lithuanian:

  [sambuːris] 'assembly'   [sampilas] 'stock'
  [sandora] 'covenant'   [santaka] 'confluence'
  [saŋkaba] 'connection'

The first syllable of all these words is a prefix that is the equivalent of *con-* in English. Notice that the place of articulation of the final nasal in this prefix is adjusted to agree with the place of articulation of the following consonant.

These examples show assimilation affecting place of articulation, but it can affect other properties of sounds equally well. Look at the data from Sudanese Arabic below:

| [kitaːb] | 'book' |
|---|---|
| [kitaːf faθi] | 'Fathi's book' |
| [bit] | 'daughter' |
| [bis samiːr] | 'Samir's daughter' |
| [biʃ ʃariːf] | 'Sharif's daughter' |
| [samak] | 'fish' |
| [samax xaːlid] | 'Khalid's fish' |

Notice that the voiced consonant at the end of [kitaːb] is made to agree in voicing with the following sound, and that the final consonant in the first word of all these phrases agrees in manner of articulation with the first consonant of the following word.

- deletion (also called *elision* and truncation) where a sound is lost from a sequence. A good example of this is found in the speech of young children acquiring English. Look at the words below:

| word | adult form | typical child form |
|---|---|---|
| *play* | [pleɪ] | [peɪ] |
| *green* | [ɡɹiːn] | [giːn] |
| *twin* | [twɪn] | [tɪn] |

The pattern shown here, in which approximant consonants are deleted when they are the second member of a word-initial cluster, is a common one in normal acquisition.

- the opposite process, insertion, puts in a sound where none was present before. A very common feature of many accents of English is called r-linking and involves inserting an r-sound of some sort between two vowels as in the words and phrases below.

*floor* [flɔː]        *flooring* [flɔːɹɪŋ]
*mother* [mʌðə]    *mother-in-law* [mʌðəɹ ɪn lɔː]
*vanilla* [vənɪlə]    *vanilla ice-cream* [vənɪləɹ aɪskɹiːm]

- lenition (also called weakening): consonants can be arranged on scales of strength:

plosive > fricative > approximant > zero
aspirated > voiceless > voiced

Thus a voiceless aspirated plosive is the strongest type of consonant, and a voiced approximant is the weakest. The scales can be summed-up by saying that a consonant is stronger the more it differs from vowels; a consonant becomes weaker the more it comes to resemble a vowel.

A lenition process affects voiced plosives between vowels in Spanish. The conventional orthography gives no indication of the changes, but the alternations are perfectly regular.

| orthography | pronunciation | meaning |
|---|---|---|
| donde | [donde] | where |

| dado | [daðo] | dice |
| todo | [toðo] | all |
| bomba | [bomba] | bomb |
| beber | [beβer] | to drink |
| bodega | [boðeɣa] | wine cellar |
| gas | [gas] | gas |
| digame | [diɣame] | hello/can I help you? |

In initial position or following a consonant we find voiced plosives, but between vowels we find the equivalent voiced fricatives. It seems reasonable to regard these fricatives as resulting from lenition of the plosives, and reasonable too that the weakening of the closure gesture for the plosive should occur in the position between two vowels.

- dissimilation: this process is the opposite of assimilation, and has the effect of preventing two similar segments occurring close together. It is much less common than assimilation, and the best examples we can give are historical ones showing its operation at some stage in the past. For example the Latin word for 'tree' [arbor] developed into Spanish [arbol] where the final [l] results from the avoidance of two r-sounds close together. The same sort of change can be seen in the development of the French word [peleʁɛ̃] 'pilgrim' from Latin [peregrinus].
- fortition: this is the opposite of lenition and involves sounds moving towards the stronger end of the scales mentioned above. An example of this comes from German, which allows both voiced and voiceless obstruents within words, but only voiceless obstruents word-finally. Comparison of alternations shows us that obstruents are getting devoiced in final position.

| Rates | [ʁaːtəs] | 'of advice' | Rat | [ʁaːt] | 'advice' |
| Rades | [ʁaːdəs] | 'of wheel' | Rad | [ʁaːt] | 'wheel' |

Here it is the final sound of the word for 'wheel' that has undergone fortition.

## Features

We can think of sounds as being specified by certain properties, called phonological features. In a sense these features summarise and formalise the phonetic description of sounds by providing a checklist of properties that can be used to classify all of the sounds in a language. In one influential version of this idea, the features are assumed to be binary – that is, they can only have the values plus (+) or minus (−).

### Some important binary features
It is beyond the scope of this book to discuss a complete list of features, but a few important ones will give an idea of how binary features are

defined and used. Some are fairly obvious, such as [+/− voice], [+/− nasal] [+/− syllabic] and [+/− lateral]. So for instance vowels are [+syllabic, + voice], nasalised vowels will be [+syllabic, +voice, +nasal], while the specification [+syllabic, +voice, −nasal] identifies specifically the class of non-nasalised vowels. Any lateral consonant will be [+lateral], while one which is also syllabic (as in one common pronunciation of the English word *bottle*) will be [+lateral, +syllabic].

For certain other features we must attend to the precise definition. The feature [+/− continuant] helps us define the category *stop*. Sounds count as stops (that is, they are [−continuant]) if they have a complete closure on the midline of the vocal tract. So plosives are [−continuant], but so are nasals (because they have a complete closure in the mouth). Plosives are thus oral stops, nasal consonants are nasal stops. Notice that 'complete closure on the midline' needn't mean that airflow is actually stopped, even in the oral cavity, so that a lateral consonant can also count as [−continuant].

The important distinction between sonorants and obstruents is handled with the feature [+/− sonorant]. All obstruents (that is, plosives, fricatives and affricates) are [−sonorant], while everything else, including vowels, is [+sonorant].

The treatment of place of articulation with binary features doesn't make use of familiar place-labels such as alveolar, velar and so on. Much of the work is done by two important features [+/− coronal] and [+/− anterior]. A sound is [+coronal] if it has an articulation in which the tongue blade is raised. So dentals, alveolars, post-alveolars, retroflexes and palatals are all [+coronal] while sounds at all other places of articulation, such as labials and velars, are [−coronal]. A sound is [+anterior] if it is produced with a constriction at, or in front of, the alveolar ridge. So labials, labiodentals, dentals and alveolars are all [+anterior], while all places of articulation further back are all [−anterior]. Note that post-alveolars, including the sounds sometimes called palato-alveolar, are in this [−anterior] class.

The examples given so far show features as applied to consonant sounds, but of course vowel sounds can also be categorised using binary features. Consonants as a class are [+consonantal], while vowels are [−consonantal, +syllabic]. The main features employed to deal with vowel quality are [+/− high], [+/− low], [+/− back] and [+/− round]. There is obviously some interaction between the features [high] and [low], since a vowel could not be both [+high] and [+low], though [−high, −low] is a reasonable way of indicating a vowel of mid height. To give an example of feature specification applied to vowels, a vowel of type [i] is [+high, −low, −back, −round]. The semivowel type of approximant will share the feature specification of the corresponding vowel, but will be [−consonantal, −syllabic]. So [j] has the same feature specification as [i] except for the value of [syllabic].

## Natural classes

We said above that the phonological processes operate on natural groupings of sounds, but what exactly are these groupings, and how do they arise? Phonological features provide a way to answer this question. Each particular sound will have its own unique list of feature-specifications, but two or more sounds that are similar in some respects will have partly overlapping feature specifications. A natural class is thus a group of sounds that is easily specified with relatively few features. So, for instance, the class of all obstruents is captured with the simple specification [−sonorant], the class of all fricatives is [−sonorant, +continuant] and so on. On the other hand, if we take a random assortment of sounds, such as [s] [e] [m] [k] we find that it is not a natural class of sounds, and there is no simple way of specifying the group using features.

## Underlying and surface forms

Pronunciations of words (the 'surface' forms) can be thought of as the output of a system of rules and representations, called the phonological component, which is internalised by speakers of a language. This starts from fairly abstract 'underlying' forms of words, in which each sound is represented as a list of feature-values, and then processes them in appropriate ways. The underlying form of a word can be different from any actual spoken form. Looking at the German example given above one can see that it makes sense to assume that the underlying form of the word 'wheel' is [ʁaːd], very much as the spelling *Rad* suggests, even though the word is never spoken with a [d] at the end. If we don't make that assumption, we can't explain why there is a [d] rather than a [t] in the inflected form [ʁaːdəs] 'of wheel'. The actual pronunciation [ʁaːt] results from putting the underlying form through a rule that forces every word-final obstruent to be voiceless in actual spoken output.

To take another example, aspiration or non-aspiration of voiceless plosives need not be shown in underlying forms in English, and need not be stored mentally for every word in which it is found. A process in the phonological component can check every word as it is produced to see if it contains any voiceless plosives in the right position (before a vowel within a stressed syllable). When it finds one, the process will add a specification of the appropriate aspiration by altering the feature representation. When the word leaves the phonological component and is spoken aloud by vocal tract movements, aspiration will appear in the correct place.

## Phonological rules

Obviously, unvoicing final obstruents in German, or adding aspiration to voiceless plosives in English, are just examples of many regularities that the phonology will have to deal with, since all other predictable characteristics will also have been removed from underlying forms. The phonological component may be visualised as a long list of rules, each one scanning for the conditions in which it must operate, and changing feature specifications where appropriate. If a certain rule doesn't apply, it passes on the input without changing it. The output of each rule becomes the input to the next, until all the rules have had a chance to operate.

There is a whole system of formalism for showing rules, and we started to use some of this earlier in this chapter when we were discussing the notion of environment. Phonological rules have the general form

$$X \rightarrow Y/A\_B$$

Here X is the input, Y the output, and A__B indicates the context. A, B, X and Y stand for sets of feature specifications, each one identifying a certain type of sound (or more usually a class of sounds). It means that if the specification X is encountered between an example of A and an example of B, then X must be changed into specification Y. Either A or B may be missing if the preceding or following context is not relevant. If both A and B are missing the rule applies regardless of context and is said to be 'context-free'. Sounds can be added or deleted as well as modified, and the symbol Ø ('zero') is used for this, and A or B can be boundaries rather than sounds; so for instance X→Ø/A__# would mean that any example of X should be deleted if it is at the end of a word and preceded by A.

The rule to devoice a final obstruent in German would thus be

$$[-\text{sonorant}] \rightarrow [-\text{voice}]/\_\#$$

It is often useful to employ this type of notation informally, with phonetic symbols or verbal descriptions instead of rigorous feature-specifications, and there are examples of this in the exercises to this chapter. The symbols C and V are used in rules with the respective meanings [+consonantal, −syllabic] and [−consonantal, +syllabic]. So

> C
> [−nasal]

means any consonant except nasals, while

> V
> [−high]

means any non-high vowel.

## The syllable

In Chapter 1, we attempted a rough definition of a phonetic syllable; there are plenty of clear examples, but the concept is hard to pin down exactly. The syllable can also be thought of as a phonological unit – that is, as a grouping of sounds in accordance with certain rules, which differ from language to language. The essential component in any syllable is a vowel, which provides the nucleus of the syllable. This may be preceded or followed by one or more consonants. Consonants before the vowel form the onset of the syllable; consonants after the vowel form the coda. There are

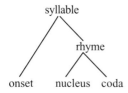

FIGURE 9.1
The structure of the syllable.

reasons for believing that the nucleus and coda together form another unit within the syllable. In English for example, two syllables are said to rhyme with each other (in verse) if they have the same nucleus and the same coda (or absence of coda). So *day* rhymes with *bay*, and *date* rhymes with *bait*. But languages seem not to make use of a unit consisting of the onset and nucleus together. The nucleus-plus-coda unit of the syllable is called the rhyme. The structure of the syllable can be shown as in Figure 9.1.

These terms can be very useful in describing the distributions of sounds. In English the velar nasal sound may appear only in the coda of syllables, never in the onset. It need not be the very last sound in a syllable, though it may be, as we see from words such as *bang, bank, banks*. Without the term coda, we would have to say that the velar nasal occurs only in the part of the syllable that follows the vowel. Similarly, the English consonants /w h j/ occur only in onsets. If the onset or the coda is missing from a particular syllable, we say that the position is 'empty'. So for instance the English word *eat* is an example of a syllable with an empty onset. (Though if we pronounce the word in isolation we may add a glottal stop at the beginning, supplying an onset that is not present in the underlying form.) A syllable with no coda is called an open syllable, whereas a syllable with at least one coda consonant is said to be closed. These terms, too, are very useful. For instance, certain English vowels (examples are [æ, e, ɒ]) have the property that they cannot occur in stressed open syllables, and this is why we know there just couldn't be any English words [bæ] or [bɒ]. With closed syllables, there's no problem: *bat* [bæt] and *box* [bɒks] are perfectly good English words.

## Phonotactics

Languages differ considerably in the types of syllables they use, and speakers of the languages have an intuitive understanding of what are, and what are not, permitted syllables in their language. To use a famous example, speakers of English will generally agree that *blick* is a 'possible' English word, while *bnick* is not. It certainly isn't the case that *bnick* is 'unpronounceable' in any general sense. It's just that [bn-] isn't a permitted syllable onset in English. In fact, no onsets of plosive consonant followed by nasal consonant are allowed in English.

A statement of the permitted combinations of phonemes into structures (often the syllable) is a statement of the phonotactics of the language. So it is quite common to find that different ranges of consonants can be used in onset and coda positions (a common pattern is for there to be a wide range of choice in the onset position, but just a few possibilities for the coda). And if sequences of consonants are permitted in the onset or coda, their length and composition is likely to be restricted. A sequence of consonants within the onset, or within the coda, is called a consonant cluster.

Onsets in English will provide an illustration of phonotactic patterning. For a single consonant, we find that any English consonant phoneme can occur, with the exception of /ŋ/ the velar nasal, which as explained above is restricted to coda position. (In plenty of other languages, of course, the velar nasal is found as an onset – for example, in Vietnamese.) When we consider two-consonant onset clusters in English, we find that it is far from being the case that any two-consonant combination will do; in fact, if you make a list and try out the hundreds of logically possible two-consonant combinations, you find that most of them are not allowed. There's no /bd-, bg-, bm-, mk-/, and so on. Those that do occur turn out to belong to one of two types. Either the first consonant is /s/ and the second is one of a group that includes chiefly /p t k m n/, or the second consonant is one of the approximants /w r l j/ and the first is drawn from a group that includes plosives, nasals and fricatives. The first type can be represented s + C, the second as C + approximant. (When searching for examples, we will sometimes find isolated instances of other onset clusters in foreign words borrowed in English. For example, English doesn't really have an onset cluster /pt-/, though some people pronounce it at the beginning of the word *pterodactyl* which is taken from Greek.)

For three-consonant onsets, we find even less choice. The first consonant is always /s/, the second generally one of /p t k/, and the third is an approximant. This gives combinations such as /str-/ in *string*, /spl-/ as in *splash*, and /skw-/ as in *squash*. Notice that these strings of three consonants always include two of the possible two-consonant onsets: /str-/ includes /st-/ and /tr-/. So the possible three-consonant onsets seem to be like two of the possible two-consonant onsets stuck together.

We have searched for onset clusters at the beginnings of English words, making the assumption that the beginning of a word must also be the beginning of a syllable. Of course onsets may be within words that have two or more syllables. For example in *construct* there is a sequence of consonants /nstr/. The first syllable has /n/ as its coda, and the second syllable appears to have the onset /str-/. If we look at the ends of words we can find 0, 1, 2, 3 or 4 consonants, as in *go, egg, friend, milked, texts*. So an English syllable can have up to three consonants in the onset, and up to four in the coda.

The situation is usually summed up in terms of a template:

$$C_0^3 \, V \, C_0^4$$

Other languages will have different templates. Maori is an example of a language that has very severe constraints on clusters. Initial clusters must consist of 0 or 1 consonant and final clusters must consist of no consonants at all. So the Maori template is:

$$C_0^1 \, V$$

Another language with a very restrictive template is Modern Standard Chinese:

$$C_0^1 \, V \, C_0^1$$

Certain languages allow very much more complex clusters than English, both in the length of clusters that are allowed and also in the permitted combinations of sound types. In Polish, for example, a word may begin with up to five consonants. And whereas it is the case in English that the affricates /tʃ ðʒ/ do not occur in onset clusters, and that no consonant ever clusters with itself, one permitted type of onset in Polish consists of two occurrences of the same affricate. Try pronouncing the examples of interesting onsets in the table below, taken from Polish and Russian.

| Polish | [ˈspstrɔw̃ɟɛm] | 'with (the) trout' |
|--------|----------------|--------------------|
|        | [vzglɔnt]      | 'respect' (noun)   |
|        | [ˈdʒdʒɪstɪ]    | 'rainy'            |
| Russian | [ˈzdrastvuj]  | 'hello/how do you do?' |
|         | [ˈmtʃatsə]    | 'to rush'          |
|         | [ˈvzmorjɪm]   | 'sea shore'        |

## Chapter summary

Contrast is the use of phonetic differences to signal the distinction between words. A pair of distinct words that differ only in one segment is a minimal pair. Two sounds that cannot mark a contrast between words may be allophones of the same basic unit (members of the same phoneme) especially if each has its own specific environments, meaning that the two are in complementary distribution. The aim of phonology is not only to establish the set of phonemes in a language, but also the patterning of these sounds, both dynamic and static. Patterns of changes in the pronunciation of words (alternations) often result from the operation of phonological processes, the same general types of process being found widely in languages. Phonological patterning can be described formally by specifying sounds (e.g. with rigorously defined features) and then writing rules that alter sound specifications. The internal or mental representation of a word (the underlying form) can be different from the observable (surface) form. The phonological syllable is a structure that specifies how sounds of different types can be combined. The rules for combinations (phonotactics) are different in different languages.

## Exercises

### Exercise 9.1
Look at the examples of minimal pairs in various languages given in Table 9.1. Try to read the words from the transcriptions given. Give phonetic labels for the two sounds that are responsible for the contrast, and say in what ways the sounds are similar and exactly how they are different.

### Exercise 9.2
Use your own pronunciation of English to search for minimal pairs among the words below. Pronounce the first word given at the left, then try each of the

others in turn to see if they make a minimal pair with the first word. When you find an example that does not a make a minimal pair, say why not.

| **dot** | dock | dog | dots | debt | doll | got |
|---------|------|-----|------|------|------|-----|
| **can** | cat | cone | cane | cape | man | mat |
| **hat** | flat | that | had | hate | at | heart |
| **green** | bean | groan | gain | grease | glean | grain |
| **shoe** | show | shoot | shrew | Sue | blue | who |

Exercise 9.3
The following forms are typical of the speech of C, an English child about three years old. The child-like patterns of pronunciation exemplified here are all frequent in normal acquisition. You may assume that other words would be similarly affected, as if the child were applying 'rules' to change the adult target form into her own version.

| brush | [bwʌs] | shop | [sɒp] |
|-------|--------|------|-------|
| change | [teɪndz] | smack | [m̥mæk] |
| class | [klɑːs] | smudge | [m̥mʌdz] |
| crunch | [kwʌnts] | sneeze | [n̥niːz] |
| dish | [dɪs] | sorry | ['sɒwi] |
| James | [deɪmz] | Spot | [pɒt] |
| judge | [dʌdz] | spring | [pwɪŋ] |
| road | [wəʊd] | stretch | [twets] |
| school | [kuːl] | watch | [wɒts] |

(a) Use a minimal pair to prove that normal adult English has a phonemic contrast between /w/ and /r/ (the latter is usually realised as [ɹ]). What is the situation in this child's speech, and what will happen to minimal pairs that depend on this contrast?

(b) Find a minimal pair to show that /s/ and /ʃ/ are in contrast in adult speech. Again, what is the situation in this child's speech, and what will happen to minimal pairs that depend on this contrast?

(c) Find all the words that in their adult versions would contain the affricates /tʃ dʒ/, and work out the pattern in the child's treatment of them. Show that the child seems to be following a rule that is 'context-sensitive'.

(d) Find all the words in the data that begin with clusters of two or three consonants in their normal adult versions (don't include affricates) and group them according to type. Explain what the child does with the different types of cluster.

(e) Write a formal rule that describes the child's treatment of /s/ in onset clusters that do not contain a nasal consonant.

(f) How is C likely to pronounce the following words? Transcribe your answers phonetically.
*Charles choose fridge juice lunch prince scratch snake stamp touch*

Exercise 9.4
Make a list of the symbols for consonant segments that are used in the child's forms in Exercise 9.3 above. Then from the list select the consonant, or group of consonants, that fit the feature specifications given.
Example [+nasal] [m n ŋ m̥ n̥]
(a) [+nasal, +voiced]
(b) [+anterior, −coronal, −continuant]

(c) [−lateral, +voiced]
(d) [−sonorant, −continuant, −nasal]
(e) [−anterior, −continuant]

## Exercise 9.5

Look at the following transcribed words of Japanese which contain examples of all of the vowel qualities employed by the language. Give statements of the distributions of the three fricatives [h ç ɸ] paying particular attention to the following vowel.

| | | | |
|---|---|---|---|
| [hoŋ] | book | [çikiɸɯne] | tugboat |
| [hako] | box | [heta] | unskilful |
| [kooçii] | coffee | [ɸɯ] | urban prefecture |
| [çi] | day | [heŋ] | vicinity |
| [çiragana] | Hiragana (writing) | [saiɸɯ] | wallet |
| [nihoŋ] | Japan | [çiroi] | wide |
| [heja] | room | [ɸɯde] | writing-brush |
| [ha] | tooth | [hai] | yes |

Do you think that the three fricatives in question are in complementary distribution? Can they be regarded as allophones of one phoneme? What indicates that [s] and [h] must be allophones of distinct phonemes?

## Exercise 9.6

The transcribed words below are from the language Campa (Peru). Notice that some items are given in two forms. This indicates that two pronunciations are used interchangeably by speakers of the language. (When it makes no difference which of two sounds is used, the sounds are said to be in free variation.) The sequence [ts] represents a voiceless alveolar affricate.

| | | |
|---|---|---|
| a kind of bird | ['ɛto] | |
| a rodent | ['ʃawo] | |
| ant | ['katstoɾi] | |
| blind | [ʃe'tɛɾi] | |
| butterfly | ['tʰampi] | ['tʰambi] |
| corn | ['siŋki] | ['siŋgi] |
| dead limb | [o'ɛmpiki] | [o'ɛmbiki] |
| egg | ['itʰoki] | |
| fish | ['siwa] | ['siwə] |
| I doubt | [nokiho'tatsi] | |
| macaw | [ha'wawo] | |
| my paddle | [no'maɾɛ] | |
| nothing | [ti'katsi] | |
| on his head | ['itoki] | |
| salt | ['tsiβi] | |
| small gourd | ['iʃko] | |
| spider monkey | [tʰo'βɛɾo] | |
| termite | [ka'ɛɾo] | |
| vine or rope | [ʃi'βitʰa] | [ʃi'βitʰə] |
| we chase | [a'kɛntiɾi] | [a'kɛndiɾi |
| your daughter | [pi'ʃinto] | [pi'ʃindo] |

(a) The data include both voiced and voiceless plosives. List them and describe them. Are voiced plosives in contrast with voiceless plosives in this language? Give evidence and discussion.

(b) Is the voiceless aspirated alveolar plosive in contrast with the voiceless unaspirated alveolar plosive in this language? Give evidence.

(c) Examine the distributions of [p b β w]. Might all of them be allophones of a single phoneme?

(d) On the evidence given here, how many different nasal consonant phonemes must be set up for this language, and what are they?

(e) List the vowel sounds that occur in the data, and give a description for each (specifying tongue and lip position). Draw a vowel quadrilateral and plot on it the approximate positions of these vowel sounds.

(f) What vowel phonemes need to be set up for this language? Explain why the number of vowel phonemes is smaller than the number of different vowel sounds that occur in the data.

Exercise 9.7
Explain in words what effect the following rules will have:

(a) V→ [+nasal]/ _ [+nasal]
(b) [−sonorant]→ [−voiced]/__#
(c) Ø → [ɹ]/ V _ V
　　　　　　[−high]

### Further reading

We have given only the most basic introduction to phonological concepts. Modern phonology is a field where there are many competing approaches, and constant innovation in theories. For some more recent ideas applied to English, see H. Giegerich, *English phonology: An introduction*, Cambridge: Cambridge University Press, 1992. A book that explains the later development of the ideas explained in this chapter is C. Gussenhoven and H. Jacobs, *Understanding phonology*, London: Arnold, 1998.

# 10 Suprasegmentals

## CHAPTER OUTLINE

In this chapter you will learn about: the use of fundamental frequency; the difference between lexical stress and rhythmic stress; lexical stress types, including fixed stress and variable stress; lexical tone languages, including contour tone and register tone languages; intonation and its role in determining the interpretation of utterances; paralinguistic features and their use in signalling speaker attitude.

## Introduction

We have looked in some detail at how speech sounds are produced, how they may influence each other and how they are organised into syllables. However, speech is not just a string of speech sounds. There are features of speech that span a number of speech sounds or a number of syllables or even whole utterances. Such features are called suprasegmental or prosodic features. They include lexical and rhythmic stress, lexical tone and intonation. In this chapter we will deal with variation in fundamental frequency and pitch and see how pitch variation is used in language to signal the difference between the meanings of words in lexical tone languages and how pitch is connected with lexical stress. Pitch variation is also very important at the level of the utterance. Intonation is used to signal how a speaker intends his or her utterances to be interpreted.

## Fundamental frequency and pitch

We saw in Chapter 2 that the vocal folds can vibrate at different rates. The typical range of rate of vibration for an adult male speaker is from about 80 Hz (80 complete cycles of vibration) to about 210 Hz. The typical range for adult female speakers is from about 150 Hz to about 320 Hz. The rate of vibration of the vocal folds determines the fundamental frequency ($F_0$) of the resulting speech sound. This is the rate at which the speech pressure waveform repeats. Figure 10.1 shows three short sections of the vowel [ɑ], pronounced by an adult male. The waveforms and a plot of the $F_0$ are given for each. Vowel (a) has a fairly constant $F_0$ of around 200 Hz. Vowel (b) has a constant $F_0$ of approximately 100 Hz. Notice that the repetition rate visible in the waveform is much lower in the second vowel. Each cycle of vibration is longer. Vowel (c) has a falling $F_0$ pattern, starting at about the same value as the first vowel and finishing a little lower than that of the second vowel.

The fundamental frequency of a sound is intimately connected with the pitch we perceive. The higher the $F_0$, the higher the pitch. So vowel (a) would sound higher in pitch than vowel (b) and vowel (c) would be heard as having a fall in pitch from high to low.

It is important to remember that it is not the absolute Hz values of a fundamental frequency contour that matter, but the relative values. So, for example, if a female speaker were to produce the vowel [ɑ] at high pitch, at low pitch and with a falling pitch, it is very likely that the Hz values would all be greater than those for the male speaker above. This is because typically women have a smaller larynx and shorter vocal folds than men.

## Stress

Stress affects whole syllables rather than single segments. The effect of stressing a syllable is to make it more prominent, more audible than neighbouring syllables. Thus, stress is a relational feature, unlike features such as place and manner features or vowel quality features. So while it

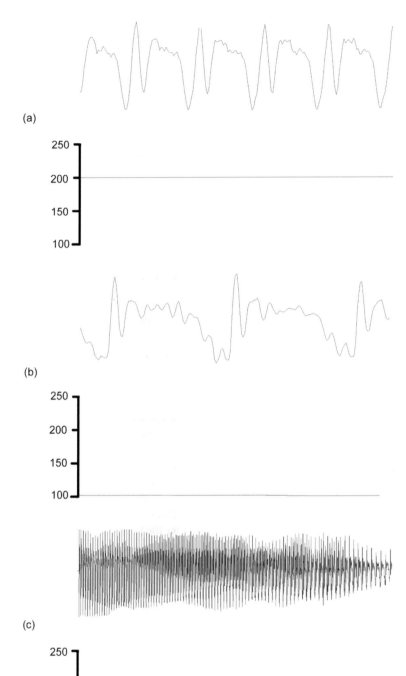

(a)

(b)

(c)

FIGURE 10.1
(a) 25 ms sample of
[ɑ] at a high pitch, and its
measured fundamental
frequency of 200 Hz;
(b) 25 ms sample of [ɑ]
at low pitch, fundamental
100 Hz; (c) a fall from
200 Hz to 100 Hz in
about 650 ms.

makes sense to ask whether an isolated consonant is, for example, alveo-lar, or whether an isolated vowel is back, it can never be sensible to ask whether an isolated syllable is stressed. The way in which a stressed sylla-ble is made more prominent than other syllables in the utterance is usually by a combination of factors: length, loudness and pitch. Thus, usu-ally a stressed syllable is longer and louder than its neighbours and may be marked by some pitch movement or new level in pitch. Look at Figure 10.2. This is a display of the speech pressure waveforms of the utterance of two English words by a male speaker. The words are *written* ['ɹɪtən] and *return* [ɹɪ'tɜːn]. Also shown is the fundamental frequency variation for these utterances. Notice that the two syllables of each of these words are clearly discernible because the consonant that separates them is a voiceless

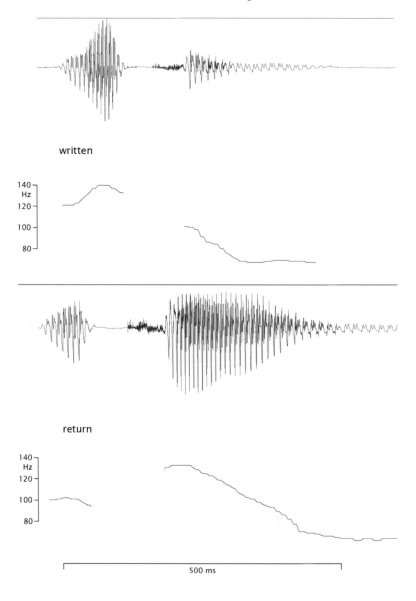

FIGURE 10.2
Waveforms and
fundamental frequency
traces for English *written*
and *return*.

**Table 10.1 Fixed penultimate stress in Welsh**

| | | | |
|---|---|---|---|
| ['mənɪð] | 'mountain' | [mə'nəðɔɪð] | 'mountains' |
| ['əsgɔɪ] | 'school' | [əs'gɔljɔn] | 'schools' |
| ['bʊrjad] | 'intention' | [bʊ'rjadi] | 'to intend' |
| ['ɬəgɔd] | 'mice' | [ɬə'gɔden] | 'mouse' |

plosive and there is no waveform activity during its hold phase. The first syllable of *written* is longer than the second and the excursion of the waveform above and below the centre line is greater for the first syllable than the second. The extent of this excursion is correlated with loudness. For *return* it is the second syllable that shows greater length and loudness. There is also a pitch difference between the utterances of these two words. The pitch of the first syllable of *written* is high and falling, while this pattern occurs on the second syllable of *return*.

## Primary and secondary stress

In words of two or three syllables it is likely that there will be only one stressed syllable. However, for longer words two or more syllables may bear stress. One of the stresses will be more prominent than the others and is called the primary stress. This is marked, as we have been doing already, with a raised vertical tick at the beginning of the syllable as in: ['pɪləʊ] and [bɪ'ləʊ]. Other stresses in a word are called secondary stresses and are marked with a lowered tick as in: [ˌkɒnsən'treɪʃn] and [ˌɪndɪˌvɪzɪ'bɪləti]. In some books, especially those published in the USA, you may see an alternative method of stress marking using diacritics over the vowel of the relevant syllables, as in [ìndɪvìzɪbíləti].

## Fixed stress

Some languages have fixed stress in the sense that most words in the language bear stress on the same syllable. Favoured places for stress in fixed stress languages are the first syllable of the word, the last syllable of the word and the penultimate syllable of the word. Look at the Welsh data in Table 10.1. In the left-hand column are words that all bear stress on the penultimate syllable. In the right-hand column the same words appear, but now with a single syllable suffix added. Notice how the stress is shifted to remain on the penultimate syllable of the new word. The vast majority of words in Welsh have stress on the penultimate syllable, although there are a few exceptional words all of which bear stress on the final syllable.

Now look at the Czech data in Table 10.2. Czech is a fixed stress language with word-initial stress. The addition of prefixes to a word makes no difference to this. The stress moves so that it is still word-initial.

One final example of a fixed stress language, this time with word-final stress, is Turkish. There are a couple of examples in Table 10.3. Again, the addition of a suffix, or even more than one suffix, does not disturb this pattern.

**Table 10.2 Fixed initial stress in Czech**

| ['mluvil] | 'he/she spoke' | ['nɛmluvil] | 'he/she didn't speak' |
|---|---|---|---|
| ['maso] | 'meat, flesh' | ['bɛzmasi] | 'fleshless' |
| ['pɔrʊtʃit] | 'to commend' | ['ɔtpɔrʊtʃit] | 'to recommend' |
| ['stali] | 'they stood' | ['nastali] | 'they arose' |

**Table 10.3 Fixed final stress in Turkish**

| [o'tel] | 'hotel' | [otel'ler] | 'hotels' | [oteller'den] | 'from the hotels' |
|---|---|---|---|---|---|
| [a'dam] | 'man' | [adam'lar] | 'men' | [adamlar'ɯn] | 'of the men' |

**Table 10.4 Variable stress in Catalan**

| [ə'stel] | 'star' | ['bensəs] | 'you defeat' | ['ɔmniβus] | 'omnibus' |
|---|---|---|---|---|---|
| [kə'laʃ] | 'drawer' | [bərə'ʒaβəm] | 'we mixed' | [de'mɔkrətə] | 'democrat' |

## Variable stress

Many languages have variable stress (sometimes called free stress). This does not mean that a particular word sometimes has one stress pattern and sometimes a different one. It means that one cannot make a simple, general statement as to which syllable of all (or most) words will be stressed. Look at the Catalan data in Table 10.4.

The words in the first column all have final stress. Those in the third column all have penultimate stress and those in the fifth column have antepenultimate stress. These are the only possibilities for Catalan. So although Catalan is a variable stress language, one can still make a generalisation about its stress placement: stress never falls more than three syllables from the end of a word. This and similar restrictions are common in variable stress languages.

## Syllable weight and stress

Many variable stress languages favour syllables of a particular type to bear stress. A heavy syllable is one that contains a long vowel or diphthong, or a short vowel followed by at least two consonants. A light syllable is one that contains a short vowel followed by one consonant or no consonants. Examples of heavy syllables in English are the first syllables of the words *beater*, *super*, *moaning*, *mighty*, *under*, *sixty*. Examples of light syllables are the final syllables in *horrid*, *hiccup*, *city*, *water*. In many variable stress languages heavy syllables in a word attract stress. Look at the English verbs in Table 10.5. If the final syllable of a verb is heavy then that syllable is stressed. If the final syllable of a verb is light then the penultimate syllable is stressed, no matter whether it itself is heavy or light.

| Table 10.5 Stress and syllable weight in English verbs | | | | | |
|---|---|---|---|---|---|
| Final heavy syllable: | believe | contend | depart | explain | resign |
| Final light syllable: | enter | edit | envelop | imagine | listen |

| Table 10.6 Stress in English Nouns | | | |
|---|---|---|---|
| Final heavy syllable: | attitude | porcupine | universe |
| Final light syllable: | aroma | asbestos | computer |
| No heavy syllables: | America | insulin | jealousy |

You should remember however that the stress system of English is very complex and it is not difficult to find exceptions to the above and to most general statements about stress in English.

## Stress and word class

Stress placement in variable stress languages may be sensitive to the lexical class of a word, that is, whether it is a noun, a verb, an adjective and so on. English is an example of such a language. Look at the English nouns in Table 10.6 and compare them with the verbs we have just looked at. The first thing to notice is that none of them have stress on the final syllable, unlike the verbs. Secondly, heavy syllables in these nouns attract stress if they are penultimate, not if they are final. Another thing to notice is that if there are no heavy syllables in a word then the antepenultimate syllable is stressed. Again, though, it is not difficult to find exceptions to this generalisation in English.

## Stress and suffixes

In the fixed stress languages we examined earlier the addition of a suffix to create a new word resulted in an adjustment of the place of the stress. In some variable stress languages, some suffixes also cause stress to shift, while other suffixes leave the stress exactly where it was before the suffix was added. The type of suffix that leaves the stress alone we will call stress-neutral suffixes and those that cause a change in the place of stress we will call stress-imposing suffixes. We will illustrate the difference using English. Look at the examples in Table 10.7. All of the suffixes in the first group (there are many more) are simply added to the word without any adjustment of the stress pattern. The suffixes in the second group (again there are more than presented here) cause the stress to shift to the syllable immediately before the suffix.

## Stress and vowel quality

In many languages the placement of stress has implications for the identity of the vowels used in the pronunciation of a word. For instance, some vowels in a language may be unable to occur in a stressed syllable. A good example of this is [ə] in many accents of English. If the addition of a suffix

### Table 10.7 Examples of English stress-neutral and stress-imposing suffixes

| Stress-neutral | | | | |
|---|---|---|---|---|
| -ed | edit | ['edɪt] | edited | ['edɪtəd] |
| -er | pretty | ['prɪti] | prettier | ['prɪtiə] |
| -est | lovely | ['lʌvli] | loveliest | ['lʌvliəst] |
| -ing | examine | [ɪg'zæmɪn] | examining | [ɪg'zæmɪnɪŋ] |
| -ive | suggest | [sə'dʒest] | suggestive | [sə'dʒestɪv] |
| -ly | rapid | ['ræpɪd] | rapidly | ['ræpɪdli] |
| Stress-imposing | | | | |
| -al | universe | ['juːnivɜːs] | universal | [juːni'vɜːsl] |
| -ic | photograph | ['fəʊtəgræf] | photographic | [fəʊtə'græfɪk] |
| -ical | hypothesis | [haɪ'pɒθəsɪs] | hypothetical | [haɪpə'θetɪkl] |
| -ity | complex | ['kɒmpleks] | complexity | [kəm'pleksəti] |

### Table 10.8 Stress minimal pairs

| Albanian | ['atə] | 'father' | [a'tə] | 'him, her' |
|---|---|---|---|---|
| Arabic | ['wasˤafaː] | 'they described' | [wa'sˤafaː] | 'and it cleared up' |
| Greek | [po'litikɔs] | 'of Constantinople' | [politi'kɔs] | 'political' |
| Italian | ['pɔrtɔ] | 'I carry' | [pɔr'tɔ] | 'he/she carried' |
| Russian | ['uʒe] | 'narrower' | [u'ʒe] | 'already' |
| Spanish | ['entre] | 'between' | [en'tre] | 'I entered' |

to a word imposes stress on a syllable that contains [ə] in the unsuffixed form, then [ə] will change to another vowel. An example is [ə] → [ɒ] in the second syllable of the words *photograph* ['fəʊtəgræf] and *photography* [fə'tɒgrəfi]. An alternative way of looking at this is to say that the shift of stress away from a syllable often causes a vowel to be weakened to [ə].

## Stress contrasts

In variable stress languages it is often possible to demonstrate that the place of stress is contrastive. That is, it is possible to find minimal pairs that differ only in the placement of stress. The two English words *import (verb)* [ɪm'pɔːt] and *import (noun)* ['ɪmpɔːt] constitute such a pair. Look at Table 10.8 where there are some more examples of stress minimal pairs from various languages.

# Rhythm

So far we have looked at stress as a property of words. This is sometimes called lexical stress. However, when words are strung together in phrases

**Table 10.9 Foot duration measurements**

| Foot | Syllable count | Duration (ms) |
|---|---|---|
| John | 1 | 406 |
| can't have for- | 3 | 542 |
| -gotten | 2 | 427 |
| Sally's | 2 | 500 |
| birthday | 2 | 676 |

or sentences some of the stressed syllables remain stressed and others may lose their stress. Let's take a simple example from English. The word *over* is stressed on the first syllable – ['əʊvə]. However, if we put this into a sentence like *The dog jumped over the fence*, we may hear that this syllable has no stress. The stress pattern of the sentence could be [ðə 'dɒg 'dʒʌmpt əʊvə ðə 'fens], with no noticeable prominence on the first syllable of the word *over*. Of course it is possible to say the sentence in a number of different ways and some of these may have may have a stress on *over*, for instance, [ðə 'dɒg dʒʌmpt 'əʊvə ðə 'fens]. So lexical stress and stress in sentences, while obviously connected, are not exactly the same thing. Here is another example of the difference between lexical stress and what is often called sentence stress or rhythmic stress. The word *afternoon* is [ˌɑːftə'nuːn], with secondary lexical stress on the first syllable and primary lexical stress on the last. However, a phrase like *afternoon tea* is likely to be pronounced as ['ɑːftənuːn 'tiː] rather than [ˌɑːftə'nuːn 'tiː]. The primary stress has moved to the first syllable of the word.

Stress in many languages is what defines the rhythm of speech. Rhythm can be defined as the pattern of occurrence in time of relatively 'strong' and relatively 'weak' events. In a language like English, the strong events are stressed syllables and the weak events are the unstressed ones. There is a tendency, and perhaps it is no more than that, for stressed syllables to occur at roughly equal intervals in time in English and in other languages. If we listen to a sentence like:

'John 'can't have for'gotten 'Sally's 'birthday

the strong beats that fall on the stressed syllables appear to be roughly equally spaced in time, athough as we can see, the number of unstressed syllables between each pair of beats varies: 0 between the first pair, 2 between the second pair, and 1 between the third and fourth pairs. In Table 10.9 are some very rough measurements in milliseconds of the durations of each stressed syllable and any following unstressed ones, taken from a recording of the sentence.

Each stressed syllable and any following syllables constitute a unit known as a foot. Compare the duration of the first and second feet. Certainly the second is longer than the first, but it is nowhere near three times as long, although there are three times as many syllables. This means that the syllable rate in the second foot must be faster than that of the first foot. The constant alteration of syllable rate to maintain a roughly equal foot duration is characteristic of many accents of English and also of other languages. These languages are sometimes called stress-timed. Not all languages, and not even all accents of English, are like this. French, for example, tends to have, or at least to sound as if it has, most syllables equal in duration. Languages like this are called syllable-timed.

This distinction between stress-timed and syllable-timed languages is very probably an oversimplification. It is probably more accurate to say that some languages make greater use of one kind of rhythm, but that both types can be found in most languages. It is also true that different accents of the same language may have different rhythmic characteristics.

### Rhythmic stress and word type

You may have noticed in the examples above that the word *the* was not marked as bearing rhythmic stress. This word is an example of what is often called a grammatical word. Other examples from English are pronouns like *he*, *she*, *him*, *her*, *us*, prepositions like *at*, *for*, *from*, modal verbs like *can*, *may*, *must*, possessives like *my*, *his*, *their* and conjunctions like *and*, *but*, *as*. Grammatical words in English and in most languages are less often rhythmically stressed than words like nouns (*book*, *John*, *honesty*), adjectives (*red*, *silly*, *international*), main verbs (*look*, *contemplate*, *understand*) and adverbs (*often*, *slowly*, *intentionally*). These sorts of words, called content words, very often do bear rhythmic stress. Here is a short passage of Welsh in phonetic symbols with a word for word translation. Notice how nearly all the content words are stressed and the grammatical words unstressed. You might like to try reading the passage out loud.

[pan oið ˈʃon ˈwiljam a i ˈdəili n ˈbuita i ˈkinjau
when was John William and his family in eating their dinner

daiθ ˈkarreg i laur o ˈbɛnː ər ˈaɬt a θruːi r ˈtoː
came rock in down from top the slope and through the roof

a disˈgənoð ar ˈdrəinʃuːr ʃoːn ˈwiljam
and fell on plate John William

a diˈvɛθθoð i ˈdattus a i ˈgiːg]
and destroyed his potatoes and his meat

Of course, grammatical words may be stressed in certain circumstances. Take for example the English sentence *Hey those are my socks, not yours!* This is likely to be pronounced with the words *my* and *yours* stressed to indicate the contrast between the two words.

## Lexical tone

The Modern Standard Chinese sentence for *I haven't got a pen* is 我沒有筆 [wo mei jou bi]. However, if you say this, you have to be careful about the pitch pattern you use, especially on the final word [bi], which means 'pen'. The pitch pattern should be a low, slightly falling then slightly rising tone.

| Table 10.10 Tonal contrasts in Modern Standard Chinese | | | | |
|--------------------|----------|---------|---------|----------|
|                    | Tone 1   | Tone2   | Tone 3  | Tone 4   |
| [fu]               | husband  | to help | rotten  | father   |
| [ma]               | mother   | hemp    | horse   | to scold |
| [tʰan]             | to try   | deep    | level   | to sigh  |

The corresponding fundamental frequency trace is shown in Figure 10.3(a). If you make a mistake and use a high rising pitch pattern instead then you would be saying *I haven't got a nose*! The fundamental frequency for [bi] meaning 'nose' is given in Figure 10.3(b).

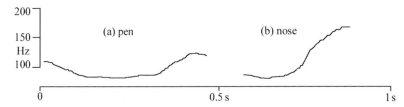

FIGURE 10.3
Fundamental frequency for MSC 'pen' and 'nose'.

Modern Standard Chinese, like nearly half the world's languages, uses pitch patterns to distinguish between one word and another. It is a lexical tone language. Lexical tone languages are found throughout Asia, in many parts of Africa and in the Americas. Some lexical tone systems are very simple, consisting of just a high level tone and a low level tone. Some are more complex. Cantonese, for example, has six distinct tone patterns.

> *Examples of tone languages from Asia, Africa and Americas*
> Asia: Chinese, Thai, Vietnamese
> Africa: Hausa, Yoruba, Xhosa, Zulu
> Americas: Mixtec, Navajo

## Contour tone

There are two kinds of tone language. The first type, of which Modern Standard Chinese is an example, have tones where the pitch movement is important and it is the difference in the pattern of pitch movement – falling, rising, falling-rising and so on – that distinguishes one word from another. There are four tones in Modern Standard Chinese: (1) high level, (2) high rising, (3) low falling-rising, (4) high falling. Table 10.10 shows some four-way tonal contrasts.

Languages such as this, where at least some of the tones have moving pitch patterns are called contour tone languages. Many lexical tone languages of Asia are of this sort.

## Register tone

In contrast to contour tone languages, some languages have tone inventories that consist entirely of level tones. Table 10.11 shows some examples of two-way and three-way contrasts, involving level tones, from various languages.

**Table 10.11 Tone contrasts in register tone languages**

| | | High | Mid | Low |
|---|---|---|---|---|
| Bafang (Cameroon) | [lox] | sleep | — | stone |
| Bole (Nigeria) | [lo] | meat | — | who |
| Karen (Burma) | [tə] | one | spoon | ant |
| Margi (Nigeria) | [ʃu] | tail | — | to dry up |
| Mixtec (Mexico) | [juku] (2nd syllable) | yoke | mountain | brush |
| Nupe (Nigeria) | [ba] | to be sour | to cut | to count |
| Yoruba (Nigeria) | [wa] | comes | looked | existed |

**Table 10.12 IPA tone transcription**

| Extra high | High | Mid | Low | Extra low | Falling | Rising | High rising | Low rising | Rising falling |
|---|---|---|---|---|---|---|---|---|---|
| ba̋ | bá | bā | bà | ba̱ | bâ | bǎ | ba᷄ | ba᷅ | ba᷈ |
| ˥ba | ˦ba | ˧ba | ˨ba | ˩ba | ˥˩ba | ˩˥ba | ˧˥ba | ˩˧ba | ˧˥˧ba |

A language that uses level tones only is known as a register tone language. Many African tonal languages are this sort, although register tones languages are found in other parts of the world too.

## Transcription and representation of tones

The chart of the IPA provides diacritics for marking tone, and these are illustrated in Table 10.12 using the syllable [ba]. Also in the table you will find what the IPA calls tone letters, which are a simple graphical way of indicating the shape of a tone.

Yet one more way to represent the shape and pitch height of a tone is by the use of superscript numbers, with 5 = extra high, 4 = high, 3 = mid, 2 = low and 1 = extra low. Usually two superscript numbers are used for each tone, the first indicating the height at the beginning of the tone and the second that at the end. So, for example, [ba⁴⁴] indicates a high level tone, while [ba⁴²] indicates a tone that falls from high to low. More complex tone shapes need three numbers, so [ba⁴³⁴] is a way of representing a high falling-rising tone.

Many of the above ways of transcribing tones suggest that contour tones are best thought of as being in some sense sequences of level tone targets, and in fact much recent work on the phonology of lexical tone has been carried out under this assumption. Modern phonological treatments of tone make use of what is known as an autosegmental representation, where the vowels and consonants of a syllable are present on one tier of the representation and the tone on an independent tier. The tiers are connected by association lines as in Figure 10.4, where H means high, M means mid and L means low.

FIGURE 10.4
The autosegmental representation of tone.

In Figure 10.4 (a) represents a high level tone, (b) a low level tone and (c) a tone that rises from low to mid. The difference between what we have called register tone languages and contour tone languages can now be thought of in a slightly different way. Register tone languages allow only one tonal target to be associated to each syllable, whereas contour tone languages allow two or more tonal targets to be associated to a syllable.

## Tones in connected speech

We have seen that vowels and consonants may turn up in different guises in different environments. This is true of tones too. If we look at Figure 10.5 which is a schematic representation of the pitch contour for the Modern Standard Chinese phrase 好不好? [hau bu hau], which means 'OK?' (literally 'good not good'), we can see that the pattern for the first occurrence of [hau] is not the same as that for the second. They both have Tone 3, low falling-rising, but the non-final occurrence has lost its rising part. So we can view Tone 3 as a toneme, in the same way as /p/ is a phoneme. Modern Standard Chinese Tone 3 has at least two variants or allotones, one that is used in final position before a pause, and the other in non-final position. The two variants are in complementary distribution.

FIGURE 10.5
Schematic representation of the pitch contour for the Modern Standard Chinese phrase 好不好 [hau bu hau].

It is also possible to find examples of the tonal equivalent of assimilation, where the actual pitch height of a tone is affected by that of a neighbouring tone. The example in Figure 10.6 is a schematic representation of the pitch heights of the syllables in the word [ód ì bó] ('banana') from Urhobo (Nigeria).

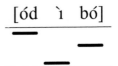

FIGURE 10.6
Tonal assimilation in Urhobo.

The first and third syllables of the word both have high tone, but the actual pitch height of the third syllable is lower than that of the first because of the low-toned syllable that precedes.

## Intonation

Languages like English, French, German, Spanish, Italian are not lexical tone languages. There are no pairs of words in these languages that are distinguished solely by the pitch pattern used to say them. However, all languages, as far as is known, use pitch variation to communicate meaning.

Let's take a simple example from Italian. The two utterances in Figure 10.7 use the same words, but (a) is a statement meaning 'It's cold' and (b) is a question meaning 'Is it cold?' As you can see, (a) ends with a falling fundamental frequency contour, while that for (b) rises at the end.

This use of pitch variation that does not affect the meanings of individual words, but that *does* affect the way in which utterances are interpreted, is known as intonation. In the rest of this section we will look at some of the main characteristics of the intonation system of English and draw a few comparisons with what goes on in other languages.

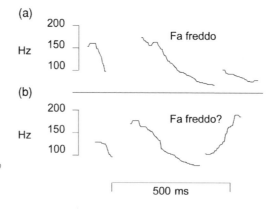

FIGURE 10.7
Fundamental frequency traces for Italian *Fa freddo* vs *Fa freddo*? ('It's cold'/'Is it cold?').

## Intonational phrases

One of the functions of intonation is to divide what we say into manageable-sized chunks known as **intonational phrases** or **IPs**. For any given bit of speech a speaker has a considerable freedom of choice about how many IPs to use and where they start and end. The two examples below are taken from recordings of the same passage by two different speakers. The symbol | indicates the boundary between two IPs and || indicates an IP boundary accompanied by a pause.

Speaker 1:   Work is scheduled to continue on both carriageways | to the south of junction seventeen | the M45 intersection || and there are more northbound lane closures | about five miles north of junction twenty | the turnoff | to Lutterworth.

Speaker 2:   Work is scheduled to continue | on both carriageways | to the south of junction seventeen | the M45 intersection || and there are more northbound lane closures | about five miles north of junction twenty | the turnoff to Lutterworth.

We shall see later on exactly how a speaker signals the end of an IP and the start of a new one, but for the time being, notice that IP boundaries are not always accompanied by a pause.

In English and other languages it is possible to use IP boundary placement to signal which of two possible meanings an utterance has. For example, the sentence *Those who spoke quickly got an angry response* is ambiguous. Is it the speaking that is quick or the response? If it is the first, then the sentence is likely to be uttered as:

Those who spoke quickly | got an angry response

but the second meaning is much more likely to be signalled by

Those who spoke | quickly got an angry response

In general, the placement of IP boundaries is used by the speaker to signal his or her judgement of what belongs with what. Here is another pair of examples:

Old men and women
Old men | and women

In the first, the hearer is likely to conclude that both the men and the women are old. In the second, the men are definitely old, but what about the women?

## Accent and nucleus

In Figure 10.8 (a ) and (b) are schematic representations of the pitch contour of two utterances of the sentence *I don't remember his telephone number*. Each is produced as one IP. The large circles represent stressed syllables and the smaller ones unstressed syllables. The tail attached to a circle indicates that there is a very noticeable glide in pitch during the production of that syllable. The upper and lower lines represent the limits of the speaker's pitch range.

(a)    I don't remember his telephone number

(b)    I don't remember his telephone number

FIGURE 10.8
Stress, accent and nucleus.

As you can see both (a) and (b) contain four stressed syllables, exactly the same ones in each case. In (a) the stressed syllables -*mem*- and *num*- are at the same pitch level as the preceding and following syllables. The syllables *don't* and *tel*-, however, are different. They both initiate a new trend in the pitch contour. They are not only stressed, but also accented. In (b) there are also two accented syllables – *don't* again and -*mem*-. The final accented syllable in an IP is known as the nucleus and its placement is very important for the interpretation of an utterance. The nucleus in (a) is *tel*- and in (b) it is -*mem*-.

Again the speaker, at least in English, has a good deal of choice where to put the nucleus within an IP. For our sentence above, the nucleus could be any of the following in addition to the two places we have already mentioned: *I*, *don't*, *his.* You might like to try sketching the pitch contours of the utterances with the nucleus in those positions and to try saying the utterances.

The main reason for choosing a particular position for the nucleus is to focus the hearer's attention on important or new information in the IP. If the speaker considers that all the information is new to the hearer (this is called broad focus), then the nucleus will be placed in a 'default' position. For most IPs in English the default position is the primary stressed syllable of the last content word. If the speaker considers that some of the information is old or unimportant because it is inferable from the context in which the conversation is taking place, then narrow focus will be used and the nucleus is likely to be placed in a position other than the default.

Let's try and make all that clearer with a couple of examples. The position of accented syllables will be indicated by using capital letters and underlining will be used to mark the nucleus. First a broad focus utterance:

Fred:    WHY are you looking so anNOYed?
Bill:    I've LOST my WALLet.

Fred's question doesn't mention losing things or wallets, so Bill's reply has broad focus and the nucleus falls on *wallet*, which is the last content word in the IP. Now a narrow focus utterance:

Sue:    LET'S go and see a MOVie.
Sally:    I CAN'T afFORD to go to the cinema.

Here Sue's utterance mentions going somewhere, so Sally avoids placing the nucleus on *go*. Sue's words *see a movie* imply going to the cinema, so that is old information too and Sally avoids placing the nucleus on *cinema*. The last piece of new information in Sally's reply is *afford*, so that is where she chooses to place the nucleus.

Accounting for nucleus placement in English, and in other languages, is a fairly complex problem and one can easily find examples of utterances where the nucleus placement is rather puzzling. Take this little conversation for example:

Mary:    Could you pass me the German dictionary, please?
Jim:    Here you are.
Mary:    Ah, I wanted the German dictionary | You've GIVen me the wrong ONE.

At least in some accents of English Mary's last IP is perfectly usual, but it is difficult to see why the nucleus should be the word *one*. It isn't a content word and it certainly isn't very informative.

Not all languages are as flexible as English when it comes to moving the nucleus around within an IP. Take for example the following utterance in Spanish (given in orthography) and compare it with the equivalent English utterance:

Con <u>LECHe</u> | o sin <u>LECHe</u>
<u>WITH</u> milk | or with<u>OUT</u> milk

English places the nuclei on the contrasting items in the two IPs, but
Spanish sticks to the last content word in both, even though it is exactly
the same word.

## Intonational tone

Both the examples in Figure 10.8 above show the nucleus as having a high
falling tone. However, this is not always the case. In Figure 10.9 we have
the same sentence, again produced as one IP, with the nucleus on the syllable *tel-*. However, this time the pitch rises from the nucleus to the end of
the IP.

I don't remember his telephone number

FIGURE 10.9
A rising nuclear tone.

Notice also that the pitch pattern of the part of the IP before the nucleus is
slightly different too. We have introduced an additional accent by making
the pitch step down slightly at the syllable *-mem-*.

A speaker of English may choose from a small number of pitch patterns
known as nuclear tones which begin at the nucleus and continue to the
end of the IP. Exactly how many nuclear tones there are and what types
there are is a matter of some debate amongst intonation analysts. Also different accents of English certainly make use of a different set of nuclear
tones.

We will not go into the fine details of the nuclear tones of English here,
but will concentrate on the sorts of meaning difference that nuclear tone
choice can signal. Before that we need to clear up a matter that we left
unresolved earlier. How does a speaker signal the end of an IP, even when
there is no pause associated with the IP boundary? The simple answer to
that question is: by using a nuclear tone. Hearers know that an IP has
come to an end because they know how IPs *can* end, rather like the way
in which we can usually tell when a musical tune has ended. If the tune
stops before its end, then we can usually tell it is incomplete, even if we
have never heard the tune before. In a similar way, we can tell that an
intonation pattern is incomplete if we haven't heard one of the patterns
of pitch that count as a nuclear tone in the accent or language we are
familiar with.

## Functions of intonational tone

One very important use of intonational tone, at least in English, is to signal the speaker's assessment of how the information in an IP fits into
the conversation she or he is taking part in. The use of a falling nuclear
tone is the speaker's signal that the information is being added to the

conversation, that it is new. A speaker can also signal that the information in an IP is already part of the background to the conversation and is
being reactivated. This is done by choosing a falling-rising nuclear tone.
Here is an example with just the IP boundary and the nuclear tones
marked. The mark \ means falling and \/ means falling and then rising.

When you go to the \/supermarket | you can call in at the \bookshop.

Here the speaker signals that (in his or her opinion) going to the supermarket is already an established fact and already part of the knowledge
that the participants in the conversation share. The new contribution is
'calling in at the bookshop'.

You can call in at the \/bookshop | when you go to the \supermarket.

In this second example, it is 'calling in at the bookshop' that is the established fact. The new bit is when this should take place.

Another important use of nuclear tone choice is to signal the attitude
that the speaker wishes to convey towards the hearer, the subject matter,
or sometimes life in general. As a simple example of the sort of attitudinal difference intonation can signal, let's imagine you have a weepy child
with you. You might say *Don't cry* or *It's all right*. If you use a pattern where
the words before the nucleus are high and level in pitch and the nucleus
itself (*cry* or *right*) falls from mid pitch to low pitch, you would sound
decidedly grumpy and unsympathetic. However, if you used a low rising
nuclear tone, again with a high level pitch preceding it, you would sound
much more soothing and sympathetic.

It isn't only nuclear tone choices that can signal attitudinal differences. Take the sentence *I'm NOT going to the SUPermarket*. With a high
level pitch from *NOT* to *the* and then a high falling nuclear tone on *SUP*,
this is simply a statement of fact. With a low level pitch on *NOT* which
then rises steadily through the following syllables as far as *the* and again
with a high falling nuclear tone on *SUP*, the utterance is not a neutral
sounding statement. The attitude conveyed is something like 'I've told
you before. I am surprised you haven't accepted the fact. I want to hear
no more about it.'

Another use of intonational tone is to signal the completeness or non-
completeness of an utterance. Some tones are used as a signal that there
is more to come. A simple example of this is a list of items like:

/carrots | /peas | /celery | po\tatoes

The rising nuclear tones on the first three items, shown with /, indicate
that the list is not yet complete and the falling tone on the last item says
that we have come to the end.

## Key

We will briefly look at another aspect of intonation known as key. Key
affects IPs as a whole and raises or lowers the pitch of all the tones in
the IP. Just as we saw that intonational tone may be used to signal non-
completeness or completeness of a list, key may be used to signal the

completeness or non-completeness of longer structures, rather like paragraphs in written language. Each of these structures deals with what the speaker considers to be a particular topic. The start of the topic is marked by a high key IP. This is then followed by a number of mid key IPs (possibly none at all). The end of the topic is marked by an IP in low key. This is sometimes very evident when newsreaders are changing from one news item to the next. See if you can spot it when you next listen to the news.

Another use of key is to mark an IP as being a parenthetical comment, rather like a bit of writing in brackets. In a sentence like:

I saw Fred Smith | you know the guy I'm talking about don't you | in the pub yesterday

the second IP is likely to be uttered with low key.

## Paralinguistic features

When we speak, we are continually giving out signals about our emotional state, our mood, our attitude towards the speakers in the conversation and towards the topic of the conversation itself. Some of these signals are non-verbal. Facial expression, posture and gesture can all tell our conversational partners how we are feeling. Some of the signals, however, are connected with the way we are actually speaking. These include the tempo of our speech, the overall loudness, the overall pitch range, the frequency of pauses and the type of phonation that we use. Such aspects of our speech are known as paralinguistic features.

If we are excited about a topic we are likely to speak more rapidly, with fewer pauses, with a wide pitch range and possibly quite loudly. If we are bored the tempo may be slower and quieter and the pitch range narrowed. Anger is often conveyed in our speech by increased loudness and wide pitch range.

# Chapter summary

In this chapter we have looked at some aspects of speech that affect units larger than a single speech sound. Such suprasegmental features include lexical stress and we distinguished between primary and secondary stress and, in variable stress languages, investigated the connection between stress and word class and syllable weight. In fixed stress languages these considerations are not an issue because stress regularly falls on the same syllable within a word.

We also looked at lexical tone which occurs in a large number of the world's languages. Words in these languages may be distinguished by their pitch pattern alone. We saw that there are two different types of tone language: contour tone languages where some of the tone patterns are falls in pitch, or rises in pitch, or sometimes more complex pitch movements. Register tone languages on the other hand use only tones that have a level pitch contour. We saw that tones, just like vowels and consonants, may have contextual variants.

Intonation is the use of pitch variation to aid the interpretation of utterances rather than to signal word meaning. We saw that speech can be divided into intonational phrases and that the choices available to the speaker in the placement of IP boundaries may affect how an utterance is interpreted. Within each IP, the speaker may choose to make certain syllables accented and the final accent, called the nucleus, is a very important way of highlighting information that the speaker considers new or significant. Accented syllables may be associated with pitch contours of different types and the choice of intonational tone is used both to signal speaker attitude and to indicate the speaker's assessment of whether the information in an IP is new or whether it is already shared knowledge. We also briefly looked at key and its role in organising speech into topics.

Finally, we introduced the concept of paralinguistic features such as tempo, pitch range, loudness, and their role in indicating the speaker's attitude or mood.

# Exercises

## Exercise 10.1

Sort the following English words into three lists. List 1 should contain all the words that have primary stress on the first syllable. List 2 should contain words with primary stress on the second syllable. List 3 is for words with primary stress on the last syllable.

kangaroo, mystery, fantasy, fantastic, recover, intention, concentrate, elephant, millionaire, understand, excitement, troublesome, crocodile, afternoon, connection, imagine, horizon, attitude, universe, puppeteer

## Exercise 10.2

The placement of stress in Maori is governed by the following principles:
(a) Stress never falls more than four syllables from the end of the word
(b) Long vowels attract stress
(c) Diphthongs attract stress except in the final syllable
(d) Long vowels take precedence over diphthongs for stress placement purposes
(e) Stress always falls as near to the beginning of the word as possible without contravening (a)–(d).

Copy out the transcriptions of the Maori words below, placing a stress mark at the beginning of the stressed syllable. Note: all vowel sequences count as diphthongs and Maori does not allow consonants to follow the vowel within the syllable. When you have done this and checked your answers, try saying the words with the correct stress.

| | | | |
|---|---|---|---|
| [atapoː] | 'early dawn' | [paːparakauta] | 'hotel' |
| [kihirimete] | 'Christmas' | [kawanataŋa] | 'government' |
| [paepae] | 'beam' | [kaumaːtua] | 'male elder' |
| [taurekareka] | 'slave' | [papakaiŋa] | 'village' |
| [marae] | 'courtyard' | [kaimoana] | 'seafood' |
| [fafai] | 'war' | [mokopuna] | 'grandchild' |

## Exercise 10.3

Below are some words from Manam, a language of Papua New Guinea.

| | | | |
|---|---|---|---|
| [aˈlaŋa] | 'reef' | [ˈmotu] | 'island' |
| [boaˈzɪŋa] | 'hole' | [waˈrige] | 'rope' |
| [malaˈboŋ] | 'flying fox' | [uˈzem] | 'I chewed' |
| [ataˈbala] | 'up' | [moaˈrepi] | 'rice' |
| [siŋaˈbaʔ] | 'bush' | [uraˈpun] | 'I waited' |
| [iˈʔint] | 'he pinched' | [ʔipoasaˈgena] | 'we are tired' |

In some words the final syllable is stressed, in others it is the penultimate syllable. What appears to determine which syllable is stressed? Try saying the above words.

## Exercise 10.4

Below are the waveforms for utterances of the two English words [ˈɪmpɔːt] and [ɪmˈpɔːt]. Can you tell which is which?
What is the duration of the initial syllable in each case?

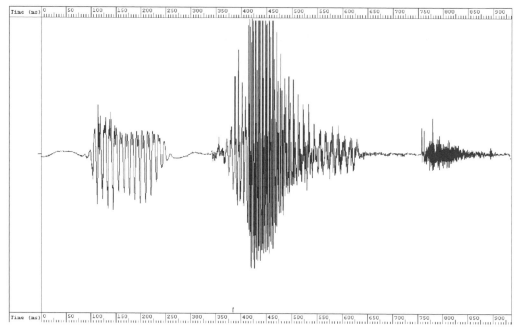

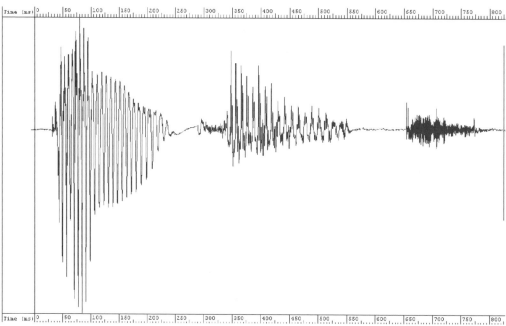

Figure for Exercise 10.4

## Exercise 10.5

The variety of Chinese spoken in Chengdu in Sichuan has four tonemes:

| I High Rising | II Low falling | III High Falling | IV Low Falling-rising |
|---|---|---|---|
| t$\int$in$^{45}$ | t$\int$in$^{21}$ | t$\int$in$^{41}$ | t$\int$in$^{213}$ |
| 'clear' | 'fine (weather)' | 'to invite' | 'to celebrate' |

Look at the following transcriptions of two-syllable sequences. In each case the syllables are given with their original tone and then the tone pattern for the sequence is given.

| | | | | | |
|---|---|---|---|---|---|
| go$\eta^{45}$ | + | fu$^{45}$ | → | go$\eta^{45}$fu$^{33}$ | 'time' |
| gue$^{21}$ | + | d$\bf z$ia$^{45}$ | → | gue$^{21}$d$\bf z$ia$^{33}$ | 'nation' |
| $\int$ia$\eta^{45}$ | + | ga$\eta^{41}$ | → | $\int$ia$\eta^{45}$ga$\eta^{41}$ | 'Hongkong' |
| fa$^{21}$ | + | d$\bf z$ia$^{21}$ | → | fa$^{21}$d$\bf z$ia$^{21}$ | 'hair clip' |
| li$^{21}$ | + | ba$^{45}$ | → | li$^{21}$ba$^{33}$ | 'fence' |
| fei$^{21}$ | + | dzau$^{213}$ | → | fei$^{21}$dzau$\textipa{P}^{211}$ | 'soap' |
| g$\ni\eta^{45}$ | + | b$\ni$n$^{41}$ | → | g$\ni\eta^{45}$b$\ni$n$^{41}$ | 'origin' |
| po$\eta^{21}$ | + | i$\ni$u$^{41}$ | → | po$\eta^{21}$i$\ni$u$^{41}$ | 'friend' |
| $\int$iau$^{41}$ | + | t$\int$$\ni$u$^{41}$ | → | $\int$iau$^{55}$t$\int$$\ni$u$^{41}$ | 'clown' |
| fu$^{213}$ | + | mu$^{41}$ | → | fu$^{213}$mu$^{41}$ | 'parents' |
| t$\int$in$^{41}$ | + | i$^{45}$ | → | t$\int$in$^{55}$i$^{33}$ | 'pyjamas' |
| $\int$iau$^{41}$ | + | t$\int$i$^{21}$ | → | $\int$iau$^{55}$t$\int$i$^{21}$ | 'small flags' |
| $\int$iau$^{41}$ | + | t$\int$i$^{213}$ | → | $\int$iau$^{55}$t$\int$i$\textipa{P}^{211}$ | 'stingy' |
| bau$^{41}$ | + | bau$^{41}$ | → | bau$^{55}$bau$^{41}$ | 'baby' |
| t$\int$i$\eta^{45}$ | + | d$\bf z$$\ni\eta^{213}$ | → | t$\int$i$\eta^{45}$d$\bf z$$\ni\eta^{211}$ | 'weight' |
| $\int$i$^{21}$ | + | guan$^{213}$ | → | $\int$i$^{21}$guan$^{211}$ | 'habit' |
| ko$\eta^{41}$ | + | pa$^{213}$ | → | ko$\eta^{55}$pa$\textipa{P}^{211}$ | 'perhaps' |
| jin$^{213}$ | + | t$\int$i$^{213}$ | → | jin$^{213}$t$\int$i$\textipa{P}^{211}$ | 'luck' |
| di$^{213}$ | + | fa$\eta^{45}$ | → | di$^{213}$fa$\eta^{45}$ | 'place' |
| $\int$ia$\eta^{213}$ | + | pi$^{21}$ | → | $\int$ia$\eta^{213}$pi$^{21}$ | 'rubber' |
| $\int$a$\eta^{213}$ | + | hai$^{41}$ | → | $\int$a$\eta^{213}$hai$^{41}$ | 'Shanghai' |
| di$^{213}$ | + | di$^{213}$ | → | di$^{213}$di$^{33}$ | 'younger brother' |

(a) Draw schematic pitch patterns (like that in Figure 10.5) for the words for 'clown' and 'pyjamas'.

(b) Comment on the occurrence of [$\textipa{P}$].

(c) Retranscribe the word for 'time' using IPA tone letters.

(d) List the variants of each toneme and state where each occurs.

## Exercise 10.6

Each of the following sentences is ambiguous. Try to work out what meanings each can have and how a particular meaning could be signalled using intonation.

(a) My sister who lives in Liverpool has just changed her job.

(b) She played and I sang the national anthem.

(c) He didn't leave because he was afraid.

## Exercise 10.7

Here is a short dialogue that has been divided into IPs for you. The place of the nucleus has been underlined in Sid's utterances. Your task is to decide where the nucleus falls in each IP of Clare's utterances.

Sid:    I've got an <u>idea</u> | Let's go out for a <u>meal</u>.
Clare:  All right | Which restaurant do you want to go to?

Sid:    There's a good <u>Chinese</u> place | near the <u>library</u>.
Clare:  I'm not terribly fond of Chinese food.

Sid:    Maybe that's because you've never had any <u>good</u> Chinese food.
Clare:  That may be true | but I think I'd prefer to try that place | some other time.

### Further reading

A very good general introduction to the study of intonation is Alan Cruttenden, *Intonation*, Cambridge: Cambridge University Press, 2nd edn, 1997. D. R. Ladd, *Intonational phonology*, Cambridge: Cambridge University Press, 1996 is an advanced treatment of up-to-date ideas in the study of intonational form. Paul Tench, *The intonation systems of English*, London: Cassell, 1996 is an excellent source of examples of intonational features and their role in signalling utterance meaning. Moira Yip, *Tone*, Cambridge: Cambridge University Press, 2002 is a wide-ranging treatment of lexical tone systems, largely in the framework of the Optimality Theory model of phonology. We have not dealt with this theory in our book, but Moira Yip's book introduces the basic concepts of the theory.

# 11 Speaker and hearer

## CHAPTER OUTLINE

In this chapter you will learn about: the human hearing mechanism; the use of visual clues in speech perception; speech perception tests – labelling and discrimination; speech development in children; hearing impairment.

## Introduction

This book has concentrated largely on how human beings produce speech and how speech sounds are organised in languages of the world. However, we usually speak for the purpose of communicating with others who must receive the acoustic signal created by movements of the speech organs. This signal must be decoded and then understood by the hearer. We begin the chapter by looking at the hearing mechanism and the supplementary use of visual cues to aid speech perception. We then describe the methods used to investigate which aspects of the acoustic signal are important for the perception of phonetic distinctions. Phoneticians are not only interested in how speech is produced by the speech organs and the acoustic properties of speech sounds, but also in how human beings receive and process the speech signal. The study of speech perception is one of the major applications of phonetics. Speech perception tests involving labelling and discrimination tasks with synthetic speech stimuli have been used in many areas of research and we look briefly at some of these, including cross-language comparison of acoustic cue perception. Next we look at the development of speech perception and production in children. The chapter concludes with an account of the ways in which hearing impairment may interfere with the perception of speech.

## The hearing mechanism

The expression 'the organs of speech' naturally calls to mind the tongue, lips, larynx and so on, which are used to produce speech. But our ears, and the hearing mechanism generally, have an equal claim to be considered organs of speech, because speech must be detected and understood, as well as produced. The characteristics and capabilities of human hearing must have shaped the evolution of human speech quite as much as the articulatory capabilities of our vocal tracts.

Hearing involves peripheral and central processing. Peripheral processing is carried out in the ear itself, central processing in the cortex. The peripheral auditory mechanism consists of three parts as shown in Figure 11.1. The

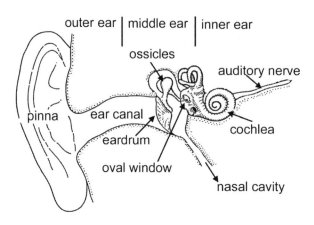

FIGURE 11.1
The hearing mechanism.

outer ear comprises the pinna (ear flap) and auditory canal (also called meatus). These collect and channel sound. The eardrum (tympanic membrane) divides the outer ear from the middle ear. In the middle ear three tiny bones (the ossicles) act as a mechanical linkage passing on vibration through another membrane (the oval window) to the inner ear. The organ of hearing proper is a spiral structure, the cochlea. It is here that conversion of vibration into electrical nerve impulses takes place, and preliminary analysis of sound according to frequency and loudness is carried out. A coded representation of the sound passes along the auditory nerve as a series of pulses.

There are considerable similarities between the human hearing mechanism and that of other mammals, the biggest difference between species being in the range of frequencies that can be heard. The lowest frequencies that we hear as sounds are in the region of 30 Hz, the highest (for a young person) around 20 kHz. Frequencies that are below our normal range of hearing are referred to as infrasound and frequencies above our normal hearing range are ultrasound, and some creatures are adapted to respond to sound in those regions. Dogs, for example, can detect frequencies higher than 20 kHz, and bats use ultrasound as a navigation system.

One can test listeners' sensitivity to sounds by presenting pure tones (sine waves) one at a time, and varying the intensity to determine when each one is just detectable. The testing must be done in a very quiet place and with carefully calibrated equipment. Young adults with good hearing tend to have a characteristic sensitivity curve like that shown in Figure 11.2(a). The horizontal axis of this graph shows the frequency of sine waves used in testing, and the vertical axis shows the intensity of sound that must be presented at each frequency for the sound to be just detectable. What the figure shows is that although we are able to detect sounds over a range of frequencies from 20 Hz to 20 kHz, very low frequencies and very high frequencies must be made very intense for us to detect them. In the middle range of frequencies, especially in the region of 1–3 kHz, our sensitivity is very much higher.

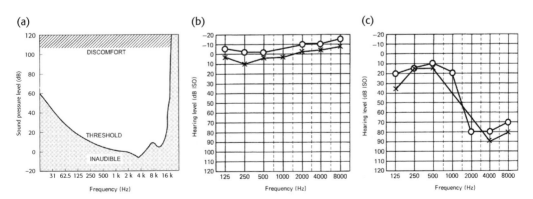

FIGURE 11.2
(a) The threshold of hearing (b) audiogram of a child aged 10 with normal hearing (X left ear, O right ear) (c) audiogram of child of similar age with high frequency loss.

If the normal threshold curve is taken as a baseline, one can determine how far an individual's hearing differs from normal by using a device called an audiometer. The results can be plotted as an audiogram. A normally hearing person will show an audiogram close to the zero line across the frequency range as in Figure 11.2(b). As people get older, their sensitivity to sound generally decreases, especially at higher frequencies, while people with seriously impaired hearing often have audiograms that look very different indeed from the normal curve. You can see an example of this in Figure 11.2(c) which shows an audiogram for a child with high frequency hearing loss in both ears.

The identification of speech sounds, syllables and words (a process generally called speech perception) takes place in the cortex of the listener's brain, and is influenced not only by the incoming sound but also by the listener's experience and linguistic knowledge. The final stage, of understanding speech and arriving at the intended interpretation, is further guided by the listener's general knowledge and expectations in the context.

## Visual cues

Although sound is the main input to the process of speech perception, it is not the only one. If we can see the speaker, we will also see some of the speech movements that he or she is making, and visual information can also influence our perception. We are accustomed to the idea that the deaf can learn to 'lip-read', but in fact even those of us with normal hearing make considerable use of visual cues. It is not at all surprising that humans make use of visual cues to aid them in the perception of speech when we remember that through most of its history spoken language has evolved for face-to-face communication.

A simple illustration of our sensitivity to visual information is how quickly we notice the small failures that sometimes occur in the synchronisation between picture and sound in a film. If we were not attending to visual cues about speech, and able to integrate them rapidly with auditory information, we would not notice the mismatch.

It has been known for a long time that visual cues help us to follow speech in a noisy situation. In one classic experiment, masking noise is mixed with a recording of speech at such a high level that subjects who hear only the noisy speech can make little sense of it. Subjects who can see the talker, but hear nothing, have to rely on lip-reading and are also unable to follow the message. So neither the sound nor the visual information is intelligible on its own. But subjects who hear the noisy speech and see the talker at the same time are able to follow the meaning quite well.

There are obvious limitations on what can be gathered about speech sounds from visual information alone. The lips are the most visible articulators. One can see if they are closed or open, and whether they are rounded or spread. If the lips are open, one can see a limited amount of what the tongue is doing in the dental/alveolar region. But back articulations such as velars are virtually impossible to see. The degree of jaw opening can also be followed visually, and this has implications for tongue height and posture and can help us make judgements about both vowels and consonants.

Even expert lip-readers can't see things that are invisible. One can't see the difference between voiced and voiceless consonants which are otherwise alike, because the vocal folds are out of sight within the larynx. Similarly, moving the soft palate up and down has no visible effect, so there's no reliable way of lip-reading the difference between a nasal consonant such as [m] and the corresponding plosives [b] or [p]. However, experienced lip-readers are often able to use the cues that are visible together with information that can be inferred from the context of the conversation to achieve very good understanding of speech.

Another illustration of our sensitivity to visual information in speech comes from what is generally called the McGurk effect, after the psychologist who first reported it. In this, experimental subjects watch a film of a talker producing a certain syllable, which has been dubbed with the wrong soundtrack. For example, the film might show the production of [ga] while the soundtrack contains the syllable [ba]. Under these conditions, many subjects report hearing the syllable [da]. The conflicting visual and auditory cues lead them to 'hear' a consonant somewhere between [ba] and [ga]. Their perception changes, however, if they close their eyes so that the visual information does not influence their perception.

## Speech perception tests

How do we know what acoustic events give rise to the perception of particular speech sounds or phonetic distinctions? There has been a long tradition of using synthetic speech, that is, an electronic simulation of human speech, to present carefully controlled speech-like stimuli to listeners in order to obtain simple judgements on their perception. Synthetic speech is used because it would be extremely difficult for a human speaker to control the acoustic properties of speech with the required degree of accuracy. Suppose we are interested in how voice onset time (VOT) is related to the perception of voicing in English plosives. We need a series of stimuli (known as a continuum) where the VOT of a plosive is increased in equal steps. It would be no use asking a human being to say a word like *bay* and then to repeat it with the VOT for the initial plosive exactly 10 ms longer and then again but with the VOT 10ms longer and so on. We do not have conscious control of our speech organs to that degree of accuracy. Using synthetic speech, our first step is to make measurements of spectrograms of a real utterance, [beɪ] say, and to use these measurements to produce a synthetic version of this syllable. From this we could produce a series of test stimuli where VOT varies in steps of 10 ms from 0 to 50 ms. The stimuli would then be used to make up a perception test, where many repetitions of the stimuli are presented in random order to a group of subjects. Such a test is called a labelling experiment. The subjects are asked to make the simple judgement of whether they hear [beɪ] or [peɪ] each time they hear a test item. The aim of such a test is to discover the VOT value at which the subjects' perception switches from [beɪ] to [peɪ]. This is done by plotting a graph of the percentage of [beɪ] responses for each VOT value. Such a graph is known as a **labelling curve** (see Figure 11.3). For this (imaginary) group of subjects [b] gives way to [p] at about 30 ms, which is where the curve crosses the 50% level. Stimuli with a VOT below 30 ms are all judged to be instances of [beɪ], while those with a VOT above 30 ms are all perceived as [peɪ].

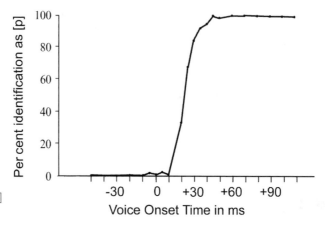

FIGURE 11.3
Labelling curve for synthetic [beɪ] versus [peɪ] stimuli.

Another sort of test we could do with these stimuli is to present pairs of adjacent VOT values, 0 and 10 ms, 10 and 20 ms and so on, and ask for same/different judgements from our subjects. We would then obtain what is known as a **discrimination curve**, which records the percentage of 'different' responses for each stimulus pair. The discrimination curve for our imaginary experiment is in Figure 11.4. There is a peak in the curve at the 30/40 ms pair of stimuli.

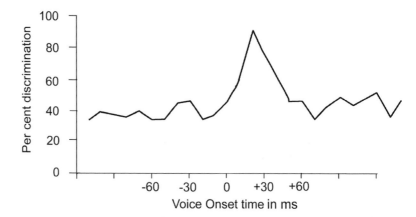

FIGURE 11.4
Discrimination function (two-step) for synthetic [beɪ] versus [peɪ] continuum.

This result together with the sharp cross over from one percept to the other in the labelling test suggests that our subjects are perceiving VOT categorically. This means that there are two perceptually well-defined areas in the VOT continuum without any intermediate percepts and that within each area subjects are unable to tell the difference between acoustically different events. Many other acoustic cues have been investigated in this way, including: burst frequency for place of articulation in plosives, direction of formant transitions for place of articulation of consonants and the relationship between F1 and F2 frequencies for vowel perception.

## Cross-language comparison of cue perception

If we extended our VOT continuum to include negative values, say from −30 ms to 50 ms, we could investigate the voiced/voiceless threshold for plosives in a language like French. French voiceless plosives are not aspirated and have a short or zero VOT value. Negative VOT values mean that the vocal folds start vibrating *before* the release of the plosive. From this we can conclude that different languages, while using the same acoustic cue to signal a phonetic distinction, may use the cue in different ways. So, for instance, plosives with a VOT in the region of 0–20 ms are categorised as voiced by English hearers, but as voiceless by French hearers.

## Cue redundancy

It is rare for a phonetic distinction to be signalled by a single acoustic cue. For instance, place of articulation for plosives is signalled simultaneously by the second formant transition (the shape of the second formant at the beginning of a following vowel) and also by the frequency of the plosive burst itself. In Figure 11.5 we can see these patterns in the forms of schematic spectrograms for the syllables [ba da ga].

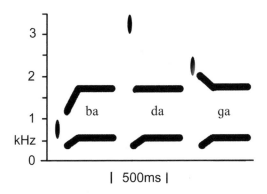

FIGURE 11.5
Schematic spectrogram
for [ba da ga].

For [ba] the burst is relatively low in frequency and the F2 transition is rising. For [da] the burst is high in frequency and the F2 transition is almost flat. [ga] has a falling F2 transition and a burst frequency between those for [ba] and [da].

This situation is known as cue redundancy – the presence of more information than is strictly necessary to distinguish phonetic events. Given perfect signal transmission, and perfect decoding, burst frequency alone, or F2 transition alone, should be enough. However, we rarely hear speech in perfect surroundings, and the redundancy of cues provides a safeguard against the effects of environmental noise and errors in processing. For example, noise in the situation might interfere with the perception of the bursts, but leave the formant transitions still audible. Speech has built into it a degree of resistance to interference by changes in listening conditions.

## Speech development

In the normal course of events, a child acquires much of its first language in the first three or four years of life and is able to communicate with other children, and with unfamiliar adults, by the time she or he goes to school. Of course, it is not uncommon for a child to be brought up in an environment where two (or even more) languages are being used, but for our purposes it will be simpler to consider the case of a child with normal cognitive and sensory abilities growing up in a monolingual environment. Obviously the child has to acquire the vocabulary and grammar of the language in question, but along with this, even before the child's first words can be uttered, must come development of the ability to identify and discriminate the sounds of the language, and to produce them.

It is usual for perception (in the sense of sound identification and discrimination) to be ahead of production in speech development. This means that children can often hear sound differences that they are not yet able to reproduce. A child learning English, for example, has to cope with a large system of fricatives, and the child's own output will certainly not at first contain all of [f θ s ʃ h] (to say nothing of the voicing difference which adds [v ð z ʒ]). The child's own speech will at first contain only one or two of these fricatives (often [f] and [h] are found early), and the distinction between [s] and [ʃ] may not appear until relatively late. But there is plenty of evidence that the child can hear and identify at least some of the sounds that are not yet present in her/his output. In a famous example, a child at a certain stage of development produced [s] for both [s] and [ʃ], saying [fɪs] for *fish*. However, when an adult spoke the form [fɪs] back to the child, the child rejected the pronunciation. This indicates clearly that the child could perceive the difference between the forms [fɪs] and [fɪʃ] but could not yet manage the distinction in production.

In general then, childlike speech is probably not the direct result of limited perceptual abilities. Whatever language they are acquiring, children begin with a simpler sound system than the adult's, adding sounds gradually as more and more difficult distinctions are mastered. It is not only a question of smaller inventories of contrasting sounds. Children also commonly simplify the phonological structures (syllables and words) they produce. For example, children acquiring English generally go through a stage of weak syllable deletion, in which words that are meant to have two, three or more syllables are simplified so as to contain fewer syllables. So the adult three-syllable word *banana* may become [nɑːnə]. The components of syllables can also be simplified. Consonant clusters, which occur in adult English as onsets and codas to syllables, are commonly reduced. So for instance a word such as *play*, which begins with the cluster [pl] for an adult, may be just [peɪ] for the child, and therefore indistinguishable from the same child's version of *pay*.

## Labelling experiments with infants

Labelling experiments of the type described earlier have been performed with very young children in order to investigate the development of perceptual abilities. Of course, it is impossible to ask a baby only a few months old to tell you what they hear, so an alternative strategy has to be used. One such strategy involves playing a stimulus repeatedly to a child and observing the child's movement. After a few repetitions of a stimulus the baby will lose interest. If the stimulus is then altered and the child does not react, by for instance turning the head, one can conclude that the difference between the two stimuli is not perceptible. If, however, the child does react when the stimulus is changed, the conclusion is that the two stimuli lie on either side of a perceptual threshold for the child.

## Hearing impairments

The discussion of speech perception, and of speech development, has so far concerned those with normal hearing. Hearing impairments can occur at various levels in the hearing mechanism. The outer ear may be temporarily blocked by wax. The middle ear can be affected by infection, or the ossicles damaged (often surgical repair is possible). But if the cochlea itself is not functioning properly the result is a permanent impairment of the ability to detect and discriminate sounds.

Different kinds of hearing loss will affect speech perception in different ways. Quite commonly, a person may have a high-frequency loss, in which higher frequencies (such as those found in fricatives and plosive bursts) are difficult to detect, while lower frequencies (such as found in the lower formants of voiced sounds), are detected quite well. A person who can hear only the very lowest frequencies may be able to respond to pitch information (tone and intonation), but hear only the first formants of vowels, so that [i] and [u], which have similar first formant frequencies, will be confused (obviously lip reading will help, if the speaker is visible).

The popular conception of deafness as loss of sensitivity to sound is only partly correct. One function of most hearing aids is indeed to amplify sounds so that they are easier to detect. But hearing impairment generally also involves some loss of the ability to discriminate sounds (to tell apart sounds of differing time and frequency composition), and hence affects speech perception directly, even if amplification makes the speech loud enough to be detected. Most hearing aids amplify and process speech so that a person can make best use of their residual hearing, but one development in the last thirty years or so has been the cochlea implant, in which one or more electrodes are introduced into a non-functioning cochlea, and electrical stimulation of the electrodes gives the otherwise entirely deaf person a degree of hearing.

The effect of hearing impairment on a person's own speech depends on when the hearing loss begins and on its severity. Those who become deaf after speech is established generally retain the ability to speak very intelligibly, whereas a child who is congenitally deaf will have severe difficulty acquiring speech, and in monitoring his or her own attempts at speaking.

## Labelling experiments with hearing-impaired subjects

Labelling experiments can also be used to investigate how people with hearing impairment perceive (or fail to perceive) speech. As an example of such an experiment, let's look at the results for a profoundly hearing-impaired fourteen-year-old subject in response to stimuli that range from an extreme rise in pitch on the syllable [əʊ] to an extreme fall in pitch on the same syllable. The subject was asked 'Do you hear a question or not?' The continuum consists of nine steps and the fifth point on the continuum is a stimulus with level pitch, as can be seen in Figure 11.6a. The results are shown in Figure 11.6b and c.

From a normally hearing subject one would expect a pretty high rate of question judgements for stimuli 1–4, all of which have rising pitch movements. Stimulus 5 should produce a response rate of about 50% and stimuli 6–9 should be judged as non-questions. However, we can see that for this subject most of the stimuli produce responses around 50%, indicating that subject's hearing loss is such that the responses are essentially random.

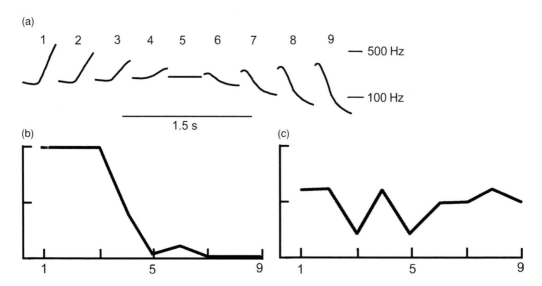

FIGURE 11.6
(a) Stimulus continuum (rising versus falling fundamental frequency), (b) Question/ Statement labelling curve for a typical normal subject, (c) labelling curve for a child with severe hearing loss. After A. J. Fourcin, 'Speech pattern tests for deaf children', *Speech and Hearing: Work in Progress*, 1976, 46–62.

## Chapter summary

The main aim of this chapter has been to provide a survey of the way in which the phonetic concepts introduced throughout the book can be applied to the investigation of speech and the areas in which phonetic knowledge is useful and important. Much of our book has been concerned with how speech is produced from the articulatory point of view and with the acoustic consequences of the movements of the speech organs. However, human speech is used for communicating information to a listener, so in this chapter we have looked at speech from the receiving end and have outlined ways in which human perception of speech may be investigated. We have pointed out the main characteristics of the hearing mechanism, shown how auditory sensitivity can be measured, and looked at some types of hearing impairment and their effect on speech perception We have seen that visual cues can be used to aid speech perception and understanding. We have also looked briefly at the way in which the ability to produce and perceive speech develops in children.

### Further reading

A very useful book covering hearing, speech acoustics and speech perception is Peter Denes and Elliot Pinson, *The speech chain*, New York: W.H. Freeman, 1993. If you wish to know about how children develop speech and what can go wrong with this process, see Pamela Grunwell, *Clinical phonology,* London: Croom Helm, 2nd edn, 1987 and David Ingram, *Phonological disability in children*, London: Arnold, 1976. For all aspects of the measurement of speech, see Katrina Hayward, *Experimental phonetics*, Harlow: Longman, 2000. For a quantitative introduction to the interrelationships between production, acoustics and perception, see Keith Johnson, *Acoustic and auditory phonetics,* Oxford: Blackwell, 2nd edn, 2003. On hearing and deafness, see John Graham and Mike Martin, *Ballantyne's deafness,* London: Whurr 6th edn, 2001. For more detail on the human hearing mechanism and its role in speech perception you should look at Brian Moore, *An introduction to the psychology of hearing,* London: Academic Press, 3rd edn, 2003.

# Glossary

| | |
|---|---|
| Accented syllable | A syllable made prominent by pitch (commonly a pitch peak). In English intonation, a stressed syllable made prominent by being accompanied by the start of a new trend in the pitch contour of the utterance. |
| Active articulator | The articulator that moves to form a constriction in the vocal tract. For example, in palatal sounds the active articulator is the front of the tongue which moves towards the hard palate. |
| Advanced | Produced slightly further forward in the vocal tract. For instance, the first consonant in the English word *keen* is an advanced velar and is produced with a closure towards the front of the velum. |
| Affricate | A consonant sound produced with a complete closure between two articulators and with velic closure preventing air escaping via the nasal cavity. The articulators part relatively slowly and the compressed air escaping between them becomes turbulent resulting in audible friction noise. [ts dʒ kx] are examples of affricates. |
| Airstream mechanism | One of a number of ways in which airflow can be created in the vocal tract for the purpose of producing speech sounds. |
| Allophone | A speech sound considered as a positional variant of a phoneme. So, for instance, in Spanish the two sounds [b] and [β] are allophones of the phoneme /b/. The bilabial fricative [β] occurs word-internally between vowels and the plosive [b] occurs in other environments. |
| Allotone | A pitch configuration considered as a positional variant of a toneme. For example, Modern Standard Chinese Tone 3 has a terminal rise in pitch when found before a pause, but lacks this terminal rise when not before a pause. These two pitch configurations can be regarded as allotones of the Tone 3 toneme. |
| Alphabetic writing system | A system of writing, like that used for English, where the symbols used represent the individual vowels and consonants of the language. |
| Alternation | The situation where a word or word-part turns up in different phonological forms in different environments. For example, the English plural ending *s* is /s/ if the preceding sound is voiceless, as in *books* /bʊks/, but it is /z/ if the preceding sound is voiced, as in *dogs* /dɑgz/. |
| Alveolar | The name of a place of articulation. The active articulator is the tip or blade of the tongue. The passive articulator is the alveolar ridge. [t s n] are examples of alveolar sounds. |
| Alveolar ridge | The front part of the roof of the mouth, just behind the upper front teeth. |
| Ambient noise | Noise in the environment which may interfere with the recording of sounds. |
| Amplitude | A measure of the up-and-down extent of a waveform (as distinct from its frequency). For a sound wave, the extent of pressure variation above or below atmospheric pressure. |
| Aperiodic | Of a waveform, one that does not have a regular repeating pattern. |

| | |
|---|---|
| Approximant | A consonant sound made with a constriction between two articulators which is not narrow enough to cause air turbulence. [w l j] are examples of approximants. |
| Articulation | A constriction of the vocal tract. |
| Articulators | The parts of the vocal tract involved in the production of speech sounds: the lips, teeth, tongue, alveolar ridge, hard palate, soft palate, uvula, pharyngeal wall and vocal folds. |
| Arytenoid cartilages | Two small cone-shaped cartilages that sit on the upper surface of the cricoid cartilage. The vocal folds are attached at the back to the arytenoids and the positioning of the cartilages is largely responsible for the position of and tension of the folds. |
| Aspiration | Weak friction noise heard on the release of a plosive sound. The noise is caused by air moving at high speed through the vocal tract. Aspiration is associated with plosives that have a long Voice Onset Time. |
| Assimilation | A phonological process that involves a change in a speech sound to make it more similar to some sound in its environment. An example from English: the word *ten* which is /ten/ in most environments may become /tem/ if the following word begins with a bilabial consonant, as for example in the phrase *ten books*, which may be pronounced /tem bʊks/. |
| Audiogram | A graph showing the sensitivity of a human subject to sounds at various frequencies. |
| Audiometer | A device capable of producing tones of precise frequency and intensity which is used to test human sensitivity to sound at various frequencies. |
| Auditory canal | The channel that leads from the outer part of the ear to the eardrum. |
| Back (of tongue) | The part of the tongue that lies below the soft palate when the tongue is at rest. |
| Bilabial | The name of a place of articulation. The articulators are the upper and lower lips. [p b m] are examples of bilabial sounds. |
| Binary | Of phonological features, taking one of two opposite values. So for example, speech sounds may be classified as [+nasal] if they are made with the velum lowered or [−nasal] if not. |
| Blade (of tongue) | The part of the tongue that lies below the alveolar ridge when the tongue is at rest. |
| Breathy voice | A type of phonation in which the pattern of vocal fold vibration allows the escape of relatively large amounts of air in each cycle of vibration, producing audible noise along with voicing. |
| Cardinal vowels | A set of agreed vowel qualities used as a reference for the purposes of describing vowels encountered in speech. |
| Categorical perception | A characteristic of the perception of certain speech sounds. Sounds are said to be perceived categorically if there is a sharp cross-over from one perceptual category to another and if, in addition, human listeners are unable to distinguish between acoustically different sounds that fall in the same category. |
| Click | A sound produced with an ingressive velaric airstream mechanism. |
| Coarticulation | The adjustments made to the articulation of a speech sound under the influence of neighbouring sounds. For instance, the first consonant in the English word *queen* [kwiːn] is likely to be produced with rounded lips because it is followed immediately by a lip-rounded sound. |

| | |
|---|---|
| Cochlea | The organ of hearing. A spiral structure in the inner ear where mechanical vibrations are converted to nerve impulses. |
| Coda | A syllable constituent consisting of any consonant sounds following the syllable nucleus. |
| Complementary distribution | Two sounds are said to be in complementary distribution in a particular language if they can never appear in the same environment as each other. For example, in English [h] can only appear in the onset of a syllable and never in the syllable coda, whereas [ŋ] can only appear in the syllable coda and never in the syllable onset. So in English [h] and [ŋ] are in complementary distribution. |
| Complex periodic tone | A sound, such as a vowel sound, whose waveform can be analysed as the sum of two or more sine waves. |
| Compression | The rise in air pressure in an enclosed space caused by a decrease in the size of the space without outflow of air. |
| Consonant | Sounds made with a relatively close constriction or complete closure in the vocal tract and that occur singly or in clusters at the edges of syllables. |
| Context-sensitive voicing | A phenomenon where the voicing of consonant sounds is determined by the context in which they appear. For example, young children often go through a stage in the development of their speech when all obstruent consonants are always voiced if they are immediately followed by a vowel and are always voiceless in other contexts. |
| Continuum | A series of synthetic speech tokens used as stimuli in a speech perception experiment. Each member of the continuum is acoustically identical to the others except in the value of the particular acoustic feature under investigation. |
| Contour tone | A lexical tone that changes in pitch. |
| Contrast | The situation where a phonetic difference is capable of signalling a difference between words in a particular language. So, for example, vowel nasalisation or lack of it in French can change the identity of a word, as can be seen with the pair of words *mot* /mo/ 'word' and *mon* /mõ/ 'my'. So there is a contrast between oral and nasalised vowels in French. English, while it has oral and nasalised vowels, never uses the difference to signal the difference between words. |
| Creaky voice | A type of phonation in which the vocal folds vibrate at a low frequency (and usually somewhat irregularly) with a very low rate of airflow through the glottis. |
| Cricoid cartilage | A ring-shaped cartilage at the top of the windpipe. It is attached to the thyroid cartilage; the arytenoid cartilages sit on its upper surface at the rear. |
| Cue redundancy | The presence of more acoustic cues than are logically necessary to signal a perceptual distinction between speech sounds. |
| CV-skeleton | A representation of the structure of a word or phrase in terms of the sequence of consonant and vowel sounds it contains. C is used to represent consonants and V to represent vowels. For instance, CVCV is the CV-skeleton for English words such as *below, city, data*. |
| Defective vowel system | A type of vowel system, found in a small number of languages, that does not conform to the Vowel Dispersion Principle, either because it lacks open vowels or because, for mid and high vowels, there is an asymmetry of front and back vowels. |

| | |
|---|---|
| Degree of stricture | The narrowness of the space between two articulators during the production of a sound. |
| Dental | The name of a place of articulation. The active articulator is the tip or blade of the tongue. The passive articulator is the upper front teeth. [θ ð] are examples of dental sounds. |
| Devoiced | Of a sound normally voiced, produced without vocal fold vibration for part or all of its duration. |
| Diacritic | A small mark placed near or attached to a phonetic symbol which is used to modify the usual meaning of the symbol or to supply further phonetic detail. For instance, [m̥] represents a voiceless bilabial nasal whereas the symbol alone without the diacritic represents a voiced bilabial nasal. |
| Diphthong | A vowel that changes quality within a single syllable. An example of a diphthong in English is [aɪ], in such words as *fine, time, sight*. |
| Discrimination curve | A graph showing how well human listeners can distinguish between adjacent stimuli on an acoustic continuum. |
| Dissimilation | The opposite of assimilation, that is a change in a sound to make it more dissimilar from some sound in its environment. |
| Distribution | The environments in which a speech sound may occur in a particular language. |
| Double articulation | An articulation in which there are two simultaneous constrictions of the vocal tract. The two constrictions are of equal narrowness. [w] is an example of a double articulation. |
| Eardrum | A membrane stretched across the auditory canal and dividing the outer ear from the middle ear. The eardrum converts pressure variation into mechanical movement. |
| Egressive | Of an airstream mechanism, one that pushes air out of the vocal tract. |
| Ejective | A sound produced with an egressive glottalic airstream mechanism. |
| Electropalatography | An instrumental technique for investigating the pattern of contact of the tongue with the roof of the mouth during speech sounds. Tongue contact is recorded by electrodes embedded in an artificial palate worn by the speaker. |
| Elision | The omission of a sound. For example, the voiceless alveolar plosive phoneme may be elided in a phrase like *last month*, giving the pronunciation /lɑːs mʌnθ/ rather than /lɑːst mʌnθ/. |
| Ending | Another term for suffix. Sounds (or letters in the written form) added to the end of a word to indicate verb tense, the plural of nouns and the like. For example, the regular plural ending for English nouns is one of /s z ɪz/, the choice depending on the last sound of the noun concerned. |
| Environment | The environment of a sound is the preceding and following sound or sounds. Statements of environments may also include the symbol #, which means a word boundary. For example, in a word like *bring* [bɹɪŋ], the environment of [ɹ] is [b] _ [ɪ] and that of [ŋ] is [ɪ] _ #. |
| Excitation | See input. |
| Feature | See phonological feature. |
| Fibrescope | A flexible bundle of light-transmitting fibres used to collect an image from inaccessible areas inside the human body. |

| | |
|---|---|
| Fixed stress language | A language where the position of the primary stress is the same for the vast majority of words. For example, Polish is a fixed stress language because nearly all words have primary stress on the penultimate syllable. |
| Flap | A consonant produced by making the active articulator strike the passive articulator in passing. [ɾ] is an example of a flap |
| Formant | A peak in the spectrum of a speech sound such as a vowel. |
| Formant frequency | The frequency at which a peak in energy occurs in the spectrum of a speech sound. |
| Fortis | Produced with increased muscular tension. Fortis speech sounds are normally voiceless. |
| Fortition | A phonological process, the opposite of lenition, which involves a change from a weaker sound to a stronger one that has a more radical obstruction to airflow. |
| Free stress | The same as variable stress. |
| Frequency | The rate of repetition of a cycle of vibration. Frequency is measured in Hertz (Hz). 1 Hz is one cycle per second, so, for example, if a periodic waveform repeats 100 times in a second, its frequency is 100 Hz. |
| Fricative | A consonant sound produced with a narrow constriction of the vocal tract which causes the airstream to become turbulent, resulting in audible friction noise. [s ʒ ɣ] are examples of fricatives. |
| Frictionless continuant | An older term for median approximant. |
| Front (of tongue) | The part of the tongue that lies below the hard palate when the tongue is at rest. |
| Glide | An older term for median approximant. |
| Glottal | The name of a place of articulation. The articulators are the vocal folds. [ʔ h] are examples of glottal sounds. |
| Glottal stop | The sound symbolised [ʔ]. It is produced by closing the vocal folds tightly, blocking the airstream from the lungs. |
| Glottalic | The name of an airstream mechanism in which the closed vocal folds initiate the airflow. Ejective consonants are produced with an egressive glottalic airstream and implosives with an ingressive one. |
| Glottis | The space between the vocal folds. |
| Heavy syllable | A syllable that contains a long vowel or diphthong, or alternatively a short vowel followed by more than one consonant. |
| Height (of vowels) | An auditory property of vowels, corresponding with the degree of raising of the highest point of the tongue during the production of a vowel. |
| Homophone | One of a pair (or larger set) of words that sound exactly the same when spoken, but which mean different things. For example, the words *write, right, rite* and *wright* are homophones in English, all being pronounced [raɪt]. |
| Homorganic | Two sounds are homorganic if they have the same place of articulation. For example, [s] and [l] are both alveolar, so they are homorganic. |
| Implosive | A sound produced with an ingressive glottalic airstream mechanism. |
| Impressionistic transcription | A transcription of speech that represents its superficial auditory effect, but is not made in accordance with a stable and economical system of symbols worked out to suit the phonological structure of the language involved. |

| | |
|---|---|
| Infrasound | Low frequency vibration below the lower frequency limits of normal human hearing. |
| Ingressive | Of an airstream, one that pulls air into the vocal tract. |
| Initiator | The part of the vocal tract that moves in order to create a rise or fall in air pressure, resulting in flow out of or into the vocal tract. For instance, in the pulmonic airstream mechanism the initiator is the walls of the lungs. |
| Input | The energy introduced into a resonating system. An alternative term is 'excitation'. The input to the vocal tract is essentially of two kinds: (1) periodic energy produced by the vibration of the vocal folds, (2) aperiodic energy produced by air turbulence caused by a narrow constriction or complete closure between two articulators. Some speech sounds, voiced fricatives especially, are produced with a combination of these two sorts of input. |
| International Phonetic Alphabet | A set of internationally agreed symbols used for representing speech sounds. |
| Intonational phrase | A group of words accompanied by a complete well-formed intonation pattern. |
| IPA | The International Phonetic Association or The International Phonetic Alphabet. |
| Key | An intonational feature that affects the pitch characteristics of a whole intonational phrase. If an intonational phrase is produced with high key, then all of the pitch values are higher. Similarly, low key makes all pitch values in the phrase lower. |
| Labelling curve | A graph showing the results of a labelling experiment. The horizontal axis shows the points in the acoustic continuum under investigation. The vertical axis shows the percentage responses for one of the two response labels for the experiment. |
| Labelling experiment | A speech perception experiment where large numbers of synthetic speech tokens are presented to human subjects. The subjects' task is to respond to each token with one of two labels. For example, the subjects might be asked whether they hear each token as the word *coat* or as the word *goat*. The stimuli for the experiment are taken from an acoustic continuum of stimuli, but are presented in random order. |
| Labialisation | A secondary articulation involving the rounding of the lips. |
| Labial-palatal | The name of a double articulation with simultaneous articulations at the lips and at the hard palate. [ɥ] is an example of a labial-palatal sound. |
| Labial-velar | The name of a double articulation with simultaneous articulations at the lips and at the velum. [w] is an example of a labial-velar sound. |
| Labiodental | The name of a place of articulation. The active articulator is the lower lip. The passive articulator is the upper front teeth. [f v] are examples of labiodental sounds. |
| Laminar flow | A characteristic of flow in a fluid such as air or water where the particles that make up the fluid move in parallel paths and there are few if any collisions between the particles. Laminar airflow does not create any sound. |
| Laryngograph | An electronic device that records vocal fold vibration by means of two electrodes placed externally on a speaker's neck. A small electric |

current is passed through the neck and the laryngograph measures the changing resistance of the neck to the passage of the current. When the vocal folds are in contact, the resistance is lower than when they are apart.

| | |
|---|---|
| Larynx | A structure made of cartilage and connective tissue at the lower end of the vocal tract and above the windpipe, containing the vocal folds. |
| Lateral | Of an approximant or fricative, produced with a complete closure on the midline of the vocal tract, but with one or both sides of the tongue lowered and not contacting the side teeth or gums, so that the air escapes over the sides of the tongue. [l ɬ] are examples of lateral sounds. |
| Lenis | Produced with reduced muscular tension. Lenis speech sounds are usually voiced. |
| Lenition | A phonological process involving the change from a stronger sound to a weaker one, where stronger sounds are defined as having a more radical obstruction to airflow than weaker ones. For example, the change from a plosive to a fricative in certain environments is lenition and so is the change from a fricative to an approximant. In addition, voiceless sounds are stronger than voiced ones. |
| Lexical tone | The use of a small number of contrasting pitch patterns to distinguish words from one another. |
| Light syllable | A syllable that contains a short vowel followed by a maximum of one consonant. |
| Location (of vowels) | The part of the tongue (front, centre or back) that is raised highest in the oral cavity for the production of a vowel sound. |
| Logographic writing system | A writing system, such as that for Chinese, where the symbols used represent whole words, rather than the sounds or syllables that make up the word. |
| Long vowel | A vowel of relatively long duration when compared to a vowel of similar or identical quality in the same vowel system. |
| Loudness | The subjective impression of the magnitude of a sound. Loudness is connected with the amplitude of the waveform of the sound. |
| Magnetic resonance imaging | A non-hazardous technique for producing images of the interior of the body. The technique involves applying a very strong magnetic field to the body, followed by a radio-frequency pulse specific to hydrogen. |
| Manner of articulation | The way in which the articulators interfere with and direct the airstream for the purposes of producing speech sounds. Manner of articulation is a complex of features such as degree of stricture, speed of articulator movement, soft palate position and the like. |
| McGurk effect | A perceptual effect demonstrating that visual cues influence speech perception. A video of the speaker's face is overdubbed with the soundtrack of an utterance different from the one that the viewer is seeing. The visual and auditory cues may be integrated by the hearer, and the resulting perception can differ from both of the speaker's utterances. |
| Meatus | Another name for the auditory canal. |
| Median | Of a fricative or approximant sound, articulated in such a way that the air escapes down the midline of the vocal tract. |

| | |
|---|---|
| Minimal pair | A pair of words that differ in only one phoneme. An example from French: *peau* /po/ 'skin' and *beau* /bo/ 'beautiful'. |
| Modal voice | A phonation type in which the vocal folds snap shut rapidly and peel apart relatively slowly. Most speech is produced with modal voice. |
| Monophthong | A vowel sound that does not change in quality. |
| Monosyllable | A word consisting of a single syllable, such as *do* and *snap* in English. |
| Nasal (stop) | A consonant sound produced with a complete closure in the mouth but without velic closure so that the airstream escapes only through the nasal cavity. [m ɲ ŋ] are examples of nasals. |
| Nasal cavity | The large cavity above the roof of the mouth, connected to the upper part of the pharynx at the rear and having the nostrils at the front. |
| Nasalised vowel | A vowel sound produced without velic closure so that air escapes simultaneously through the oral cavity and the nasal cavity. |
| Neutralisation | The suspension, in certain environments, of a phonetic contrast normally found in a language. For example, voicing is contrastive for obstruent consonants in German, except at the end of words, where only voiceless consonants are permitted. |
| Non-pulmonic | Of airstream mechanisms, not involving the lungs as an initiator. The two non-pulmonic airstream mechanisms used for speech sounds are glottalic and velaric. |
| Nuclear tone | One of a small number of pitch configurations associated with the nucleus and any following syllables in the intonational phrase. |
| Nucleus | (1) The syllable that bears the last accent in an intonational phrase. (2) The only obligatory component of a syllable. |
| Obstruent | A sound that is produced with a constriction narrow enough to cause an appreciable rise in air pressure inside the vocal tract. Plosives, affricates and fricatives are all obstruents. |
| Octave | An interval between two musical notes in a scale. If the frequency of any note is doubled, the result is the same note, but one octave higher. |
| Onset | A syllable constituent consisting of any consonant sounds preceding the syllable nucleus. |
| Oral | A sound produced with velic closure to prevent nasal escape of air, so that the airstream escapes through the oral cavity alone. |
| Oral cavity | The mouth. The cavity bounded by the lips at the front and joined to the pharynx at the rear. |
| Oral vowel | A vowel sound where all of the air escapes via the oral cavity and where there is no nasal airflow. |
| Ossicles | The three small bones of the middle ear which act as a linkage between the eardrum and the oval window. |
| Oval window | An opening into the cochlea, covered by a membrane, to which mechanical movement is transmitted from the eardrum via the ossicles. |
| Palatal | The name of a place of articulation. The active articulator is the front of the tongue. The passive articulator is the hard palate. [j ɲ] are examples of palatal sounds. |
| Palatalisation | A secondary articulation in which the front of the tongue is raised towards the hard palate. |
| Palatogram | A record of the pattern of contact between the tongue and the roof of the mouth during the production of a speech sound. |

| | |
|---|---|
| Paralinguistic feature | A feature of speech, such as loudness or voice quality, used to convey speaker attitude rather than linguistic meaning. |
| Parametric diagram | A diagram showing the estimated movements or activity of various parts of the vocal tract such as the soft palate and the vocal folds. |
| Passive articulator | The stationary articulator involved in forming a constriction in the vocal tract. For instance, the hard palate is the passive articulator for both palatal and retroflex sounds. |
| Periodic | Of a waveform, regularly repeating in time. |
| Pharyngeal | The name of a place of articulation. The active articulator is the root of the tongue. The passive articulator is the rear wall of the pharynx. [ħ ʕ] are examples of pharyngeal sounds. |
| Pharyngealisation | A secondary articulation in which the root of the tongue is retracted and approaches the rear wall of the pharynx. |
| Pharynx | The part of the vocal tract immediately above the larynx. |
| Phonation | The generation of voice in the larynx, by vibration of the vocal folds. |
| Phoneme | A set of speech sounds that form a basic contrastive unit in a language. For example in English, the set which contains the sounds [l ɫ ĩ ɨ], amongst others, is the /l/ phoneme. The members (or allophones) do not contrast with one another in the language in question. |
| Phonetic symbol | A symbol representing a speech sound. |
| Phonetic transcription | The representation of speech using phonetic symbols. |
| Phonological feature | One of a small set of labels used to specify an aspect of the articulation (or of the acoustic properties) of a speech sound or a set of speech sounds. For example, the phonological feature [anterior] is used to distinguish those sounds produced on or in front of the alveolar ridge from those sounds produced further back in the vocal tract. |
| Phonological process | A widespread phonological phenomenon such as assimilation, elision or lenition. |
| Phonotactics | The patterning of permissible phoneme sequences in syllables. |
| Pinna | The outer, visible part of the ear. |
| Pitch | The perceptual attribute of a sound that enables the hearer to locate the sound on a scale from high to low. The physical correlate of pitch is the frequency of the sound. |
| Place of articulation | The point within the vocal tract where a constriction is formed to produce a consonant sound. The place of articulation is defined by the active and passive articulators involved. |
| Plosive | A consonant sound produced with a complete closure between two articulators and with velic closure preventing air escaping via the nasal cavity. The articulators part rapidly allowing rapid release of the compressed air without any accompanying friction noise. [p d c q] are examples of plosive sounds. |
| Postalveolar | The name of a place of articulation. The active articulator is the tip or blade of the tongue. The passive articulator is the rear of the alveolar ridge. [ɹ ʃ ʒ] are examples of postalveolar sounds. |
| Pre-fortis clipping | The reduction in duration of sonorant sounds when followed in the same syllable by a fortis consonant. For example, the vowel in the English word *seat* [siːt] is clipped, whereas that in *seed* [siːd] is not. |

| | |
|---|---|
| Pressure | The molecules that make up a gas such as air are constantly moving and colliding with the surface of objects that contain the gas. The force created by the sum of these collisions is the pressure of the gas. Pressure is measured in force per unit area. |
| Primary articulation | The narrowest constriction in the vocal tract during the production of a speech sound. |
| Primary stress | See stress. |
| Prosodic | The same as suprasegmental. |
| Pulmonic | The name of an airstream mechanism in which the lungs initiate the airflow. The majority of sounds of human speech are produced with a pulmonic egressive airstream. |
| Pure tone | The sound associated with a sine wave. |
| Rarefaction | The fall in air pressure in an enclosed space caused by an increase in the size of the space without inflow of air. |
| Register tone | A lexical tone with a level pitch contour. |
| Resonant frequency | The frequency at which an acoustic system vibrates when excited by input energy. |
| Retracted | Produced slightly further back in the vocal tract. For instance, the first consonant in the English word *trip* is a retracted alveolar and is produced at the back of the alveolar ridge. |
| Retroflex | The name of a place of articulation. The active articulator is the tip of the tongue. The passive articulator is the hard palate. [ʈ ɖ ʂ] are examples of retroflex sounds. |
| Rhyme | A syllable constituent consisting of the syllable nucleus plus the coda. |
| Roll | Another term for trill. |
| Root (of tongue) | The very back part of the tongue which faces the rear wall of the pharynx. |
| Rounded | Of a vowel, produced with rounded lips. [y u o ɔ] are examples of rounded vowels. |
| Rule | A statement of a phonological phenomenon in terms of the input (the sounds affected), the output (the changes made), and the context in which the change occurs. An example is: [−son] → [−voi] / _ [−voi]. This means: any obstruent (the input) becomes voiceless (the output) before another voiceless sound (the context). |
| Sampling rate | The frequency that samples are taken from a waveform for the purposes of digitising speech. For example, a sampling rate of 10 kHz means that each second of the waveform is represented by 10,000 equally spaced samples. |
| Secondary articulation | A constriction of the vocal tract that takes place at the same time as a narrower constriction elsewhere. [ɫ] is an example of a sound where the secondary articulation is formed by the tongue back being raised towards the soft palate while at the same the tongue tip makes the primary articulation (a complete closure on the alveolar ridge). |
| Secondary stress | See stress. |
| Segment | Another term for speech sound. |
| Semivowel | A type of approximant sound, like [w] or [j], whose articulation is very similar to that of a vowel. |
| Short vowel | A vowel of relatively short duration when compared to a vowel of similar or identical quality in the same vowel system. |

| | |
|---|---|
| Sine wave | A waveform with a simple shape and a single constant frequency and constant amplitude. |
| Soft palate | The rear part of the roof of the mouth. |
| Sonorant | An articulation where the constriction is not so narrow, or is not of sufficient duration, as to cause an appreciable rise in air pressure inside the vocal tract. Vowels, nasals, approximants, taps, flaps and trills are all sonorants. |
| Spectrum | A visual display of the relative amplitudes of the different frequency components of a sound such as a vowel. |
| Stop | A consonant sound that involves a complete closure in the oral cavity. Plosives, affricates and nasals are all stops. |
| Stress | The relative prominence of syllables. In many languages one (or more) syllables in a word are produced louder and longer than others. These syllables are said to be stressed. Examples from English: *butter*, *teaching* (first syllable stressed) and *resign*, *unsure* (second syllable stressed). In many languages there is more than one degree of stress. So, for example, in the English word *international* there is a primary stress on the third syllable and a secondary stress on the first syllable: [ˌɪntəˈnæʃnəl]. |
| Stress-timed language | A language whose rhythm shows perceptually equal time intervals between stressed syllables. |
| Suprasegmental | A name for features such as stress, lexical tone and intonation, which affect more than one segment. |
| Syllabary | A system of writing where the symbols used represent whole syllables rather than the individual consonants and vowels that make up the syllable. |
| Syllabic | Of a speech sound, capable of forming the core of a syllable. In most languages vowels are the only syllabic sounds, but some consonants, mainly sonorants, are also used as syllabic sounds in some languages. |
| Syllable | A phonological structure composed of speech sounds. Words are made up of syllables. The syllable is the domain of association for such phenomena as stress and lexical tone. |
| Syllable-timed language | A language whose rhythm is based on perceptually equal duration of syllables. |
| Synthetic speech | An electronic simulation of human speech. |
| Tap | A consonant sound produced by making the active articulator strike the passive articulator for a very brief duration. [ɾ] is an example of a tap. |
| Thyroid cartilage | The largest cartilage of the larynx. It is attached to the cricoid cartilage below and is supported by muscles attached to the bones of the skull. The front ends of the vocal folds are attached to its inner surface. |
| Tip (of tongue) | The extreme front end of the tongue. |
| Tone | See lexical tone. |
| Toneme | A group of pitch configurations that are functionally equivalent in a particular lexical tone language. |
| Trill | A consonant sound where the active articulator vibrates rapidly striking the passive articulator repeatedly. [r ʀ] are examples of trills. |
| Turbulent flow | A characteristic of flow in a fluid such as air or water where the particles that make up the fluid move in a chaotic, unpredictable |

fashion. The particles collide with each other and the energy created by these collisions is heard as noise.

| | |
|---|---|
| Tympanic membrane | Another name for the eardrum. |
| Ultrasound | High frequency vibration above the upper frequency limit of normal human hearing. |
| Unrounded | Of a vowel, produced without rounding of the lips. [i a ɯ] are examples of unrounded vowels. |
| Uvula | The fleshy protuberance that hangs from the end of the soft palate. |
| Uvular | The name of a place of articulation. The active articulator is the back of the tongue. The passive articulator is the uvula. [q ɢ ɴ] are examples of uvular sounds. |
| Variable stress language | A language where the primary stress is not fixed to a particular position in a word. |
| Velar | The name of a place of articulation. The active articulator is the back of the tongue. The passive articulator is the soft palate. [k g ŋ] are examples of velar sounds. |
| Velaric | The name of an airstream mechanism in which the airflow is intitiated by a closure of the back of the tongue on the velum. Clicks are produced with a velaric ingressive airstream. |
| Velarisation | A secondary articulation in which the back of the tongue is raised towards the velum. |
| Velic closure | The closure formed by raising the soft palate to contact the rear wall of the pharynx. Oral sounds are produced with velic closure, which prevents air escaping via the nasal cavity. |
| Velopharyngeal | The same as velic. |
| Velum | Another name for the soft palate. |
| Vocal cords | An older term for the vocal folds. |
| Vocal folds | Two folds of tissue with embedded muscle and ligaments found inside the larynx. They are attached at the back to the arytenoid cartilages and at the front to the inner surface of the thyroid cartilage. Their vibration is the source of the periodic energy for human speech sounds. |
| Vocal tract | The oral cavity, nasal cavity, pharynx and larynx. |
| Voice Onset Time | The time lapse, measured in milliseconds, between the release of a plosive sound and the onset of voicing for the following sound. Voice onset time is an important perceptual cue for voicing of plosives. |
| Voiced | Produced with accompanying vocal fold vibration or, for plosives, produced with a short or zero voice onset time. |
| Voiceless | Produced without accompanying vocal fold vibration or, for plosives, produced with a relatively long voice onset time. |
| VOT | The abbreviation for Voice Onset Time. |
| Vowel | A sound produced without a close obstruction in the vocal tract and which forms the centre of a syllable. |
| Vowel Dispersion Principle | The tendency for vowel systems to consist of qualities that are widely and evenly dispersed in perceptual space. |
| Vowel system | The set of contrastive vowel qualities found in a particular language. |
| Wav file | One common format for storing sounds as computer files. |
| Waveform | A visual representation of the variation of air pressure caused by a sound. The horizontal axis represents time and the vertical axis represents pressure variation above and below atmospheric pressure. |

# Solutions to the exercises

## Exercise 1.1

1  box XXXX
2  sorry XXXX
3  possess XXXXX
4  knees XXX
5  quickly XXXXXX

6  rhyme XXX
7  climb XXXX
8  gnaw XX
9  mushroom XXXXX
10  elephants XXXXXXXX

## Exercise 1.2

1  damp        CVCC
2  fox         CVCC
3  friend      CCVCC
4  unit        CVCVC
5  talker      CVCV

6  physics     CVCVCC
7  knowledge   CVCVC
8  spaghetti   CVCVCV
9  columnist   CVCVCVCC
10  ghastliness  CVCCCVCVC

5 Is CVCVC in some accents of English where the final *r* is pronounced.

## Exercise 1.4

1  CV       *he to the you to too*
2  CVC      *height but would not reach lot said man shook his head had keys have much*
3  CVCC     *lost*
4  VC       *of it in*
5  VCC      *aren't old and*
6  CVCV     *ladder*
7  CCVC     *tried still break*
8  CCVCC    *smiled*
9  CVCVC    *having Colin patted causing damage*
10  CVCCVC   *success wanted*

## Exercise 1.5

The number below each word indicates the number of segments. If you get a different figure, it may be because you pronounce that word differently.

The first time I drove a car in Europe was in Italy.  We picked up a car at
2 3 3 14 12 2 5 3 2 5 2 4 2 1 3 2
the airport and drove to the place we were staying. It took us about five
2 4 3 4 2 2 4 2 2 5 2 3 2 4 3
and a half hours.  I had a bit of trouble with the gears and spent the first
3 1 3 3 1 3 1 3 2 5 3 2 3 3 4 2 4
couple of miles stuck in third, but after I got the hang of it, we got along
4 2 4 4 2 3 3 4 1 3 2 3 2 2 2 3 4
fine.  The next day was a different matter.  I suppose it was
3 2 5 2 3 1 7 4 1 4 2 3

overconfidence or something, but we nearly had a terrible disaster.  We
11                    1 6              3   2   4       3   1 6        7            2
set off to see some sight or other, I forget now where we were going.
3   2   2 2   3      3      2 3      1 5      2      2       2 2      4
Suddenly my wife screamed out that I was driving on the wrong side of
6          2  3   6          2   3   1 3   6       2 2  3        3   2
the road.  I managed to get back to the correct side just in time to miss
2   3      1 6          2 3  3     2 2  5        3    4  2 3      2 3
a large lorry which appeared round the bend in front of us. It would have
1 3     4    3      4          4      2  4       2 5    2 2  2 3      3
been a very nasty accident and I was extremely careful for the rest of the
3      1 4    5      7        3   1 3   9          4       2   2  4   2 2
holiday.
6

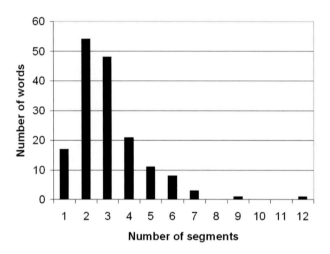

Exercise 1.6
As an example, here is an analysis of the passage in exercise 1.5, which
contains 166 words. The syllable count is as follows

| | |
|---|---|
| 1 syllable | 133 words |
| 2 syllables | 25 words |
| 3 syllables | 7 words |
| 5 syllables | 1 word |

There are some problematic words: *correct, hours, suppose* could be viewed
as having 1 syllable or 2 and *different* can be pronounced with 2 syllables or
with 3.

Exercise 1.9
Waveform A is the word *potato*. There are three separate sections of high
amplitude waveform, corresponding to the three syllables in the word.
Waveform B is the word *pepper*. There are only two sections of high
amplitude waveform here, corresponding to the two syllables in this word.

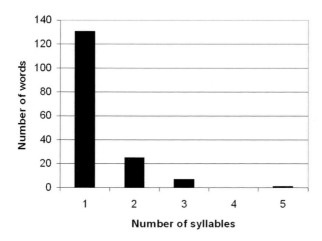

**Exercise 2.1**

|  | The first segment is a: |
| --- | --- |
| Monday | voiced consonant |
| Tuesday | voiceless consonant |
| Wednesday | voiced consonant |
| Thursday | voiceless consonant |
| Friday | voiceless consonant |
| Saturday | voiceless consonant |
| Sunday | voiceless consonant |
| January | voiced consonant |
| February | voiceless consonant |
| March | voiced consonant |
| April | vowel |
| May | voiced consonant |
| June | voiced consonant |
| July | voiced consonant |
| August | vowel |
| September | voiceless consonant |
| October | vowel |
| November | voiced consonant |
| December | voiced consonant |
| one | voiced consonant |
| two | voiceless consonant |
| three | voiceless consonant |
| four | voiceless consonant |
| five | voiceless consonant |
| six | voiceless consonant |
| seven | voiceless consonant |
| eight | vowel |
| nine | voiced consonant |

**Exercise 2.2**

| 1 | bus | voiceless | 7 | buzz | voiced |
| --- | --- | --- | --- | --- | --- |
| 2 | use (noun) | voiceless | 8 | use (verb) | voiced |
| 3 | as | voiced | 9 | teeth | voiceless |
| 4 | breathe | voiced | 10 | rule | voiced |

| 5 | has | voiced | 11 | of | voiced |
| 6 | off | voiceless | 12 | booth | voiceless for some speakers, voiced for others |

## Exercise 2.4

|  | adult pronunciation | child's form |
|---|---|---|
| bag | [bæg] | [bæk] |
| boot | [buːt] | [buːt] |
| beaker | [biːkə] | [biːgə] |
| can | [kæn] | [gæn] |
| coach | [kəʊtʃ] | [gəʊtʃ] |
| pad | [pæd] | [bæt] |
| Paddy | [pædi] | [bædi] |
| jug | [dʒʌg] | [dʒʌk] |
| father | [fɑːðə] | [vɑːðə] |
| footpath | [fʊtpɑːθ] | [vʊtbɑːθ] |
| Jack | [dʒæk] | [dʒæk] |
| motor | [məʊtə] | [məʊdə] |
| rabbit | [ræbɪt] | [ræbɪt] |
| song | [sɒŋ] | [zɒŋ] |
| shop | [ʃɒp] | [ʒɒp] |
| teatime | [tiːtaɪm] | [diːdaɪm] |

## Exercise 3.1
(a) [ʃ] is postalveolar, the rest are alveolar
(b) [f ] is labiodental, the rest are bilabial
(c) [ɢ] is uvular, the rest are velar

## Exercise 3.2
(a) *fight*: kite
(b) *take*: shake, Jake, rake
(c) *bathe*: base, baize, bale, bait, bate, bane, bayed

## Exercise 3.3
(b) sent: all alveolar
(c) palm: all bilabial, the l is silent
(d) align: all alveolar, the g is silent
(e) lazy: all alveolar, the y represents a vowel

## Exercise 3.4
(a, b)

| Adult | Child |
|---|---|
| bilabial | bilabial |
| dental | labiodental |
| alveolar | alveolar |
| postalveolar | palatal |
| velar | alveolar |

(c) This happens at the end of a word.
(d) This happens at the beginning or in the middle of a word.

## Exercise 3.5
(A) labiodental (B) palatal (C) bilabial (D) uvular

## Exercise 3.6

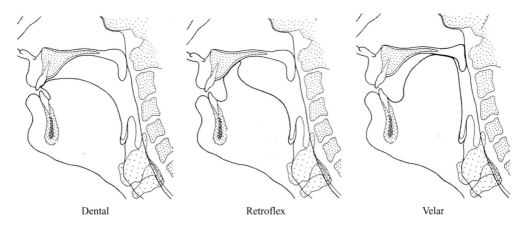

Dental                    Retroflex                    Velar

## Exercise 3.7
It is possible to form an articulation involving the tongue and the upper lip. This is actually reported in a few languages and is called a linguolabial articulation. It is just about possible to make the tongue tip articulate with the velum, but this is not known to occur in any language. The lower lip can be drawn back to approach or touch the alveolar ridge, but again this type of articulation does not occur regularly in any language.

## Exercise 4.1
The consonants are all fricatives.

## Exercise 4.2
talked, sky, cows, captive, chalk

## Exercise 4.3
(a) They are all voiceless plosives.
(b) Mutation I changes them to the equivalent voiced plosives.
(c) Mutation II changes them into homorganic voiceless fricatives, or in the case of [p] into a near-homorganic voiceless fricative.
(d) The initial consonants are all voiced plosives. In the case of the bilabial and alveolar plosives, Mutation I changes them into near-homorganic voiced fricatives and in the case of the velar the consonant is deleted.

## Exercise 4.4
A is a plosive. B is a fricative. C is a trill.

## Exercise 4.5
lorry = [lɒli], shoes = [tuːd], yellow = [leləʊ], woolly = [lʊli], silly = [tɪli], puzzle = [pʌdl], swallow = [tlɒləʊ], umbrella = [ʌmblelə]
You could write either [iː] or [ɪ] instead of the symbol [i] which we have used at the ends of words here.

## Exercise 4.6
sixty = [ɬɪkɬti], amusing = [əmjuːɮɪŋ], results = [ɹɪɮʌltɬ], cousins = [kʌɮənɮ], sensible = [ɬenɬəbl]

### Exercise 4.7

*dramar* = [dramaʁ], *taran* = [taɾan], *garsat* = [gaʁsat], *rakra* = [rakra],
*aramard* = [aɾamaʁd]

### Exercise 4.8

| | |
|---|---|
| [slamb] | This is possible. |
| [flant] | This is possible. |
| [gwalm] | This not possible because [m] is a sonorant, so the word contravenes (c). |
| [spats] | This is not possible because [p] is an obstruent, so the word contravenes (b). |
| [twalf] | This is possible. |
| [kjaŋg] | This is possible. |
| [blams] | This is not possible. The word contravenes (d). $C_3$ is a bilabial nasal so $C_4$ must be a bilabial plosive. [s] is an alveolar fricative. |
| [ljalʃ] | This word is not possible. [l] is a sonorant, so the word contravenes (a). |
| [zjalt] | This is possible. |
| [kramd] | This is not possible. The word contravenes (d). $C_3$ is a bilabial nasal so $C_4$ must be a bilabial plosive. [d] is an alveolar plosive. |
| [dlaps] | This is possible. |
| [snand] | This is possible. |

### Exercise 4.9

(a)

| | bilabial | alveolar | palatal | velar | uvular |
|---|---|---|---|---|---|
| voiceless plosive | p | t | c | k | q |
| voiced plosive | b | d | ɟ | g | ɢ |
| voiced nasal | m | n | ɲ | ŋ | ɴ |

(b)

| | bilabial | alveolar | palatal | velar | uvular |
|---|---|---|---|---|---|
| voiceless fricative | ɸ | s | ç | x | χ |
| voiced fricative | β | z | ʝ | ɣ | ʁ |

(c)

(i) All consonants in a word are hormoganic.
   This is false.
   [zaβa], [gaʁuŋ], [baɸam], [nusaɸ], [ɲiɣax], [ceʁaç] and [ɢaɟuχ] are all words that disprove the statement.

(ii) Stops may not occur between vowels.
   This is true. All the intervocalic consonants are fricatives.

(iii) The only obstruent consonants permitted word-finally are voiceless fricatives.
   This is true.

(iv) Front consonants (articulated on the alveolar ridge or further forward) may not occur in the same word as back consonants.
   This is true.

(v) Voiced fricatives may not occur word-initially.
   This is false. [zaβa] is the single word that disproves the statement.

### Exercise 4.10
A pharyngeal nasal is impossible because a nasal consonant requires airflow through the nasal cavity while the oral cavity is completely blocked. While it is possible, though not particularly easy, to form a complete closure by drawing back the root of the tongue to contact the rear wall of the pharynx, this closure would prevent air flowing through the nasal cavity. The closure would be below the point where the vocal tract divides into oral and nasal cavities

### Exercise 4.11

|     | Keyword | Voice | Place | Manner |
|-----|---------|-------|-------|--------|
| p   | pie     | *voiceless* | *bilabial* | *plosive* |
| t   | tie     | *voiceless* | *alveolar* | *plosive* |
| k   | key     | *voiceless* | *velar* | *plosive* |
| b   | buy     | *voiced* | *bilabial* | *plosive* |
| d   | die     | *voiced* | *alveolar* | *plosive* |
| g   | guy     | *voiced* | *velar* | *plosive* |
| m   | my      | *voiced* | *bilabial* | *nasal* |
| n   | no      | *voiced* | *alveolar* | *nasal* |
| ŋ   | sing    | *voiced* | *velar* | *nasal* |
| f   | fee     | *voiceless* | *labiodental* | *fricative* |
| v   | van     | *voiced* | *labiodental* | *fricative* |
| θ   | thigh   | *voiceless* | *dental* | *fricative* |
| ð   | though  | *voiced* | *dental* | *fricative* |
| s   | so      | *voiceless* | *alveolar* | *fricative* |
| z   | zoo     | *voiced* | *alveolar* | *fricative* |
| ʃ   | she     | *voiceless* | *postalveolar* | *fricative* |
| ʒ   | measure | *voiced* | *postalveolar* | *fricative* |
| tʃ  | chip    | *voiceless* | *postalveolar* | *affricate* |
| dʒ  | jam     | *voiced* | *postalveolar* | *affricate* |
| w   | wet     | *voiced* | *labial-velar* | *median approximant* |
| ɹ   | red     | *voiced* | *postalveolar* | *median approximant* |
| l   | let     | *voiced* | *alveolar* | *lateral approximant* |
| j   | yes     | *voiced* | *palatal* | *median approximant* |
| h   | hat     | *voiceless* | *glottal* | *fricative* |

### Exercise 4.12
(a) singing = [sɪgɪg], onion = [ʌdjəd], murmur = [bɜːbə]
(b) [n̥i̥ːn̥aĩm] = *teatime*, [m̥ẽĩm̥ə̃] = *paper*, [mẽĩŋ̊ĩŋ] = *baking or making*

### Exercise 5.1
(a) [ɔ] is the odd one out, because it is the only rounded vowel
(b) [u] is the odd one out, because it is the only back vowel
(c) [œ] is the odd one out, because it is the open-mid and the others are close

### Exercise 5.2

| | |
|---|---|
| [ɛ̝] | lowered open-mid front unrounded |
| [e] | close mid front unrounded |
| [e̞] | lowered close mid front unrounded |
| [ë̝] | raised centralised close-mid front unrounded |
| [ə̝] | raised mid central unrounded |

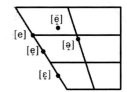

**Exercise 5.3**
[almadan] [tokojdon] [yjdøn] [køldøn] [etten] [tuzdon] [iʃten] [ʒɯldan]

**Exercise 5.4**
Words (a) and (c) contain monophthongs. They show much less change in formant frequencies than words (b) and (d). The words are: (a) *seat* (b) *sight* (c) *seed* (d) *side*.

**Exercise 5.5**
The durations are approximately as follows:
(a) 130 ms
(b) 180 ms
(c) 330 ms
(d) 335 ms

The ratio of (a) to (c) is 0.39
The ratio of (b) to (d) is 0.54

**Exercise 5.6**
Spectrogram (a) is [kil] and (b) is [kyl]. The lower F2 frequency in (b) is a sign that the vowel is rounded.

**Exercise 5.7**
(a) Hindi
(b) Farsi
(c) Hindi, Igbo
(d) Japanese
(e) Hindi

**Exercise 6.1**

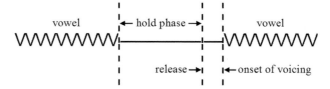

**Exercise 6.2**
(a) [jɔː njuː kredɪt kɑːd ʃʊd əraɪɣ suːn]
(b) [ʃɒpɪŋ ɪn seɪlz ɪz ə gʊd weɪ tə get b̥ɑːgɪnz̥]

**Exercise 6.3**
The vertical lines on the diagram mark the start and end of the VOT which is approximately 65 ms.

**Exercise 6.4**
The velar plosives in the words *kite* and *occur* are likely to have a longer VOT than those in *sky*, *baker* and *basket*.

**Exercise 6.5**
Waveforms (a), (c) and (f) show examples of normal voice at different fundamental frequencies. Waveform (b) shows a low-frequency double-pulsing excitation which sounds creaky. Waveform (e), with very short closures, is breathy. In waveform (d) the rate of closing is slower than that of opening. It was made on an inward flow of air.

## Exercise 6.6
(b) feet
(c) feast
(f) felt

## Exercise 6.7
(a) please
(c) quick
(d) crown
(f) pure

## Exercise 7.1
(a) a voiceless alveolar lateral click
(b) a voiced velar implosive

## Exercise 7.2
The larynx must rise to cause the increase in air pressure. The soft palate must be in a raised position throughout, sealing off the nasal cavity, otherwise there will be no increase in pressure because air will escape via the nose.

## Exercise 7.3
(a) The soft palate is raised shutting off nasal airflow. The glottis is closed tightly. The tongue tip makes a firm closure on the alveolar ridge and the sides of the tongue contact the upper side teeth and gums. The larynx moves upwards compressing the air in the mouth and pharynx. The tongue rapidly breaks its contact with the alveolar ridge and the compressed air escapes. Shortly afterwards the glottis opens.

(b) The lips are closed. The back of the tongue makes firm contact with the velum. The centre of the tongue moves down, enlarging the space between the two closures and the air pressure in the oral cavity decreases. The lips part and air rushes into the oral cavity.

(c) The tongue tip makes a firm closure with the very front of the alveolar ridge and the back of the upper front teeth. The rims of the tongue make firm contact with the upper side teeth and gums. The back of the tongue makes firm contact with the soft palate. The soft palate itself is lowered, allowing nasal airflow. The vocal folds are held loosely closed. The lungs push air up the trachea, causing the vocal folds to vibrate. The tongue centre moves down, enlarging the enclosed space between the dental and velar closures and causing a decrease in air pressure. The dental closure is released and air rushes into the oral cavity.

## Exercise 7.4
(a) voiceless alveolar lateral fricative: pulmonic egressive
(b) voiced bilabial implosive: pulmonic egressive + glottalic ingressive
(c) voiceless dental click: velaric ingressive
(d) voiceless alveolar ejective affricate: glottalic egressive
(e) voiced nasalised postalveolar click: velaric ingressive + pulmonic egressive
(f) voiceless velar ejective affricate: glottalic egressive
(g) voiceless aspirated velar plosive: pulmonic egressive
(h) voiced alveolar lateral click: velaric ingressive + pulmonic egressive
(i) voiceless velar ejective stop (unaffricated): glottalic egressive
(j) voiced bilabial nasal: pulmonic egressive

### Exercise 7.5

(a) Watch what you're doing     [wɒtʃ' wɒt' jɔː ɗuːɪʤ]
(b) Can I get a glass of milk?   [k'æɗ aɪ ʤet' ə ɡlɑːs' əv ɓɪlk']
(c) Is it five past nine?        [ɪz ɪt' f'aɪv p'ɑːs't' ɗaɪd]

### Exercise 8.1

At the beginning of the utterance the organs of speech are in a position of rest. The glottis is open for quiet breathing and the soft palate is lowered. The lips are closed and the tongue fills most of the oral cavity. The word is produced on a pulmonic egressive airstream. The lips open. The soft palate rises to form a closure with the back wall of the pharynx preventing air from escaping via the nose. The tongue tip approaches the alveolar ridge and forms a narrow constriction. The rims of the tongue are in firm contact with the upper side teeth and gums, preventing lateral escape of air. The lips are rounded in anticipation of the following rounded sound. As the air passes through the alveolar constriction, it becomes turbulent and generates friction noise for the first segment [sʷ]. The tongue tip moves away from the alveolar ridge and the back of the tongue rises towards the soft palate to form a wide approximation. The lips remain rounded. The vocal folds are drawn together loosely and begin to vibrate soon after the friction noise dies away. They continue to vibrate for the rest of the utterance. The lips lose their rounded shape and the back of the tongue moves away from the soft palate. Simultaneously, the front of the tongue rises towards the hard palate for the production of the vowel [ĩ]. During the production of the vowel the soft palate begins to fall in anticipation of the following nasal segment. This allows air to escape through the nasal cavity and the vowel is nasalised. The lips close, shutting off the oral airflow, so that the airstream can escape only through the nasal cavity for the nasal stop [m]. The vocal folds stop vibrating and the organs of speech return to their rest position.

Exercise 8.2

(a)

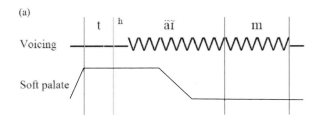

(b)

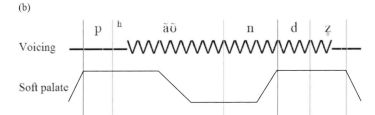

(c)

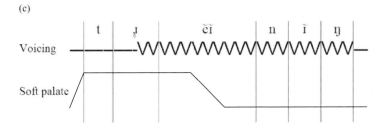

(d)

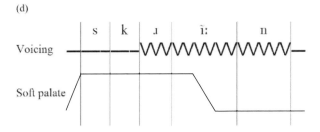

(e)

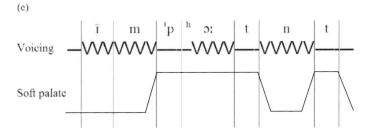

### Exercise 8.3

(a) *camp* fits the diagram. The number of segments is correct and there is a nasal stop in position 3 as shown in the diagram.

(b) *cold* does not fit, as it contains no nasal segment.

(c) *mission* does not fit. Although the word may be pronounced with 4 segments [mɪʃn], the first and last of these need the soft palate to be lowered. The diagram shows segments 1 and 4 with a raised soft palate. Furthermore, [ʃ] is produced with the soft palate raised but the diagram shows segment 3 with a lowered soft palate.

(d) *elms* fits. The [l] in this word will be nasalised as is shown for segment 2 in the diagram.

(e) *film* does not fit. The nasal is in the wrong place.

### Exercise 8.4

The sequences of plosives where release masking is likely are underlined in the passage.

The cha<u>p g</u>rinned, pi<u>ck</u>ed himself up off the floor and ru<u>bb</u>ed his knee. U<u>p t</u>ill that moment the atmosphere ha<u>d b</u>een quite relaxed. Everyone started to loo<u>k t</u>ense. Maybe he wouldn'<u>t b</u>e able to do it.

### Exercise 8.5

We estimate the duration of the [s] in *sigh* to be 235 ms and the [s] in *sky* to be 165 ms.

### Exercise 9.1

| | |
|---|---|
| Burmese: | The two sounds involved are [m] voiced bilabial nasal and [m̥] voiceless bilabial nasal. For the first the vocal folds are vibrating and for the second the glottis open and there is no vibration. |
| Ewe: | The sounds are [f] voiceless labiodental fricative and [ɸ] voiceless bilabial fricative. For the first of these the articulators are the top front teeth and the lower lip. For the second the articulators are the upper and lower lips. |
| German: | The sounds are [d] and [t] voiced and voiceless alveolar plosives. The difference is the presence versus absence of vocal fold vibration. |
| Italian: | The sounds are both voiceless alveolar plosives. The plosive in the word for *done* has a much longer hold phase. |
| Korean: | The two sounds are [p] voiceless unaspirated bilabial plosive and [pʰ] voiceless aspirated bilabial plosive. The second has a much longer VOT. |
| Spanish: | The sounds are [r] voiced alveolar trill and [ɾ] voiced alveolar tap. For the first the tongue tip vibrates against the alveolar ridge, making a series of rapid closures. For the second the tongue tip strikes the alveolar ridge just once. |
| Welsh: | The sounds involved are both close, front, unrounded vowels. The vowel in the word for *white* has a longer duration. |

### Exercise 9.2

The words that make minimal pairs with the first word are underlined

| | | | | | | |
|---|---|---|---|---|---|---|
| **dot** | <u>dock</u> | <u>dog</u> | <u>dots</u> | <u>debt</u> | <u>doll</u> | <u>got</u> |
| **can** | <u>cat</u> | <u>cone</u> | <u>cane</u> | cape | <u>man</u> | mat |
| **hat** | flat | <u>that</u> | <u>had</u> | <u>hate</u> | <u>at</u> | <u>heart</u> |

| **green** | bean | groan | gain | grease | glean | grain |
|---|---|---|---|---|---|---|
| **shoe** | show | shoot | shrew | Sue | blue | who |

Can/cape is not a minimal pair because there is more than a single segment difference between the words /kæn/ and /keɪp/. The same is true of the pair can/mat /kæn/ – /mæt/.

Hat/flat is not a minimal pair because the second word has an extra segment and the initial segments are different.

Green/bean is not a minimal pair because the initial segments are different and the second word has one fewer segments. Green/gain is not a minimal pair because there is a mismatch in the number of segments and the vowels are different too.

Shoe/blue is not a minimal pair because there is a mismatch in the number of segments and the initial segments are different.

### Exercise 9.3

(a) An example of a minimal pair for /w/ versus /r/ is *went* and *rent*. The child produces only [w], so all minimal pairs depending on the contrast will be homophones in the child's speech. The child would say, for example, [went] for both *went* and *rent*.

(b) An example of a minimal pair for /s/ versus /ʃ/ is *bus* and *bush*. The child produces only [s], so again all minimal pairs depending on the contrast will be homophones in the child's speech. The child would say [bʌs] for both *bus* and *bush*, for example.

(c) The adult words that contain affricates are: *change, crunch, James, judge, smudge, stretch, watch*. Sometimes, the child produces an affricate, but an alveolar one rather than a postalveolar one like the adult target. This happens at the end of a word. At the beginning of a word, the child uses an alveolar plosive instead of an affricate. The voicing of the child's consonants matches that of the adult target.

(d)

- Words beginning with a cluster of /s/ + a plosive: *school, spot*. The child deletes the /s/.
- Words beginning with a cluster of /s/ + plosive + approximant: *spring, stretch*. Again the child deletes the /s/, but retains the approximant, although as we have seen it is [w] rather than [ɹ].
- Words beginning with a cluster of a plosive + approximant: *brush, class, crunch*. Both segments are retained by the child.
- Words beginning with a cluster of /s/ + nasal: *smack, smudge, sneeze*. Here the first segment is not deleted, but is produced as a voiceless nasal at the same place of articulation as the following nasal.

(e) /s/ ⟶ ø /# __ C
            [-nasal]

(f) *Charles* [tɑːlz], *choose* [tuːz], *fridge* [fwɪdz], *juice* [duːs], *lunch* [lʌnts], *prince* [pwɪns], *scratch* [kwæts], *snake* [n̥neɪk], *stamp* [tæmp], *touch* [tʌts]

### Exercise 9.4

The child's consonants are p b m m̥ t d n n̥ s z ts dz k ŋ w l

(a) [+nasal, +voiced]: m n ŋ

(b) [+anterior, −coronal, −continuant]: **p b m m̥**
(c) [−lateral, +voiced]: **b m d n z dz ŋ w**
(d) [−sonorant, −continuant, −nasal]: **p b t d ts dz k**
(e) [−anterior, −continuant]: **k ŋ**

## Exercise 9.5

The three fricative sounds are all voiceless [h] glottal, [ç] palatal, [ɸ] bilabial. None of these occurs word finally, but all occur both word initially and between vowels in the middle of a word. [ç] only occurs immediately preceding [i]. [ɸ] only occurs immediately preceding [ɯ]. [h] occurs immediately preceding all the other vowels [e a o], but not before [i] or [ɯ]. They are therefore in complementary distribution because where one can occur the other two cannot. As they are also phonetically quite similar they can be regarded as allophones of the same phoneme. As [h] has the widest distribution this single phoneme is best symbolised as /h/.

[s] and [h] on the other hand are not in complementary distribution. Both occur immediately before [a], as can be seen in the words for *tooth* and *wallet*. This indicates that they should be regarded as allophones of two distinct phonemes.

## Exercise 9.6

(a) The plosive sounds in the data are

[p] voiceless bilabial plosive
[b] voiced bilabial plosive
[t] voiceless alveolar plosive
[tʰ] voiceless aspirated alveolar plosive
[k] voiceless velar plosive
[g] voiced velar plosive

Both voiced and voiceless plosives occur immediately after a homorganic nasal, but elsewhere plosives are all voiceless. The occurrence of voiced plosives only in words where they are in free variation with the corresponding voiceless plosive (*butterfly*, *corn*, *dead limb*, *we chase*, *your daughter*) indicates that the voicing distinction is not contrastive for plosives in Campa.

(b) [t] and [tʰ] are in contrast in Campa. The minimal pair [itoki] on *his head* and [itʰoki] *egg* proves this.

(c) We have already established that there is no contrast between [p] and [b]. As these are phonetically similar, we may safely conclude that they are allophones of the same phoneme. As [p] has the wider distribution, let us represent the phoneme as /p/. Notice also that [p] does not occur between two vowels, but only word-initially or in the middle of a word preceded by a consonant. As we saw [b] occurs in this latter environment. Both [w] and [β] only occur between two vowels. Moreover, [β] only occurs immediately before the front vowels [i] and [e], while [w] only occurs before other vowels [a], [o] and [ə]. These two sounds are therefore in complementary distribution, both with each other and with [p] and [b]. As the sounds are all labial ([p b β] are bilabial and [w] is labial-velar), it would be reasonable to conclude that they are all allophones of the /p/ phoneme.

(d) It is clear that [n] and [ŋ] are in complementary distribution. [ŋ] only occurs before velar plosives, whereas [n] nevers occurs in this environment. We can then conclude that these two sounds are allophones of a single phoneme /n/ and that the occurrence of [ŋ] be dealt with by an assimilation rule. Turning to [m], we can see that two instances of this sound are immediately before a bilabial plosive and we might be tempted to deal with these using an assimilation rule too. However there is another occurrence of [m] in the word [noˈmarɛ] *my paddle*. This cannot be accounted for by assimilation. We must therefore conclude that there are two nasal phonemes in Campa: /m/ and /n/.

(e) The vowel sounds are:

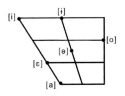

[i] front, close, unrounded
[ɨ] central, close, unrounded
[ɛ] front, open-mid unrounded
[ə] central, between close-mid and open-mid, unrounded
[a] front, open, unrounded
[o] back, close-mid rounded

(f) The vowel phonemes of Campa are /i ɛ a o/. They are fewer in number than the vowel sounds for the following reasons:

- [a] and [ə] are in free variation. A word may end in either of these two vowels and no meaning difference is signalled. [a] has a wider distribution than [ə], so these two sounds may be assigned to the /a/ phoneme.
- [i] and [ɨ] are in complementary distribution. [ɨ] only occurs immediately following [s] or [ts]. [i] never occurs in this environment. They are both allophones of the /i/ phoneme.

## Exercise 9.7

(a) V→ [+nasal]/__[+nasal]
    A vowel is nasalised before an immediately following nasal (or nasalised sound).
(b) [−sonorant]→ [−voiced]/__#
    Any obstruent (plosive, fricative or affricate) is voiceless if it occurs word-finally.
(c) ø → [ɹ]/     V __ V
            [−high]
    [ɹ] is inserted between a mid or low vowel and any following vowel.

## Exercise 10.1
List 1 Words with primary stress on the first syllable:
*attitude, concentrate, crocodile, elephant, fantasy, mystery, troublesome, universe*

List 2 Words with primary stress on the second syllable:
*connection, excitement, fantastic, horizon, imagine, intention, recover*

List 3 Words with primary stress on the last syllable:
*afternoon, kangaroo, millionaire, puppeteer, understand*

## Exercise 10.2
Maori stress

| | | | |
|---|---|---|---|
| [ataˈpoː] | 'early dawn' | [paːparaˈkauta] | 'hotel' |
| [kiˈhirimete] | 'Christmas' | [kaˈwanataŋa] | 'government' |
| [ˈpaepae] | 'beam' | [kauˈmaːtua] | 'male elder' |

| | | | |
|---|---|---|---|
| [tauˈrekareka] | 'slave' | [papaˈkaiŋa] | 'village' |
| [ˈmarae] | 'courtyard' | [ˈkaimoana] | 'seafood' |
| [ˈfafai] | 'war' | [ˈmokopuna] | 'grandchild' |

### Exercise 10.3

Manam stress: If the final syllable ends in a vowel, then the penultimate syllable is stressed. Otherwise the final syllable is stressed.

### Exercise 10.4

Waveform (a) is of an utterance of [ɪmˈpɔːt] *import* (verb) and the duration of the first syllable is 154 ms. Waveform (b) is [ˈɪmpɔːt] *import* (noun) and the initial syllable duration is 191 ms.

### Exercise 10.5

Chengdu tones

(a)

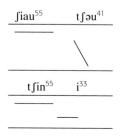

(b) Glottal stop appears at the end of the following words:

fei²¹dzau$ʔ^{211}$ 'soap', ʃiau⁵⁵ tʃi$ʔ^{211}$ 'stingy', jin²¹³ tʃi$ʔ^{211}$ 'luck', koŋ⁵⁵ pa$ʔ^{211}$ 'perhaps'

For all of these, the citation form of the second element ends in a vowel sound and has the falling rising toneme.

(c) goŋ⁴⁵fu³³ 'time'   ˥goŋ ˧fu

(d) I High Rising

Citation: 45        Variant: 33 in second element except after 213

II Low Falling

Citation: 21        No variants

III High Falling

Citation: 41        Variant: 55 in first element

IV Low Falling-rising

Citation: 213       Variant: 33 in second element following another 213
                    Variant: 211 in second element after other tones

### Exercise 10.6

Underlining indicates the place of nuclear syllables

(a)   My sister who lives in <u>Liverpool</u> | has just changed <u>her job</u>.
      (This would probably be interpreted as meaning that I have more than one sister and I am telling you which one I am talking about.)

My <u>sis</u>ter | who lives in <u>Liverpool</u> | has just changed her <u>job</u>.
(This is the equivalent of 'My sister lives in Liverpool and she has just changed her job'.)

(b)   She <u>played</u> | and I sang the national <u>anthem</u>.
(She played something, not even a musical instrument necessarily.)

She <u>played</u> | and I <u>sang</u> the national <u>anthem</u>.
(She played the national anthem and I sang it.)

(c)   He didn't leave because he was <u>afraid</u>.
(He left for some other reason.)

He didn't <u>leave</u> | because he was <u>afraid</u>.
(Being afraid was the reason for his not leaving.)

## Exercise 10.7

| | |
|---|---|
| Sid: | I've got an <u>idea</u> | Let's go out for a <u>meal</u>. |
| Clare: | All <u>right</u> | Which <u>restaurant</u> do you want to go to? |
| | OR |
| Clare: | All <u>right</u> | Which restaurant do you want to <u>go</u> to? |
| Sid: | There's a good Chi<u>nese</u> place | near the <u>library</u>. |
| Clare: | I'm not terribly <u>fond</u> of Chinese food. |
| Sid: | Maybe that's because you've never had any <u>good</u> Chinese food. |
| Clare: | That may be <u>true</u> | but I think I'd prefer to try <u>that</u> place | some <u>other</u> time. |
| | OR |
| Clare: | That may be <u>true</u> | but I think I'd prefer to try <u>that</u> place | some other <u>time</u>. |

# Index